THE
GUIDEPOSTS
TREASURY
OF
INSPIRATIONAL
CLASSICS

BANTAM BOOKS
TORONTO • NEW YORK • LONDON

*This low-priced Bantam Book
has been completely reset in a type face
designed for easy reading, and was printed
from new plates. It contains the complete
text of the original hard-cover edition.*
NOT ONE WORD HAS BEEN OMITTED.

GUIDEPOSTS TREASURY OF INSPIRATIONAL CLASSICS
*A Bantam Book / published by arrangement with
Doubleday & Co., Inc.*

PRINTING HISTORY
*Doubleday edition published February 1980
3 printings through March 1980*
Bantam edition / February 1981

ISBN 0-553-14271-2

Published simultaneously in the United States and Canada

PRINTED IN THE UNITED STATES OF AMERICA

0 9 8 7 6 5 4 3 2 1

CONTENTS

I

THE GREATEST THING IN
THE WORLD

Henry Drummond

page 1

II

ACRES OF DIAMOND

Russell Conwell

page 31

III

AS A MAN THINKETH

James Allen

page 69

IV

THE PRACTICE OF THE
PRESENCE OF GOD

Brother Lawrence

page 103

V

THE IMITATION OF CHRIST

Thomas a Kempis

page 137

ABOUT THESE BOOKS

From time to time Guideposts magazine has presented excerpts from each of the five books presented in this volume. Now we take pleasure in publishing these great Christian classics in their complete form. Though the works span four centuries, the message in each is timeless and dateless, as vital and vibrant as when first written.

Arbitrarily, we have ordered them from latest to earliest, beginning with three 19th century-written books—Henry Drummond's *The Greatest Thing in the World*, Russell Conwell's *Acres of Diamonds* and James Allen's *As a Man Thinketh*. Whatever might be said about those three books would be inadequate. Each is a Christian giant which has had tremendous impact on millions of people. Each is filled with passages worthy of memorization and repeated meditation. Each speaks simply, yet movingly and profoundly. Each is a lifelong guide for a rich life.

The fourth book in the set is Brother Lawrence's *The Practice of the Presence of God*. As with the three writers who proceed him, Brother Lawrence's 15th century work is no less simply presented, nor more filled with spiritual wisdom. That ode to contentment from a humble French friar who did his praying and meditating in a monastery kitchen should strike a particularly helpful chord for Christians of today. People buffeted by the ever-changing currents of our times will find reaffirming faith in Brother Lawrence's example.

We conclude this volume with Thomas à Kempis'

much heralded *The Imitation of Christ*. Written in 1426 it represents the oldest book of the lot, but time has done nothing except underscore the great message of that inspired German priest. Its four sections are divided into 114 chapters, each a devotional in itself. Next to the Bible, many scholars have cited it as the most important religious book to be written. Full of rich meaning and beautiful expression, Thomas à Kempis' *The Imitation of Christ* has instructed and counseled serious Christians for more than five centuries and interest in it shows little sign of abating.

Guideposts believes these five titles are worthy of space on your bookshelves. More important, we hope their messages find space in your heart.

The Editors

I

THE GREATEST THING IN THE WORLD

HENRY DRUMMOND

ABOUT
THE AUTHOR

Henry Drummond (1851-1897) was born in Stirling, Scotland, educated at Edinburgh and in 1877 became a lecturer on natural science at Glasgow College. In 1883, he wrote *Natural Law in the Spiritual World* which set forth his premise that the scientific principle of continuity expanded from the physical world to the spiritual. But it was not his scientific writings which caught the eye of evangelist Dwight L. Moody, but rather a discussion Drummond led on the 13th chapter of First Corinthians. Moody was so excited by his friend's remarks on the "love" chapter that he invited the professor to Northfield to address the students. Later, Drummond's speech was published under the title of *The Greatest Thing in the World* and by the time of his death in 1897, it had achieved classic status around the world.

INTRODUCTION

I was staying with a party of friends in a country house during my visit to England in 1884. On Sunday evening as we sat around the fire, they asked me to read and expound some portion of Scripture. Being tired after the services of the day, I told them to ask Henry Drummond, who was one of the party. After some urging he drew a small Testament from his hip pocket, opened it at the 13th chapter of I Corinthians, and began to speak on the subject of Love.

It seemed to me that I had never heard anything so beautiful, and I determined not to rest until I brought Henry Drummond to Northfield to deliver that address. Since then I have requested the principals of my schools to have it read before the students every year. The one great need in our Christian life is love, more love to God and to each other. Would that we could all move into that Love chapter, and live there.

D.L. Moody.

Though I speak with the tongues of men and of angels, and have not love, I am become as sounding brass, or a tinkling cymbal.

And though I have the gift of prophecy, and understand all mysteries, and all knowledge; and though I have all faith, so that I could remove mountains, and have not love, I am nothing.

And though I bestow all my goods to feed the poor and though I give my body to be burned, and have not love, it profiteth me nothing.

Love suffereth long, and is kind; love envieth not; love vaunteth not itself, is not puffed up,

Doth not behave itself unseemly, seeketh not her own, is not easily provoked, thinketh no evil;

Rejoiceth not in iniquity, but rejoiceth in the truth;

Beareth all things, believeth all things, hopeth all things, endureth all things.

Love never faileth: but whether there be prophecies, they shall fail; whether there be tongues, they shall cease; whether there be knowledge, it shall vanish away.

For we know in part, and we prophesy in part.

But when that which is perfect is come, then that which is in part shall be done away.

When I was a child, I spake as a child, I understood as a child, I thought as a child: but when I became a man, I put away childish things.

For now we see through a glass, darkly; but then face to face: now I know in part; but then shall I know even as also I am known.

And now abideth faith, hope, love, these three; but the greatest of these is love.

LOVE:
The Greatest Thing in the World

Everyone has asked himself the great question of antiquity as of the modern world: What is the *summum bonum*—the supreme good? You have life before you. Once only you can live it. What is the noblest object of desire, the supreme gift to covet?

We have been accustomed to be told that the greatest thing in the religious world is faith. That great word has been the keynote for centuries of the popular religion; and we have easily learned to look upon it as the greatest thing in the world. Well, we are wrong. If we have been told that, we may miss the mark. In the 13th chapter of I Corinthians, Paul takes us to Christianity at its source; and there we see, "The greatest of these is love."

It is not an oversight. Paul was speaking of faith just a moment before. He says, "If I have all faith, so that I can remove mountains, and have not love, I am nothing." So far from forgetting, he deliberately contrasts them, "Now abideth faith, hope, love," and with a moment's hesitation the decision falls, "The greatest of these is love."

And it is not prejudice. A man is apt to recommend to others his own strong point. Love was not Paul's strong point. The observing student can detect a beautiful tenderness

9

growing and ripening all through his character as Paul gets old; but the hand that wrote, "The greatest of these is love," when we meet it first, is stained with blood.

Nor is this letter to the Corinthians peculiar in singling out love as the *summum bonum*. The masterpieces of Christianity are agreed about it. Peter says, "Above all things have fervent love among yourselves." *Above all things*. And John goes farther, "God is love."

"You remember the profound remark which Paul makes elsewhere, "Love is the fulfilling of the law." Did you ever think what he meant by that? In those days men were working the passage to heaven by keeping the Ten Commandments, and the hundred and ten other commandments which they had manufactured out of them. Christ came and said, "I will show you a more simple way. If you do one thing, you will do these hundred and ten things without ever thinking about them. If you *love*, you will unconsciously fulfill the whole law."

You can readily see for yourselves how that must be so. Take any of the commandments. "Thou shalt have no other gods before me." If a man love God, you will not require to tell him that. Love is the fulfilling of that law. "Take not his name in vain." Would he ever dream of taking His name in vain if he loved Him? "Remember the Sabbath day to keep it holy." Would he not be too glad to have one day in seven to dedicate more exclusively to the object of his affection? Love would fulfill all these laws regarding God.

And so, if he loved man, you would never think of telling him to honor his father and mother. He could not do anything else. It would be preposterous to tell him not to kill. You could only insult him if you suggested that he should not steal—how could he steal from those he loved? It would be superfluous to beg him not to bear false witness against his neighbor. If he loved him it would be the last thing he would do. And you would never dream of urging him not to covet what his neighbors had. He would rather they possessed it than himself. In this way "love is the fulfilling of the law." It is the rule for fulfilling all rules, the new commandment for keeping all the old commandments, Christ's one secret of the Christian life.

Now Paul has learned that; and in this noble eulogy he has given us the most wonderful and original account extant of the *summum bonum*. We may divide it into three parts. In the beginning of the short chapter we have love *contrasted*; in the heart of it, we have love *analyzed*; toward the end, we have love *defended* as the supreme gift.

THE CONTRAST

Paul begins by contrasting love with other things that men in those days thought much of. I shall not attempt to go over these things in detail. Their inferiority is already obvious.

He contrasts it with *eloquence*. And what a noble gift it is, the power of playing upon the souls and wills of men, and rousing them to lofty purposes and holy deeds! Paul says, "If I speak with the tongues of men and of angels, and have not love, I am become sounding brass, or a tinkling cymbal." We all know why. We have all felt the brazenness of words without emotion, the hollowness, the unaccountable unpersuasiveness, of eloquence behind which lies no love.

He contrasts it with *prophecy*. He contrasts it with *mysteries*. He contrasts it with *faith*. He contrasts it with *charity*. Why is love greater than faith? Because the end is greater than the means. And why is it greater than charity? Because the whole is greater than the part.

Love is greater than faith, because the end is greater than the means. What is the use of having faith? It is to connect the soul with God. And what is the object of connecting man with God? That he may become like God. But God is love. Hence faith, the means, is in order to love, the end. Love, therefore, obviously is greater than faith. "If I have all faith, so as to remove mountains, but have not love, I am nothing."

It is greater than charity, again, because the whole is

12

greater than a part. Charity is only a little bit of love, one of the innumerable avenues of love, and there may even be, and there is, a great deal of charity without love. It is a very easy thing to toss a copper to a beggar on the street; it is generally an easier thing than not to do it. Yet love is just as often in the withholding. We purchase relief from the sympathetic feelings roused by the spectacle of misery, at the copper's cost. It is too cheap—too cheap for us, and often too dear for the beggar. If we really loved him we would either do more for him, or less. Hence, "If I bestow all my good to feed the poor, but have not love it profiteth me nothing."

Then Paul contrasts it with *sacrifice* and *martyrdom*: "If I give my body to be burned, but have not love, it profiteth me nothing." Missionaries can take nothing greater to the heathen world than the impress and reflection of the love of God upon their own character. That is the universal language. It will take them years to speak in Chinese, or in the dialects of India. From the day they land, that language of love, understood by all, will be pouring forth its unconscious eloquence.

It is the man who is the missionary, it is not his words. His character is his message. In the heart of Africa, among the great Lakes, I have come across black men and women who remembered the only white man they ever saw before— David Livingstone; and as you cross his footsteps in that dark continent, men's faces light up as they speak of the kind doctor who passed there years ago. They could not understand him; but they felt the love that beat in his heart. They knew that it was love, although he spoke no words.

Take into your sphere of labor, where you also mean to lay down your life, that simple charm, and your lifework must succeed. You can take nothing greater, you need take nothing less. You make take every accomplishment; you may be braced for every sacrifice; but if you give your body to be burned, and have not love, it will profit you and the cause of Christ *nothing*.

THE ANALYSIS

After contrasting love with these things, Paul, in three very short verses, gives us an amazing analysis of what this supreme thing is.

I ask you to look at it. It is a compound thing, he tells us. It is like light. As you have seen a man of science take a beam of light and pass it through a crystal prism, as you have seen it come out on the other side of the prism broken up into its component colors—red, blue, yellow, violet, orange, and all the colors of the rainbow—so Paul passes this thing, love, through the magnificent prism of his inspired intellect, and it comes out on the other side broken up into its elements.

In these few words we have what one might call the spectrum of love, and analysis of love. Will you observe what its elements are? Will you notice that they have common names; that they are virtues which we hear about every day; that they are things which can be practiced by every man in every place in life; and how, by a multitude of small things and ordinary virtues the supreme thing, the *summum bonum*, is made up?

The spectrum of love has nine ingredients:

Patience . . . . Love suffereth long.
Kindness . . . . And is kind.
Generosity . . . Love envieth not.
Humility . . . . Love vaunteth not itself, is not puffed up.

Courtesy . . . . Doth not behave itself unseemly.

Unselfishness . . Seeketh not its own.

Good temper . . Is not provoked.

Guilelessness . . Taketh not account of evil.

Sincerity . . . . Rejoiceth not in unrighteousness, but rejoiceth with the truth.

Patience, kindness, generosity, humility, courtesy, unselfishness, good temper, guilelessness, sincerity—these make up the supreme gift, the stature of the perfect man.

You will observe that all are in relation to men, in relation to life, in relation to the known today and the near tomorrow, and not to the unknown eternity. We hear much of love to God; Christ spoke much of love to man. We make a great deal of peace with heaven; Christ made much of peace on earth. Religion is not a strange or added thing, but the inspiration of the secular life, the breathing of an eternal spirit through this temporal world. The supreme thing, in short, is not a thing at all, but the giving of a further finish to the multitudinous words and acts which make up the sum of every common day.

Patience. This is the normal attitude of love; love passive, love waiting to begin; not in a hurry; calm; ready to do its work when the summons comes, but meantime wearing the ornament of a meek and quiet spirit. Love suffers long; bareth all things; believeth all things; hopeth all things. For love understands, and therefore waits.

Kindness. Love active. Have you ever noticed how much of Christ's life was spent in doing kind things—in *merely* doing kind things? Run over it with that in view, and you will find that He spent a great proportion of His time simply in making people happy, in doing good turns to people. There is only one thing greater than happiness in the world, and that is holiness; and it is not in our keeping; but what God *has* put in our power is the happiness of those about us, and that is largely to be secured by our being kind to them.

"The greatest thing," says someone, "a man can do for his Heavenly Father is to be kind to some of His other children." I wonder why it is that we are not all kinder than we are? How much the world needs it! How easily it is done! How instantaneously it acts! How infallibly it is remembered! How superabundantly it pays itself back—for there is no debtor in the world so honorable, so superbly honorable, as love. "Love never faileth." Love is success, love is happiness, love is life. "Love," I say with Browning, "is energy of life."

> For life, with all it yields of joy or woe
> And hope and fear,
> Is just our chance o' the prize of learning love,—
> How love might be, hath been indeed, and is.

Where love is, God is. He that dwelleth in love dwelleth in God. God is love. Therefore *love*. Without distinction, without calculation, without procrastination, love. Lavish it upon the poor, where it is very easy; especially upon the rich, who often need it most; most of all upon our equals, where it is very difficult, and for whom perhaps we each do least of all. There is a difference between *trying to please* and *giving pleasure*. Give pleasure. Lose no chance of giving pleasure; for that is the ceaseless and anonymous triumph of a truly loving spirit. "I shall pass through this world but once. Any good thing, therefore, that I can do, or any kindness that I can show to any human being, let me do it now. Let me not defer it or neglect it, for I shall not pass this way again."

Generosity. "Love envieth not." This is love in competition with others. Whenever you attempt a good work you will find other men doing the same kind of work, and probably doing it better. Envy them not. Envy is a feeling of ill will to those who are in the same line as ourselves, a spirit of covetousness and detraction. How little Christian work even is a protection against unchristian feeling! That most despicable of all the unworthy moods which cloud a Christian's soul assuredly waits for us on the threshold of every work, unless we are fortified with this grace of magnanimity. Only one thing truly need the Christian envy—the large, rich, generous soul which "envieth not."

Humility. And then, after having learned all that, you have to learn this further thing, humility—to put a seal upon your lips and forget what you have done. After you have been kind, after love has stolen forth into the world and done its beautiful work, go back into the shade again and say nothing about it. Love hides even from itself. Love waives even self-satisfaction. "Love vaunteth not itself, is not puffed up." Humility—love hiding.

Courtesy. The fifth ingredient is a somewhat strange one to find in this *summum bonum*: courtesy. This is love in society, love in relation to etiquette. "Love does not behave itself unseemly."

Politeness has been defined as love in trifles. Courtesy is said to be love in little things. And the one secret of politeness is to love.

Love *cannot* behave itself unseemly. You can put the most untutored persons into the highest society, and if they have a reservoir of love in their hearts they will not behave themselves unseemly. They simply cannot do it. Carlisle said of Robert Burns that there was no truer gentleman in Europe than the ploughman-poet. It was because he loved everything—the mouse, and the daisy, and all the things, great and small, that God had made. So with this simple passport he could mingle with any society and enter courts and palaces from his little cottage on the banks of the Ayr.

You know the meaning of the word "Gentleman." It means a gentle man—a man who does things gently, with love. That is the whole art and mystery of it. The gentle man cannot in the nature of things do an ungentle, an ungentlemanly thing. The ungentle soul, the inconsiderate, unsympathetic nature, cannot do any thing else. "Love doth not behave itself unseemly."

Unselfishness. "Love seeketh not her own." Observe: seeketh not even that which is her own. In Britain the Englishman is devoted, and rightly, to his rights. But there come times when a man may exercise even the higher right of giving up his rights.

Yet Paul does not summon us to give up our rights. Love strikes much deeper. It would have us not seek them at all, ignore them, eliminate the personal element altogether from our calculations.

It is not hard to give up our rights. They are often enternal. The difficult thing is to give up *ourselves*. The more difficult thing still is not to seek things for ourselves at all. After we have sought them, bought them, won them, deserved them, we have taken the cream off them for ourselves already. Little cross then to give them up. But not to seek them, to look every man not on his own things, but on the things of others—that is the difficulty. "Seekest thou great things for thyself?" said the prophet: "*seek them not.*" Why? Because there is no greatness in *things*. Things cannot be great. The only greatness is unselfish love. Even self-denial in itself is nothing, is almost a mistake. Only a great purpose or a mightier love can justify the waste.

It is more difficult, I have said, not to seek our own at all than having sought it, to give it up. I must take that back. It is only true of a partly selfish heart. Nothing is a hardship to love, and nothing is hard. I believe that Christ's "yoke" is easy. Christ's yoke is just His way of taking life. And I believe it is an easier way than any other. I believe it is a happier way than any other. The most obvious lesson in Christ's teaching is that there is no happiness in having and getting anything, but only in giving. I repeat, *there is no happiness in having or in getting, but only in giving.* Half the world is on the wrong scent in pursuit of happiness. They think it consists in having and getting, and in being served by others. It consists in giving, and in serving others. "He that would be great among you," said Christ, "let him serve." He that would be happy, let him remember that there is but one way—"It is more blessed, it is more happy, to give than to receive."

Good temper. The next ingredient is a very remarkable one: "love is not provoked." Nothing could be more striking than to find this here. We are inclined to look upon bad temper as a very harmless weakness. We speak of it as a mere infirmity of nature, a family failing, a matter of temperament, not a thing to take into very serious account in estimating a man's character. And yet here, right in the heart of this analysis of love, it finds a place; and the Bible again, and again returns to condemn it as one of the most destructive elements in human nature.

The peculiarity of ill temper is that it is the vice of the virtuous. It is often the one blot on an otherwise noble character. You know men who are all but perfect, and women who would be entirely perfect, but for an easily ruffled, quick-tempered, or "touchy" disposition. This compatibility of ill temper with high moral character is one of the strangest and saddest problems of ethics. The truth is, there are two great classes of sins—sins of the *body* and sins of the *disposition.* The Prodigal Son may be taken as a type of the first, the Elder Brother of the second. Now, society has no doubt whatever as to which of these is the worse. Its brand falls, without a challenge, upon the Prodigal. But are we right? We have no balance to weigh one another's sins, and coarser and finer are but human words; but faults in the higher nature may be less venal than those in the lower, and to the eye of

Him who is love, a sin against love may seem a hundred times more base. No form of vice, not worldliness, not greed of gold, not drunkenness itself, does more to unchristianize society than evil temper. For embittering life, for breaking up communities, for destroying the most sacred relationships, for devastating homes, for withering up men and women, for taking the bloom of childhood, in short, for sheer gratuitous misery-producing power this influence stands alone.

Look at the Elder Brother—moral, hardworking, patient, dutiful—let him get all credit for his virtues—look at this man, this baby, sulking outside his own father's door. "He was angry," we read, "and would not go in." Look at the effect upon the father, upon the servants, upon the happiness of the guests. Judge of the effect upon the Prodigal—and how many prodigals are kept out of the kingdom of God by the unlovely character of those who profess to be inside. Analyze, as a study in temper, the thunder-cloud itself as it gathers upon the Elder Brother's brow. What is it made of? Jealousy, anger, pride, uncharity, cruelty, self-righteousness, touchiness, doggedness, sullenness—these are the ingredients of this dark and loveless soul. In varying proportions, also, these are the ingredients of all ill temper. Judge if such sins of the disposition are not worse to live in, and for others to live with, than the sins of the body. Did Christ indeed not answer the question Himself when He said, "I say unto you that the publicans and the harlots go into the kingdom of God before you"? There is really no place in heaven for a disposition like this. A man with such a mood could only make heaven miserable for all the people in it. Except, therefore, such a man be born again, he cannot, simply *cannot*, enter the kingdom of heaven.

You will see then why temper is significant. It is not in what it is alone, but in what it reveals. This is why I speak of it with such unusual plainness. It is a test for love, a symptom, a revelation of an unloving nature at bottom. It is the intermittent fever which bespeaks unintermittent disease within; the occasional bubble escaping to the surface which betrays some rottenness underneath; a sample of the most hidden products of the soul dropped involuntarily when off one's guard; in a word, the lightning form of a hundred hideous and unchristian sins. A want of patience, a want of kindness, a want of generosity, a want of courtesy, a want of unselfishness, are all instantaneously symbolized in one flash of temper.

Hence it is not enough to deal with the temper. We must go to the source and change the inmost nature, and the angry humors will die away of themselves. Souls are made sweet not by taking the acid fluids out but by putting something in—a great love, a new spirit, the Spirit of Christ. Christ, the Spirit of Christ, interpenetrating ours, sweetens, purifies, transforms all. This only can eradicate what is wrong, work a chemical change, renovate and regenerate, and rehabilitate the the inner man. Will power does not change men. Time does not change men. Christ does. Therefore, "Let that mind be in you which was also in Christ Jesus."

Some of us have not much time to lose. Remember, once more, that this is a matter of life or death. I cannot help speaking urgently for myself, for yourselves. "Whoso shall offend one of these little ones, which believe in me, it were better for him that a millstone were hanged about his neck, and that he were drowned in the depth of the sea." That is to say, it is the deliberate verdict of the Lord Jesus that it is better not to live than not to love. *It is better not to live than not to love.*

Guilelessness and *Sincerity* may be dismissed almost without a word. Guilelessness is the grace for suspicious people. The possession of it is the great secret of personal influence.

You will find, if you think for a moment, that the people who influence you are people who believe in you. In an atmosphere of suspicion men shrivel up; but in that atmosphere they expand, and find encouragement and educative fellowship.

It is a wonderful thing that here and there in this hard uncharitable world there should still be left a few rare souls who think no evil. This is the great unworldliness. Love "thinketh no evil," imputes no motive, sees the bright side, puts the best construction on every action. What a delightful state of mind to live in! What a stimulus and benediction even to meet with it for a day! To be trusted is to be saved. And if we try to influence or elevate others, we shall soon see that success is in proportion to their belief of our belief in them. The respect of another is the first restoration of the self-respect a man has lost; our ideal of what he is becomes to him the hope and pattern of what he may become.

"Love rejoiceth not in unrighteousness, but rejoiceth with

the truth." I have called this sincerity, from the words rendered in the Authorized Version by "rejoiceth in the truth." And, certainly, were this the real translation, nothing could be more just; for he who loves will love truth not less than men. He will rejoice in the truth—rejoice not in what he has been taught to believe; not in this church's doctrine or in that; not in this ism or in that ism; but *"in the truth."* He will accept only what is real; he will strive to get at facts; he will search for truth with a humble and unbiased mind, and cherish whatever he finds at any sacrifice. But the more literal translation of the Revised Version calls for just such a sacrifice for truth's sake here. For what Paul really meant is, as we there read, "Rejoiceth not in unrighteousness, but rejoiceth with the truth," a quality which probably no one English word—and certainly not "sincerity"—adequately defines. It includes, perhaps more strictly, the self-restraint which refuses to make capital out of others' faults; the charity which delights not in exposing the weakness of others, but "covereth all things"; the sincerity of purpose which endeavors to see things as they are, and rejoices to find them better than suspicion feared or calumny denounced.

So much for the analysis of love. Now the business of our lives is to have these things fitted into our characters. That is the supreme work to which we need to address ourselves in this world, to learn love. Is life not full of opportunities for learning love? Every man and woman every day has a thousand of them. The world is not a playground; it is a schoolroom. Life is not a holiday, but an education. And the one eternal lesson for us all is *how better we can love.*

What makes a man a good cricketer? Practice. What makes a man a good artist, a good sculptor, a good musician? Practice. What makes a man a good linguist, a good stenographer? Practice. What makes a man a good man? Practice. Nothing else. There is nothing capricious about religion. We do not get the soul in different ways, under different laws, from those in which we get the body and the mind. If a man does not exercise his arm he develops no biceps muscle; and if a man does not exercise his soul, he acquires no muscle in his soul, no strength of character, no vigor of moral fibre, no beauty of spiritual growth. Love is not a thing of enthusiastic emotion. It is a rich, strong, manly, vigorous expression of the whole round Christian character—the Christlike nature in its fullest development. And the constituents of this great character are only to be built up by ceaseless practice.

What was Christ doing in the carpenter's shop? Practicing. Though perfect, we read that He *learned* obedience, and grew in wisdom and in favor with God. Do not quarrel, therefore, with your lot in life. Do not complain of its never-ceasing cares, its petty environment, the vexations you have to stand, the small and sordid souls you have to live and work with. Above all, do not resent temptation; do not be perplexed because it seems to thicken round you more and more, and ceases neither for effort nor for agony nor prayer. That is your practice. That is the practice which God appoints you; and it is having its work in making you patient, and humble, and generous, and unselfish, and kind, and courteous. Do not grudge the hand that is moulding the still too shapeless image within you. It is growing more beautiful, though you see it not; and every touch of temptation may add to its perfection. Therefore keep in the midst of life. Do not isolate yourself. Be among men and other things, and among troubles, and difficulties, and obstacles. You remember Goethe's words: "Talent develops itself in solitude; character in the stream of life." Talent develops itself in solitude—the talent of prayer, of faith, of meditation, of seeing the unseen; character grows in the stream of the world's life. That chiefly is where the men are to learn love.

How? Now, how? To make it easier, I have named a few of the elements of love. But these are only elements. Love itself can never be defined. Light is a something more than the sum of its ingredients—a glowing, dazzling, tremulous ether. And love is something more than all its elements—a palpitating, quivering, sensitive, living thing. By synthesis of all the colors, men man make whiteness; they cannot make light. By synthesis of all the virtues, men can make virtue; they cannot make love. How then are we to have this transcendent living whole conveyed into our souls? We brace our wills to secure it. We try to copy those who have it. We lay down rules about it. We watch. We pray. But these things alone will not bring love into our nature. Love is an *effect*. And only as we fulfill the right condition can we have the effect produced. Shall I tell you what the *cause* is?

If you turn to the Revised Version of the First Epistle of John you find these words: "We love because he first loved us." "We love," not "We love *him*." That is the way the old version has it, and it is quite wrong. "We *love*—because he first loved us." Look at that word "because." It is the *cause* of which I have spoken. "*Because* he first loved us," the effect follows that we love, we love Him, we love all men. We cannot help it. Because He loved us, we love, we love everybody. Our heart is slowly changed. Contemplate the love of Christ, and you will love. Stand before that mirror, reflect Christ's character, and you will be changed into the same image from tenderness to tenderness. There is no other way. You cannot love to order. You can only look at the lovely object, and fall in love with it, and grow into likeness to it. And so look at this Perfect Character, this Perfect Life. Look at the great sacrifice as He laid down Himself, all through life, and upon the Cross of Calvary; and you must love Him. And loving Him, you most become like Him. Love begets love. It is a process of induction. Put a piece of iron in the presence of an electrified body, and that piece of iron for a time becomes electrified. It is changed into a temporary magnet in the mere presence of a permanent magnet, and as long as you leave the two side by side, they are both magnets alike. Remain side by side with Him who loved us, and gave Himself for us, and you, too will become a permanent magnet, a permanently attractive force; and like Him you draw all men unto you, like Him you will be drawn unto all men. That is the inevitable effect of love. Any man who fulfills that cause must have that effect produced in him.

Try to give up the idea that religion comes to us by chance, or by mystery, or by caprice. It comes to us by natural law, or by supernatural law, for all law is Divine.

Edward Irving went to see a dying boy once, and when he entered the room he just put his hand on the sufferer's head, and said, "My boy, God loves you," and went away. The boy started from his bed, and called out to the people in the house,

"God loves me! God loves me!"

One word! It changed that boy. The sense that God loved him overpowered him, melted him down, and began the creating of a new heart in him. And that is how the love of God melts down the unlovely heart in man and begets in him the new creature, who is patient and humble and gentle and unselfish. And there is no other way to get it. There is no mystery about it. We love others, we love everybody, we love enemies, *because He first loved us.*

THE DEFENSE

Now I have a closing sentence or two to add about Paul's reason for singling out love as the supreme possession.

It is a very remarkable reason. In a single word it is this: *it lasts*. "Love," urges Paul, "never faileth." Then he begins again one of his marvelous lists of the great things of the day, and exposes them one by one. He runs over the things that men thought were going to last, and shows that they are all fleeting, temporary, passing away.

"Whether there be *prophecies*, they shall be done away." It was the mother's ambition for her boy in those days that he should become a prophet. For hundreds of years God had never spoken by means of any prophet, and at that time the prophet was greater than the king. Men waited wistfully for another messenger to come, and hung upon his lips when he appeared, as upon the very voice of God, Paul says, "Whether there be prophecies, they shall fail." The Bible is full of prophecies. One by one they have "failed"; that is, having been fulfilled, their work is finished; they have nothing more to do now in the world except to feed a devout man's faith.

Then Paul talks about *tongues*. That was another thing that was greatly coveted. "Whether there be tongues, they shall cease." As we all know, many, many centuries have passed since tongues have been known in this world. They have ceased. Take it in any sense you like. Take it, for illustration merely, as languages in general—a sense which was not in Paul's mind at all, and which though it cannot give us the specific lesson, will point the general truth. Consider the words in which these chapters were written—Greek. It has gone. Take the Latin, the other great tongue of those days. It ceased long ago. Look at the Indian language. It is ceasing. The language of Wales, of Ireland, of the Scottish Highlands is dying before our eyes. The most popular book in the English tongue at the present time, except the Bible, is one of Dickens' works, his *Pickwick Papers*. It is largely written in the language of London street-life; and experts assure us that in fifty years it will be unintelligible to the average English reader. [The author was writing before the advent of the twentieth century.]

Then Paul goes farther, and with even greater boldness adds, "Whether there be *knowledge*, it shall be done away." The wisdom of the ancients, where is it? It is wholly gone. A schoolboy today knows more than Sir Isaac Newton knew; his knowledge has vanished away. You put yesterday's newspaper in the fire: its knowledge has vanished away. You buy the old editions of the great encyclopedias for a few cents: their knowledge has vanished away. Look how the coach has been superseded by the use of steam. Look how electricity has superseded that, and swept a hundred almost new inventions into oblivion. "Whether there be knowledge, it shall vanish away." At every workshop you will see, in the back yard, a heap of old iron, a few wheels, a few levers, a few cranks, broken and eaten with rust. Twenty years ago that was the pride of the city. Men flocked in from the country to see the great invention; now it is superseded, its day is done. And all the boasted science and philosophy of this day will soon be old.

In my time, in the university of Edinburgh, the greatest figure in the faculty was Sir James Simpson, the discoverer of chloroform. Recently his successor and nephew, Professor Simpson, was asked by the librarian of the university to go to the library and pick out the books on his subject (midwifery) that were no longer needed. His reply to the librarian was this:

"Take every textbook that is more than ten years old and put it down in the cellar."

Sir James Simpson was a great authority only a few years

ago: men came from all parts of the earth to consult him; and almost the whole teaching of that time is consigned by the science of today to oblivion. And in every branch of science it is the same. "Now we know in part. We see through a glass darkly." Knowledge does not last.

Can you tell me anything that is going to last? Many things Paul did not condescend to name. He did not mention money, fortune, fame; but he picked out the great things of his time, the things the best men thought had something in them, and brushed them peremptorily aside. Paul had no charge against these things in themselves. All he said about them was that they would not last. They were great things, but not supreme things. There were things beyond them. What we are stretches past what we do, beyond what we possess. Many things that men denounce as sins are not sins; but they are temporary. And that is a favorite argument of the New Testament. John says of the world, not that it is wrong, but simply that it "passeth away." There is a great deal in the world that is delightful and beautiful; there is a great deal in it that is great and engrossing; but it will not last. All that is in the world, the lust of the eye, the lust of the flesh, and the pride of life, are but for a little while. Love not the world therefore. Nothing that it contains is worth the life and consecration of an immortal soul. The immortal soul must give itself to something that is immortal. And the only immortal things are these: "Now abideth faith, hope, love, but the greatest of these is love."

Some think the time may come when two of these three things will also pass away—faith into sight, hope into fruition. Paul does not say so. We know but little now about the conditions of the life that is to come. But what is certain is that love must last. God, the Eternal God, is love. Covet, therefore, that everlasting gift, that one thing which it is certain is going to stand, that one coinage which will be current in the universe when all the other coinages of all the nations of the world shall be useless and unhonored. You will give yourselves to many things; give yourself first to love. Hold things in their proportion. *Hold things in their proportion.* Let at least the first great object of our lives be to achieve the character defended in these words, the character—and it is the character of Christ—which is built around love.

I have said this thing is eternal. Did you ever notice how continually John associates love and faith with eternal life? I

was not told when I was a boy that "God so
that he gave his only-begotten Son, that whos
in him should have everlasting life." What
remember, was, that God so loved the world that,
in Him, I was to have a thing called peace, or I w   nave
rest, or I was to have joy, or I was to have safety. But I had
to find out for myself that whosoever trusteth in Him—that
is, whosoever loveth Him, for trust is only the avenue to
love—hath everlasting life. The gospel offers a man a life.
Never offer men a thimbleful of gospel. Do not offer them
merely joy or merely peace, or merely rest, or merely safety;
tell them how Christ came to give men a more abundant life
than they have, a life abundant in love, and therefore abundant in salvation for themselves, and large in enterprise for
the alleviation and redemption of the world. Then only can
the gospel take hold of the whole of a man, body, soul and
spirit, and give to each part of his nature its exercise and reward. Many of the current gospels are addressed only to a
part of man's nature. They offer peace, not life; faith, not
love; justification, not regeneration. And men slip back again
from such religion because it has never really held them.
Their nature was not all in it. It offered no deeper and glad-
der life-current than the life that was lived before. Surely it
stands to reason that only a fuller love can compete with the
love of the world.

To love abundantly is to live abundantly, and to love forever is to live forever. Hence, eternal life is inextricably
bound up with love. We want to live forever for the same
reason that we want to live tomorrow. Why do we want to
live tomorrow? Is it because there is someone who loves you,
and whom you want to see tomorrow, and be with, and love
back? There is no other reason why we should live on than
that we love and are beloved. It is when a man has no one to
love him that he commits suicide. So long as he has friends,
those who love him and whom he loves, he will live, because
to live is to love. Be it but the love of a dog, it will keep him
in life; but let that go, he has no contact with life, no reason
to live. He dies by his own hand.

Eternal life also is to know God, and God is love. This is
Christ's own definition. Ponder it. "This is life eternal, that
they might know thee the only true God, and Jesus Christ
whom thou has sent." Love must be eternal. It is what God
is. On the last analysis, then, love is life. Love never faileth,

life never faileth, so long as there is love. That is the philosophy of what Paul is showing us; the reason why in the nature of things love should be the supreme thing—because it is going to last; because in the nature of things it is an eternal life. It is a thing that we are living now, not that we get when we die; that we shall have a poor chance of getting when we die unless we are living now. No worse fate can befall a man in this world than to live and grow old alone, unloving and unloved. To be lost is to live in an unregenerate condition, loveless and unloved; and to be saved is to love; and he that dwelleth in love dwelleth already in God. For God is love.

Now I have all but finished. How many of you will join me in reading this chapter once a week for the next three months? A man did that once and it changed his whole life. Will you do it? It is for the greatest thing in the world. You might begin by reading it every day, especially the verses which describe the perfect character. "Love suffereth long, and is kind; love envieth not; love vaunteth not itself." Get these ingredients into your life. Then everything that you do is eternal. It is worth doing. It is worth giving time to. No man can become a saint in his sleep; and to fulfill the condition required demands a certain amount of prayer and meditation and time, just as improvement in any direction, bodily or mental, requires preparation and care. Address yourselves to that one thing; at any cost have this transcendent character exchanged for yours.

You will find as you look back upon your life that the moments that stand out, the moments when you have really lived, are the moments when you have done things in a spirit of love. As memory scans the past, above and beyond all the transitory pleasures of life, there leap forward those supreme hours when you have been enabled to do unnoticed kindnesses to those round about you, things too trifling to speak about, but which you feel have entered into your eternal life. I have seen almost all the beautiful things God has made; I have enjoyed almost every pleasure that He has planned for man; and yet as I look back I see standing out above all the life that has gone, four or five short experiences when the love of God reflected itself in some poor imitation, some small act of love of mine, and these seem to be the things which alone of all one's life abide. Everything else in all our lives is transitory. Every other good is visionary. But the acts of love which no man knows about, or can ever know about—they never fail.

In the Book of Matthew, where the Judgment Day is depicted for us in the imagery of One seated upon a throne and dividing the sheep from the goats, the test of a man then is not, "How have I believed?" but "How have I loved?" The test of religion, the final test of religion, is not religiousness, but love. I say the final test of religion at that great Day is not religiousness, but love; not what I have done, not what I have believed, not what I have achieved, but how I have discharged the common charities of life. Sins of commission in that awful indictment are not even referred to. By what we have not done, *by sins of omission*, we are judged. It could not be otherwise. For the withholding of love is the negation of the Spirit of Christ, the proof that we never knew Him, that for us He lived in vain. It means that He suggested nothing in all our thoughts, that He inspired nothing in all our lives, that we were not once near enough to Him to be seized with the spell of His compassion for the world. It means that—

> I lived for myself, I thought for myself,
> For myself, and none beside—
> Just as if Jesus had never lived,
> As if He had never died.

Thank God the Christianity of today is coming nearer the world's need. Live to help that on. Thank God men know better, by a hair's breadth, what religion is, what God is, who Christ is, where Christ is. Who is Christ? He who fed the hungry, clothed the naked, visited the sick. And where is Christ? Where? "Whoso shall receive a little child in my name receiveth me." And who are Christ's? "Every one that loveth is born of God."

II

ACRES
OF DIAMONDS

RUSSELL CONWELL

ABOUT
THE AUTHOR

Russell Conwell (1843-1925) was 19 and a student at Yale when the Civil War began. To help the Union cause, he returned home to Berkshire, Massachusetts, where he joined a group of volunteers in training for service. It was a move which was to change his entire life.

During a battle late in the war, a company commanded by Conwell was taken by surprise by the Confederates. Fleeing across a bridge, Conwell found himself with neither gun nor sword. His orderly, a frail teenager named Johnny Ring, impetuously ran back to get his commander's sword. By the time the boy returned, the bridge was ablaze but he courageously fought his way across, arriving on the other side afire himself. Two hours later just before he died he told Conwell that he was not afraid of death because of his Christian faith. Conwell, an avowed atheist, was so deeply moved that he became a Christian and pledged himself to a life of 16 hours-a-day work—eight for himself, eight for Johnny.

He kept his word, eventually leaving a Boston law practice to go into the ministry. After serving a church in Lexington, he accepted a call to a rundown parish in Philadelphia. He was to see the church, Temple Baptist, become one of the largest, best known in the country. While ministering at Temple Baptist Church he founded Temple University and later Samaritan Hospital. To raise money to support the school, Conwell delivered over 200 speeches a year, most on the subject of succeeding where you are with what you have at hand. He told his audiences, "You have riches in your own backyard," and he called the speech "Acres of Diamonds."

ACRES
OF DIAMONDS

When going down the Tigris and Euphrates rivers many years ago with a party of English travelers I found myself under the direction of an old Arab guide whom we hired up at Bagdad, and I have often thought how that guide resembled our barbers in certain mental characteristics. He thought that it was not only his duty to guide us down those rivers, and do what he was paid for doing, but also to entertain us with stories curious and weird, ancient and modern, strange and familiar. Many of them I have forgotten, and I am glad I have, but there is one I shall never forget.

The old guide was leading my camel by its halter along the banks of those ancient rivers, and he told me story after story until I grew weary of his story-telling and ceased to listen. I have never been irritated with that guide when he lost his temper as I ceased listening. But I remember that he took off his Turkish cap and swung it in a circle to get my attention. I could see it through the corner of my eye, but I determined not to look straight at him for fear he would tell another story. But although I am not a woman, I did finally look, and as soon as I did he went right into another story.

Said he, "I will tell you a story now which I reserve for my particular friends." When he emphasized the words "particular friends," I listened, and I have ever been glad I did. I really feel devoutly thankful that there are 1,674 young men who have been carried through college by this lecture who are also glad that I did listen. The old guide told me that there once lived not far from the River Indus an ancient Persian by the name of Ali Hafed. He said that Ali Hafed owned a very large farm, that he had orchards, grainfields, and gardens; that he had money at interest, and was a wealthy and contented man. He was contented because he was wealthy, and wealthy because he was contented. One day there visited the old Persian farmer one of those ancient Buddhist priests, one of the wise men of the East. He sat down by the fire and told the old farmer how this world of ours was made. He said that this world was once a mere bank of fog, and that the Almighty thrust His finger into this bank of fog, and began slowly to move His finger around, increasing the speed until at last He whirled this bank of fog into a solid ball of fire. Then it went rolling through the universe, burning its way through other banks of fog, and condensed the moisture without, until it fell in floods of rain upon its hot surface, and cooled the outward crust. Then the internal fires bursting outward through the crust threw up the mountains and hills, the valleys, the plains and prairies of this wonderful world of ours. If this internal molten mass came bursting out and cooled very quickly it became granite; less quickly copper, less quickly silver, less quickly gold, and, after gold, diamonds were made.

Said the old priest, "A diamond is a congealed drop of sunlight." Now that is literally scientifically true, that a diamond is an actual deposit of carbon from the sun. The old priest told Ali Hafed that if he had one diamond the size of his thumb he could purchase the county, and if he had a mine of diamonds he could place his children upon thrones through the influence of their great wealth.

Ali Hafed heard all about diamonds, how much they were worth, and went to bed that night a poor man. He had not lost anything, but he was poor because he was discontented, and discontented because he feared he was poor. He said, "I want a mine of diamonds," and he lay awake all night.

Early in the morning he sought out the priest. I know by experience that a priest is very cross when awakened early in the morning, and when he shook that old priest out of his dreams, Ali Hafed said to him:

"Will you tell me where I can find diamonds?"

"Diamonds! What do you want with diamonds?" "Why, I wish to be immensely rich." "Well, then, go along and find them. That is all you have to do; go and find them, and then you have them." "But I don't know where to go." "Well, if you will find a river that runs through white sands, between high mountains, in those white sands you will always find diamonds." "I don't believe there is such river." "Oh yes, there are plenty of them. All you have to do is to go and find them, and then you have them." Said Ali Hafed, "I will go."

So he sold his farm, collected his money, left his family in charge of a neighbor, and away he went in search of diamonds. He began his search, very properly to my mind, at the Mountains of the Moon. Afterward he came around into Palestine, then wandered on into Europe, and at last when his money was all spent and he was in rags, wretchedness, and poverty, he stood on the shore of that bay at Barcelona, in Spain, when a great tidal wave came rolling in between the pillars of Hercules, and the poor, afflicted, suffering, dying man could not resist the awful temptation to cast himself into that incoming tide, and he sank beneath its foaming crest, never to rise in this life again.

When that old guide had told me that awfully sad story he stopped the camel I was riding on and went back to fix the baggage that was coming off another camel, and I had an opportunity to muse over his story while he was gone. I remember saying to myself, "Why did he reserve that story for his 'particular friends'?" There seemed to be no beginning, no middle, no end, nothing to it. That was the first story I had ever heard told in my life, and would be the first one I ever read, in which the hero was killed in the first chapter. I had but one chapter of that story, and the hero was dead.

When the guide came back and took up the halter of my camel, he went right ahead with the story, into the second chapter, just as though there had been no break. The man who purchased Ali Hafed's farm one day led his camel into the garden to drink, and as that camel put its nose into the shallow water of that garden brook, Ali Hafed's successor noticed a curious flash of light from the white sands of the stream. He pulled out a black stone having an eye of light reflecting all the hues of the rainbow. He took the pebble into the house and put it on the mantel which covers the central fires, and forgot all about it.

A few days later this same old priest came in to visit Ali

Hafed's successor, and the moment he opened that drawing-room door he saw that flash of light on the mantel, and he rushed up to it, and shouted: "Here is a diamond! Has Ali Hafed returned?" "Oh no, Ali Hafed has not returned, and that is not a diamond. That is nothing but a stone we found right out here in our own garden." "But," said the priest, "I tell you I know a diamond when I see it. I know positively that is a diamond."

Then together they rushed out into that old garden and stirred up the white sands with their fingers, and lo! there came up other more beautiful and valuable gems than the first. "Thus," said the guide to me, and, friends, it is historically true, "was discovered the diamond mine of Golconda, the most magnificent diamond mine in all the history of mankind, excelling the Kimberly itself. The Kohinoor, and the Orloff of the crown jewels of England and Russia, the largest on earth, came from that mine."

When that old Arab guide told me the second chapter of his story, he then took off his Turkish cap and swung it around in the air again to get my attention to the moral. Those Arab guides have morals to their stories, although they are not always moral. As he swung his hat, he said to me, "Had Ali Hafed remained at home and dug in his own cellar, or underneath his own wheat fields, or in his own garden, instead of wretchedness, starvation, and death by suicide in a strange land, he would have had 'acres of diamonds.' For every acre of that old farm, yes, every shovelful, afterward revealed gems which since have decorated the crowns of monarchs."

When he had added the moral to his story I saw why he reserved it for "his particular friends." But I did not tell him I could see it. It was that mean old Arab's way of going around a thing like a lawyer, to say indirectly what he did not dare say directly, that "in his private opinion there was a certain young man then traveling down the Tigris River that might better be at home in America." I did not tell him I could see that, but I told him his story reminded me of one, and I told it to him quickly, and I think I will tell it to you.

I told him of a man out in California in 1847, who owned a ranch. He heard they had discovered gold in southern California, and so with a passion for gold he sold his ranch to Colonel Sutter, and away he went, never to come back. Colonel Sutter put a mill upon a stream that ran through that ranch, and one day his little girl brought some wet sand from the raceway into their home and sifted it through her fingers before the fire, and in that falling sand a visitor saw the first shining scales of real gold that were ever discovered in California. The man who had owned that ranch wanted gold, and he could have secured it for the mere taking. Indeed, thirty-eight millions of dollars have been taken out of a very few acres since then. About eight years ago I delivered this lecture in a city that stands on that farm, and they told me that a one-third owner for years and years had been getting one hundred and twenty dollars in gold every fifteen minutes, sleeping or waking, without taxation. You and I would enjoy an income like that—if we didn't have to pay an income tax.

But a better illustration really than that occurred here in our own Pennsylvania. If there is anything I enjoy above another on the platform, it is to get one of these German audiences in Pennsylvania before me, and fire that at them, and I enjoy it tonight. There was a man living in Pennsylvania, not unlike some Pennsylvanians you have seen, who owned a farm, and he did with that farm just what I should do with a farm if I owned one in Pennsylvania—he sold it. But before he sold it he decided to secure employment collecting coal oil for his cousin, who was in business in Canada, where they first discovered oil on this continent. They dipped it from the running streams at that early time. So this Pennsylvania farmer wrote to his cousin asking for employment. You see, friends, this farmer was not altogether a foolish man. No, he was not. He did not leave his farm until he had something else to do. *Of all the simpletons the stars shine on I don't know of a worse one than the man who leaves one job before he has gotten another.* That has especial reference to my profession, and has no reference whatever to a man seeking a divorce. When he wrote to his cousin for employment, his cousin replied, "I cannot engage you because you know nothing about the oil business."

Well, then the old farmer said, "I will know," and with most commendable zeal (characteristic of the students of Temple University) he set himself at the study of the whole subject. He began away back at the second day of God's creation when this world was covered thick and deep with that rich vegetation which since has turned to the primitive beds of coal. He studied the subject until he found that the drainings really of those rich beds of coal furnished the coal that was worth pumping, and then he found how it came up with the living springs. He studied until he knew what it looked like, smelled like, tasted like, and how to refine it. Now said he in his letter to his cousin, "I understand the oil business." His cousin answered, "All right, come on."

So he sold his farm, according to the county record, for $833 (even money, "no cents"). He had scarcely gone from that place before the man who purchased the spot went out to arrange for the watering of the cattle. He found the previous owner had gone out years before and put a plank across the brook back of the barn, edgewise into the surface of the water just a few inches. The purpose of that plank at that sharp angle across the brook was to throw over to the other bank a dreadful-looking scum through which the cattle would not put their noses. But with that plank there to throw it all over to one side, the cattle would drink below, and thus that man who had gone to Canada had been himself damming back for twenty-three years a flood of coal oil which the state geologists of Pennsylvania declared to us ten years later was even then worth a hundred millions of dollars to our state, and four years ago our geologist declared the discovery to be worth to our state a thousand millions of dollars. The man who owned that territory on which the city of Titusville now stands, and those Pleasantville valleys, had studied the subject from the second day of God's creation clear down to the present time. He studied it until he knew all about it, and yet he is said to have sold the whole of it for $833, and again I say, "no sense."

But I need another illustration. I found it in Massachusetts, and I am sorry I did because that is the state I came from. This young man in Massachusetts furnishes just another phase of my thought. He went to Yale College and studied mines and mining, and became such an adept as a mining engineer that he was employed by the authorities of the university to train students who were behind their classes. During his senior year he earned $15 a week for doing that work. When he graduated they raised his pay from $15 to $45 a week, and offered him a professorship, and as soon as they did he went home to his mother. *If they had raised that boy's pay from $15 to $15.60 he would have stayed and been proud of the place, but when they put it up to $45 at one leap, he said, "Mother, I won't work for $45 a week. The idea of a man with a brain like mine working for $45 a* *week!* Let's go out in California and stake out gold mines and silver mines, and be immensely rich."

Said his mother, "Now, Charlie, it is just as well to be happy as it is to be rich."

"Yes," said Charlie, "but it is just as well to be rich and happy, too." And they were both right about it. As he was an only son and she a widow, of course he had his way. They always do.

They sold out in Massachusetts, and instead of going to California they went to Wisconsin, where he went into the employ of the Superior Copper Mining Company at $15 a week again, but with the proviso in his contract that he should have an interest in any mines he should discover for the company. I don't believe he ever discovered a mine, and if I am looking in the face of any stockholder of that copper company, you wish he had discovered something or other. I have friends who are not here because they could not afford a ticket, who did have stock in that company at the time this young man was employed there. This young man went out there, and I have not heard a word from him. I don't know what became of him, and I don't know whether he found any mines or not, but I don't believe he ever did.

But I do know the other end of the line. He had scarcely gotten out of the old homestead before the succeeding owner went out to dig potatoes. The potatoes were already growing in the ground when he bought the farm, and as the old farmer was bringing in a basket of potatoes it hugged very tight between the ends of the stone fence. You know in Massachusetts our farms are nearly all stone wall. There you are obliged to be very economical of front gateways in order to have some place to put the stone. When that basket hugged so tight he set it down on the ground, and then dragged on one side, and pulled on the other side, and as he was dragging that basket through this farmer noticed in the upper and outer corner of that stone wall right next the gate, a block of native silver eight inches square. That professor of mines, mining, and mineralogy, who knew so much about the subject that he would not work for $45 a week, when he sold that homestead in Massachusetts sat right on that silver to make the bargain. He was born on that homestead, was brought up there, and had gone back and forth rubbing the stone with his sleeve until it reflected his countenance, and seemed to say, "Here is a hundred thousand dollars right down here just for the taking." But he would not take it. It was in a home in Newburyport, Massachusetts, and there was no silver there, all away off—well, I don't know where, and he did not, but somewhere else, and he was a professor of mineralogy.

My friend, that mistake is very universally made, and why should we even smile at him. I often wonder what has become of him. I do not know at all, but I will tell you what I "guess" as a Yankee. I guess that he sits out there by his fireside tonight with his friends gathered around him, and he is saying to them something like this: "Do you know that man Conwell who lives in Philadelphia?" "Oh yes, I have heard of him." "Do you know that man Jones who lives in Philadelphia?" "Yes, I have heard of him, too."

Then he begins to laugh, and shakes his sides, and says to his friends, "Well, they have done just the same thing I did, precisely"—and that spoils the whole joke, for you and I have done the same thing he did, and while we sit here and laugh at him he has a better right to sit out there and laugh at us. I know I have made the same mistakes, but, of course, that does not make any difference, because we don't expect the same man to preach and practice, too.

As I come here tonight and look around this audience I am seeing again what through these fifty years I have continually seen—men that are making precisely that same mistake. I often wish I could see the younger people, and would that the Academy had been filled tonight with our high-school scholars and our grammar-school scolars, that I could have them to talk to. While I would have preferred such an audience as that, because they are most susceptible, as they have not grown up into their prejudices as we have, they have not gotten into any custom that they cannot break, they have not met with any failures as we have; and while I could perhaps do such an audience as that more good than I can do grown-up people, yet I will do the best I can with the material I have. I say to you that you have "acres of diamonds" in Philadelphia right where you now live. "Oh," but you will say, "you cannot know much about your city if you think there are any 'acres of diamonds' here."

I was greatly interested in that account in the newspaper of the young man who found that diamond in North Carolina. It was one of the purest diamonds that has ever been discovered, and it has several predecessors near the same locality. I went to a distinguished professor in mineralogy and asked him where he thought those diamonds came from. The professor secured the map of the geologic formations of our continent, and traced it. He said it went either through the underlying carboniferous strata adapted for such production, westward through Ohio and the Mississippi, or in more probability came eastward through Virginia and up the shore of the Atlantic Ocean. It is a fact that the diamonds were there, for they have been discovered and sold; and that they were carried down there during the drift period, from some northern locality. Now who can say but some person going down with his drill in Philadelphia will find some trace of a diamond mine yet down here? Oh, friends! you cannot say that you are not over one of the greatest diamond mines in the world, for such a diamond as that only comes from the most profitable mines that are found on earth.

But it serves simply to illustrate my thought, which I emphasize by saying if you do not have the actual diamond mines literally you have all that they would be good for to you. Because now that the Queen of England has given the greatest compliment ever conferred upon American woman for her attire because she did not appear with any jewels at all at the late reception in England, it has almost done away with the use of diamonds anyhow. All you would care for would be the few you would wear if you wish to be modest, and the rest you would sell for money.

Now then, I say again that the opportunity to get rich, to attain unto great wealth, is here in Philadelphia now, within the reach of almost every man and woman who hears me speak tonight, and I mean just what I say. I have not come to this platform even under these circumstances to recite something to you. I have come to tell you what in God's sight I believe to be the truth, and if the years of life have been of any value to me in the attainment of common sense, I know I am right; that the men and women sitting here, who found it difficult perhaps to buy a ticket to this lecture or gathering tonight, have within their reach "acres of diamonds," opportunities to get largely wealthy. There never was a place on earth more adapted than the city of Philadelphia today, and never in the history of the world did a poor man without capital have such an opportunity to get rich quickly and honestly as he has now in our city. I say it is the truth, and I want you to accept it as such; for if you think I have come to simply recite something, then I would better not be here. I have no time to waste in any such talk, but to say the things I believe, and unless some of you get richer for what I am saying tonight my time is wasted.

I say that you ought to get rich, and it is your duty to get rich. How many of my pious brethren say to me, "Do you, a Christian minister, spend your time going up and down the country advising young people to get rich, to get money?" "Yes, of course I do." They say, "Isn't that awful! Why don't you preach the gospel instead of preaching about man's making money?" "Because to make money honestly is to preach the gospel." That is the reason. The men who get rich may be the most honest men you find in the community.

"Oh," but says some young man here tonight, "I have been told all my life that if a person has money he is very dishonest and dishonorable and mean and contemptible." My friend, that is the reason why you have none, because you have that idea of people. The foundation of your faith is altogether false. Let me say here clearly, and say it briefly, though subject to discussion which I have not time for here, ninety-eight out of one hundred of the rich men of America are honest. That is why they are rich. That is why they are trusted with money. That is why they carry on great enterprises and find plenty of people to work with them. It is because they are honest men.

Says another young man, "I hear sometimes of men that get millions of dollars dishonestly." Yes, of course you do, and so do I. But they are so rare a thing in fact that the newspapers talk about them all the time as a matter of news until you get the idea that all the other rich men got rich dishonestly.

My friend, you take and drive me—if you furnish the auto—out into the suburbs of Philadelphia, and introduce me to the people who own their homes around this great city, those beautiful homes with gardens and flowers, those magnificent homes so lovely in their art, and I will introduce you to the very best people in character as well as in enterprise in our city, and you know I will. A man is not really a true man until he owns his own home, and they that own their homes are made more honorable and honest and pure, and true and economical and careful, by owning the home.

For a man to have money, even in large sums, is not an inconsistent thing. We preach against covetousness, and you know we do, in the pulpit, and oftentimes preach against it so long and use the terms about "filthy lucre" so extremely that Christians get the idea that when we stand in the pulpit we believe it is wicked for any man to have money—until the collection basket goes around, and then we almost swear at the people because they don't give more money. Oh, the inconsistency of such doctrines as that!

Money is power, and you ought to be reasonably ambitious to have it. You ought because you can do more good with it than you could without it. Money printed your Bible, money builds your churches, money sends your missionaries, and money pays your preachers, and you would not have many of them, either, if you did not pay them. I am always willing that my church should raise my salary, because the church that pays the largest salary always raises it the easiest. You never knew an exception to it in your life. The man who gets the largest salary can do the most good with the power that is furnished to him. Of course he can if his spirit is right to use it for what it is given to him.

I say, then, you ought to have money. If you can honestly attain unto riches in Philadelphia, it is your Christian and godly duty to do so. It is an awful mistake of these pious people to think you must be awfully poor in order to be pious.

Some men say, "Don't you sympathize with the poor people?" Of course I do, or else I would not have been lecturing these years. I won't give in but what I sympathize with the poor, but the number of poor who are to be sympathized with is very small. To sympathize with a man whom God has punished for his sins, thus to help him when God would still continue a just punishment, is to do wrong, no doubt about it, and we do that more than we help those who are deserving. While we would sympathize with God's poor—that is, those who cannot help themselves—let us remember there is not a poor person in the United States who was not made poor by his own shortcomings, or by the shortcomings of someone else. It is all wrong to be poor, anyhow. Let us give in to that argument and pass that to one side.

A gentleman gets up back there, and says, "Don't you think there are some things in this world that are better than money?" Of course I do, but I am talking about money now. Of course there are some things higher than money. Oh yes, I know by the grave that has left me standing alone that there are some things in this world that are higher and sweeter and purer than money. Well do I know there are some things higher and grander than gold. Love is the grandest thing on God's earth, but fortunate the lover who has plenty of money. Money is power, money is force, money will do good as well as harm. In the hands of good men and women it could accomplish, and it has accomplished, good.

I hate to leave that behind me. I heard a man get up in a prayer-meeting in our city and thank the Lord he was "one of God's poor." Well, I wonder what his wife thinks about that? She earns all the money that comes into that house, and he smokes a part of that on the veranda. I don't want to see any more of the Lord's poor of that kind, and I don't believe the Lord does. And yet there are some people who think in order to be pious you must be awfully poor and awfully dirty. That does not follow at all. While we sympathize with the poor, let us not teach a doctrine like that.

Yet the age is prejudiced against advising a Christian man (or, as a Jew would say, a godly man) from attaining unto wealth. The prejudice is so universal and the years are far enough back, I think, for me to safely mention that years ago at Temple University there was a young man in our theological school who thought he was the only pious student in that department. He came into my office one evening and sat down by my desk, and said to me: "Mr. President, I think it is my duty sir, to come in and labor with you." "What has happened now?" Said he, "I heard you say at the Academy, at the Peirce School commencement, that you thought it was an honorable ambition for a young man to desire to have wealth, and that you thought it made him temperate, made him anxious to have a good name, and made him industrious. You spoke about man's ambition to have money helping to make him a good man. Sir, I have come to tell you the Holy Bible says that 'money is the root of all evil.'"

I told him I had never seen it in the Bible, and advised him to go out into the chapel and get the Bible, and show me the place. So out he went for the Bible, and soon he stalked into my office with the Bible open, with all the bigoted pride of the narrow sectarian, or of one who founds his Christianity on some misinterpretation of Scripture. He flung the Bible down on my desk, and fairly squealed into my ear: "There it is, Mr. President; you can read it for yourself." I said to him: "Well, young man, you will learn when you get a little older that you cannot trust another denomination to read the Bible for you. You belong to another denomination. You are taught in the theological school, however, that emphasis is exegesis. Now, will you take that Bible and read it yourself, and give the proper emphasis to it?"

He took the Bible, and proudly read, " 'The love of money is the root of all evil.' "

Then he had it right, and when one does quote aright from that same old Book he quotes the absolute truth. I have lived through fifty years of the mightiest battle that old Book has ever fought, and I have lived to see its banners flying free; for never in the history of this world did the great minds of earth so universally agree that the Bible is true—all true—as they do at this very hour.

So I say that when he quoted right, of course he quoted the absolute truth. "The love of money is the root of all evil." He who tried to attain unto it too quickly, or dishonestly, will fall into many snares, no doubt about that. The love of money. What is that? It is making an idol of money, and idolatry pure and simple everywhere is condemned by the Holy Scriptures and by man's common sense. The man that worships the dollar instead of thinking of the purposes for which it ought to be used, the man who idolizes simply money, the miser that hordes his money in the cellar, or hides it in his stocking, or refuses to invest it where it will do the world good, that man who hugs the dollar until the eagle squeals has in him the root of all evil.

I think I will leave that behind me now and answer the question of nearly all of you who are asking, "Is there opportunity to get rich in Philadelphia?" Well, now, how simple a thing it is to see where it is, and the instant you see where it is it is yours. Some old gentleman gets up back there and says, "Mr. Conwell, have you lived in Philadelphia for thirty-one years and don't know that the time has gone by when you can make anything in this city?" "No, I don't think it is." "Yes, it is; I have tried it." "What business are you in?" "I kept a store here for twenty years, and never made over a thousand dollars in the whole twenty years."

"Well, then, you can measure the good you have been to this city by what this city has paid you, because a man can judge very well what he is worth by what he receives; that is, in what he is to the world at this time. If you have not made a thousand dollars in twenty years in Philadelphia, it would

have been better for Philadelphia if they had kicked you out
of the city nineteen years and nine months ago. A man has
no right to keep a store in Philadelphia twenty years and not
make at least five hundred thousand dollars, even though it
be a corner grocery uptown." You say, "You cannot make
five thousand dollars in a store now." Oh, my friends, if you
will just take only four blocks around you, and find out what
the people want and what you ought to supply and set them
down with your pencil, and figure up the profits you would
make if you did supply them, you would very soon see it.
There is wealth right within the sound of your voice.

Someone says: "You don't know anything about business.
A preacher never knows a thing about business." Well, then,
I will have to prove that I am an expert. I don't like to do
this, but I have to do it because my testimony will not be
taken if I am not an expert. My father kept a country store,
and if there is any place under the stars where a man gets all
sorts of experience in every kind of mercantile transactions, it
is in the country store. I am not proud of my experience, but
sometimes when my father was away he would leave me in
charge of the store, though fortunately for him that was not
very often. But this did occur many times, friends: A man
would come in the store and say to me, "Do you keep jackknives?" "No, we don't keep jackknives," and I went off
whistling a tune. What did I care about that man, anyhow?
Then another farmer would come in and say, "Do you keep
jackknives?" "No, we don't keep jackknives." Then I went
away and whistled another tune. Then a third man came
right in the same door and said, "Do you keep jackknives?"
"No. Why is everyone around here asking for jackknives? Do
you suppose we are keeping this store to supply the whole
neighborhood with jackknives?" Do you carry on your store
like that in Philadelphia?" The difficulty was I had not then
learned that the foundation of godliness and the foundation
principle of success in business are both the same precisely.
The man who says, "I cannot carry my religion into business"
advertises himself either as being an imbecile in business, or
on the road to bankruptcy, or a thief, one of the three, sure.
He will fail within a very few years. He certainly will if he
doesn't carry his religion into business. If I had been carrying
on my father's store on a Christian plan, godly plan, I would
have had a jackknife for the third man when he called for it.
Then I would have actually done him a kindness, and I

would have received a reward myself, which it would have been my duty to take.

There are some overpious Christian people who think if you take any profit on anything you sell that you are an unrighteous man. On the contrary, you would be a criminal to sell goods for less than they cost. You have no right to do that. You cannot trust a man with your money who cannot take care of his own. You cannot trust a man in your family that is not true to his own wife. You cannot trust a man in the world that does not begin with his own heart, his own character, and his own life. It would have been my duty to have furnished a jackknife to the third man, or the second, and to have sold it to him and actually profited myself. I have no more right to sell goods without making a profit on them than I have to overcharge him dishonestly beyond what they are worth. But I should so sell each bill of goods that the person to whom I sell shall make as much as I make.

To live and let live is the principle of the gospel, and the principle of everyday common sense. Oh, young man, hear me; live as you go along. Do not wait until you have reached my years before you begin to enjoy anything of this life. If I had the millions back, or fifty cents of it, which I have tried to earn in these years, it would not do me anything like the good that it does me now in this almost sacred presence tonight. Oh, yes, I am paid over and over a hundredfold tonight for dividing as I have tried to do in some measure as I went along through the years. I ought not speak that way, it sounds egotistic, but I am old enough now to be excused for that. I should have helped my fellow men, which I have tried to do, and everyone should try to do, and get the happiness of it. The man who goes home with the sense that he has stolen a dollar that day, that he has robbed a man of what was his honest due, is not going to sweet rest. He arises tired in the morning, and goes with an unclean conscience to his work the next day. He is not a successful man at all, although he may have laid up millions. But the man who has gone through life dividing always with his fellow men, making and demanding his own rights and his own profits, and giving to every other man his rights and profits, lives every day, and not only that, but it is the royal road to great wealth. The history of the thousands of millionaires show that to be the case.

The man over there who said he could not make anything

in a store in Philadelphia has been carrying on his store on the wrong principle. Suppose I go into your store tomorrow morning and ask, "Do you know neighbor A, who lives one square away, at house No. 1240?" "Oh yes, I have met him. He deals here at the corner store." "Where did he come from?" "I don't know." "How many does he have in his family?" "I don't know." "What ticket does he vote?" "I don't know." "What church does he go to?" "I don't know, and don't care. What are you asking all these questions for?"

If you had a store in Philadelphia would you answer me like that? If so, then you are conducting your business just as I carried on my father's business in Worthington, Massachusetts. You don't know where your neighbor came from when he moved to Philadelphia, and you don't care. If you had cared you would be a rich man now. If you had cared enough about him to take an interest in his affairs, to find out what he needed, you would have been rich. But you go through the world saying, "No opportunity to get rich," and there is the fault right at your own door.

But another young man gets up over there and says, "I cannot take up the mercantile business." (While I am talking of trade it applies to every occupation.) "Why can't you go into the mercantile business?" "Because I haven't any capital." Oh, the weak and dudish creature that can't see over its collar! It makes a person weak to see these little dudes standing around the corners and saying, "Oh, if I had plenty of capital, how rich I would get." "Young man, do you think you are going to get rich on capital?" "Certainly." Well, I say, "Certainly not." If your mother has plenty of money, and she will set you up in business, you will "set her up in business," supplying you with capital.

The moment a young man or woman gets more money than he or she has grown to by practical experience, that moment he has gotten a curse. It is no help to a young man or woman to inherit money. It is no help to your children to leave them money, but if you leave them education, if you leave them Christian and noble character, if you leave them a wide circle of friends, if you leave them an honorable name, it is far better than that they should have money. It would be worse for them, worse for the nation, that they should have any money at all. Oh, young man, if you have inherited money, don't regard it as a help. It will curse you through your years, and deprive you of the very best things of human life. There is no class of people to be pitied so much as the inexperienced sons and daughters of the rich of our generation. I pity the rich man's son. He can never know the best things in life.

One of the best things in our life is when a young man has earned his own living, and when he becomes engaged to some lovely young woman, and makes up his mind to have a home of his own. Then with that same love comes also that divine inspiration toward better things, and he begins to save his money. He begins to leave off his bad habits and put money in the bank. When he has a few hundred dollars he goes out in the suburbs to look for a home. He goes to the savings bank, perhaps, for half of the value, and then goes for his wife, and when he takes his bride over the threshold of that door for the first time he says in words of eloquence my voice can never touch: "I have earned this home myself. It is all mine, and I divide with thee." That is the grandest moment a human heart may ever know.

But a rich man's son can never know that. He takes his bride into a finer mansion, it may be, but he is obliged to go all the way through it and say to his wife, "My mother gave me that, my mother gave me that, and my mother gave me this," until the wife wishes she had married his mother. I pity the rich man's son.

The statistics of Massachusetts showed that not one rich man's son out of seventeen ever dies rich. I pity the rich man's sons unless they have the good sense of the elder Vanderbilt, which sometimes happens. He went to his father and said, "Did you earn all your money?" "I did, my son. I began to work on a ferryboat for twenty-five cents a day." "Then," said his son, "I will have none of your money," and he, too, tried to get employment on a ferryboat that Saturday night. He could not get one there, but he did get a place for three dollars a week. Of course, if a rich man's son will do that, he will get the discipline of a poor boy that is worth more than a university education to any man. He would then be able to take care of the millions of his father. But as a rule the rich men will not let their sons do the very thing that made them great. As a rule, the rich man will not allow his son to work—and his mother! Why, she would think it was a social disgrace if her poor, weak, little lily-fingered, sissy sort of a boy had to earn his living with honest toil. I have no pity for such rich men's sons.

I remember one at Niagara Falls. I think I remember one a great deal nearer. I think there are gentlemen present who were at a great banquet, and I beg pardon of his friends. At a banquet here in Philadelphia there sat beside me a kind-hearted young man, and he said, "Mr. Conwell, you have been sick for two or three years. When you go out, take my limousine, and it will take you up to your house on Broad Street." I thanked him very much, and perhaps I ought not to mention the incident in this way, but I follow the facts. I got onto the seat with the driver of that limousine, outside, and when we were going up I asked the driver, "How much did this limousine cost?" "Six thousand eight hundred, and he had to pay the duty on it." "Well," I said, "does the owner of this machine ever drive it himself?" At that the chauffeur laughed so heartily that he lost control of his machine. He was so surprised at that question that he ran up on the sidewalk, and around a corner lamp post out into the street again. And when he got out into the street he laughed till the whole machine trembled. He said: "He drive this machine! Oh, he would be lucky if he knew enough to get out when we get there."

I must tell you about a rich man's son at Niagara Falls. I came in from the lecture to the hotel, and as I approached the desk of the clerk there stood a millionaire's son from New York. He was an indescribable specimen of anthropologic impotency. He had a skullcap on one side of his head, with a gold tassel in the top of it, and a gold-headed cane under his arm with more in it than in his head. It is a difficult thing to describe that young man. He wore an eyeglass that he could not see through, patent-leather boots that he could not walk in, and pants that he could not sit down in——dressed like a grasshopper. This human cricket came up to the clerk's desk just as I entered, adjusted his unseeing eyeglass, and spake in this wise to the clerk. You see, he thought it was "Hinglish, you know," to lisp. "Thir, will you have the kindneth to thupply me with thome papah and enwelophs!" The hotel clerk measured that man quick, and he pulled the envelopes and paper out of a drawer, threw them across the counter toward the young man, and then turned away to his books. You should have seen that young man when those envelopes came across that counter. He swelled up like a gobbler turkey, adjusted his unseeing eyeglass, and yelled: "Come right back here. Now thir, will you order a thervant

to take that papah and enwelophs to yondah dethk." Oh, the
poor, miserable, contemptible American monkey! He could
not carry paper and envelopes twenty feet. I suppose he
could not get his arms down to do it. I have no pity for such
travesties upon human nature. If you have not capital, young
man, I am glad of it. What you need is common sense, not
copper cents.

The best thing I can do is to illustrate by actual facts well-
known to you all. A. T. Stewart, a poor boy in New York,
had $1.50 to begin life on. He lost 87½ cents of that on the
very first venture. How fortunate that young man who loses
the first time he gambles. That boy said, "I will never gamble
again in business," and he never did. How came he to lose
87½ cents? You probably all know the story how he lost it—
because he bought some needles, threads, and buttons to sell
which people did not want, and had left them on his hands, a
dead loss. Said the boy, "I will not lose any more money in
that way." Then he went around first to the doors and asked
the people what they did want. Then when he had found out
what they wanted he invested his 62½ cents to supply a
known demand. Study it wherever you choose—in business,
in your profession, in your housekeeping, whatever your life,
that one thing is the secret of success. You must first know
the demand. You must first know what people need, and then
invest yourself where you are most needed. A. T. Steward
went on that principle until he was worth what amounted afterward to forty millions of dollars, owning the very store in
which Mr. Wanamaker carries on his great work in New
York. His fortune was made by losing something, which
taught him the great lesson that he must only invest himself
or his money in something that people need. When will you
salesmen learn it? When will you manufacturers learn that
you must know the changing needs of humanity if you would
succeed in life? Apply yourselves, all you Christian people, as
manufacturers or merchants or workmen to supply that human need. It is a great principle as broad as humanity and as
deep as the Scripture itself.

The best illustration I ever heard was of John Jacob Astor.
You know that he made the money of the Astor family when
he lived in New York. He came across the sea in debt for his
fare. But that poor boy with nothing in his pocket made the
fortune of the Astor family on one principle. Some young
man here tonight will say, "Well, they could make those for-

tunes over in New York, but they could not do it in Philadelphia!" My friends, did you ever read that wonderful book of Riis (his memory is sweet to us because of his recent death), wherein is given his statistical account of the records taken in 1889 of 107 millionaires of New York? If you read the account you will see that out of the 107 millionaires only seven made their money in New York. Out of the 107 millionaires worth ten million dollars in real estate then, 67 of them made their money in towns of less than 3,500 inhabitants. The richest man in this country today, if you read the real estate values, has never moved away from a town of 3,500 inhabitants. It makes not so much difference where you are as who you are. But if you cannot get rich in Philadelphia you certainly cannot do it in New York.

Now John Jacob Astor illustrated what can be done anywhere. He had a mortgage once on a millinery store, and they could not sell bonnets enough to pay the interest on his money. So he foreclosed that mortgage, took possession of the store, and went into partnership with the very same people, in the same store, with the same capital. He did not give them a dollar of capital. They had to sell goods to get money. Then he left them alone in the store just as they had been before, and he went out and sat down on a bench in the park in the shade. What was John Jacob Astor doing out there, and in partnership with people who had failed on his own hands? He had the most important and, to my mind, the most pleasant part of that partnership on his hands. For as John Jacob Astor sat on that bench he was watching the ladies as they went by; and where is the man who would not get rich at that business? As he sat on the bench if a lady passed him with her shoulders back and head up, and looked straight to the front, as if she did not care if all the world did gaze on her, then he studied her bonnet, and by the time it was out of sight he knew the shape of the frame, the color of the trimmings, and the crinklings in the feather. I sometimes try to describe a bonnet, but not always. I would not try to describe a modern bonnet. Where is the man that could describe one? This aggregation of all sorts of driftwood stuck on the back of the head, or the side of the neck, like a rooster with only one tail feather left. But in John Jacob Astor's day there was some art about the millinery business, and he went to the millinery store and said to them: "Now put into the show window just such a bonnet as I describe to you, be-

cause I have already seen a lady who likes such a bonnet.
Don't make up any more until I come back." Then he went
out and sat down again, and another lady passed him of a
different form, of different complexion, with a different shape
and color of bonnet. "Now," said he, "put such a bonnet as
that in the show window." He did not fill his show window
uptown with a lot of hats and bonnets to drive people away,
and then sit on the back stairs and bawl because people went
to Wanamaker's to trade. He did not have a hat or a bonnet
in that show window but what some lady liked before it was
made up. The tide of custom began immediately to turn in,
and that has been the foundation of the greatest store in New
York in that line, and still exists as one of three stores. Its
fortune was made by John Jacob Astor after they had failed
in business, not by giving them any more money, but by finding out what the ladies liked for bonnets before they wasted
any material in making them up. I tell you if a man could
foresee the millinery business he could foresee anything under
heaven!

Suppose I were to go through this audience tonight and ask
you in this great manufacturing city if there are not opportunities to get rich in manufacturing. "Oh yes," some young
man says, "there are opportunities here still if you build with
some trust and if you have two or three millions of dollars to
begin with as capital." Young man, the history of the breaking up of the trusts by that attack upon "big business" is only
illustrating what is now the opportunity of the smaller man.
The time never came in the history of the world when you
could get rich so quickly manufacturing without capital as
you can now.

But you will say, "You cannot do anything of the kind.
You cannot start without capital." Young man, let me illustrate for a moment. I must do it. It is my duty to every
young man and woman, because we are all going into
business very soon on the same plan. Young man, remember
if you know what people need you have gotten more
knowledge of a fortune than any amount of capital can give
you.

There was a poor man out of work living in Hingham,
Massachusetts. He lounged around the house until one day
his wife told him to get out and work, and, as he lived in
Massachusetts, he obeyed his wife. He went out and sat down
on the shore of the bay, and whittled a soaked shingle into a

wooden chain. His children that evening quarreled over it, and he whittled a second one to keep peace. While he was whittling the second one a neighbor came in and said: "Why don't you whittle toys and sell them? You could make money at that." "Oh," he said, "I would not know what to make." "Why don't you ask your own children right here in your own house what to make?" "What is the use of trying that?" said the carpenter. "My children are different from other people's children." (I used to see people like that when I taught school.) But he acted upon the hint, and the next morning when Mary came down the stairway, he asked, "What do you want for a toy?" She began to tell him she would like a doll's bed, a doll's washstand, a doll's carriage, a little doll's umbrella, and went on with a list of things that would take him a lifetime to supply. So, consulting his own children, in his own house, he took the firewood, for he had no money to buy lumber, and whittled those strong, unpainted Hingham toys that were for so many years known all over the world. That man began to make those toys for his own children, and then made copies and sold them through the boot-and-shoe store next door. He began to make a little money, and then a little more, and Mr. Lawson, in his *Frenzied Finance* says that man is the richest man in old Massachusetts, and I think it is the truth. And that man is worth a hundred millions of dollars today, and has been only thirty-four years making it on that one principle—that one must judge that what his own children like at home other people's children would like in their homes, too; to judge the human heart by oneself, by one's wife or by one's children is the royal road to success in manufacturing. "Oh," but you say, "didn't he have any capital?" Yes, a penknife, but I don't know that he had paid for that.

I spoke thus to an audience in New Britain, Connecticut, and a lady four seats back went home and tried to take off her collar, and the collar button stuck in the buttonhole. She threw it out and said, "I am going to get up something better than that to put on collars." Her husband said: "After what Conwell said tonight, you see there is a need of an improved collar fastener that is easier to handle. There is a human need; there is a great fortune. Now, then, get up a collar button and get rich." He made fun of her, and consequently made fun of me, and that is one of the saddest things which comes over me like a deep cloud of midnight sometimes—although I have worked so hard for more than a century, yet how little I have ever really done. Notwithstanding the greatness and the handsomeness of your compliment tonight, I do not believe there is one in ten of you that is going to make a million of dollars because you are here tonight; but it is not my fault, it is yours. I say that sincerely. What is the use of my talking if people never do what I advise them to do? When her husband ridiculed her, she made up her mind she would make a better collar button, and when a woman makes up her mind "she will," and does not say anything about it, she does it. It was that New England woman who invented the snap button which you can find anywhere now. It was first a collar button with a spring cap attached to the outer side. Any of you who wear modern waterproofs know the button that simply pushes together, and when you unbotton it you simply pull it apart. That is the button to which I refer, and which she invented. She afterward invented several other buttons, and then invested in more, and then was taken into partnership with great factories. Now that woman goes over the sea every summer in her private steamship—yes, and takes her husband with her! If her husband were to die, she would have money enough left now to buy a foreign duke or count or some such title as that at the latest quotations.

Now what is my lesson in that incident? It is this: I told her then, though I did not know her, what I now say to you, "Your wealth is too near to you. You are looking right over it"; and she had to look over it because it was right under her chin.

I have read in the newspaper that a woman never invented anything. Well, that newspaper ought to begin again. Of course, I do not refer to gossip—I refer to machines—and if I did I might better include the men. That newspaper could never appear if women had not invented something. Friends, think. Ye women, think! You say you cannot make a fortune because you are in some laundry, or running a sewing machine, it may be, or walking before some loom, and yet you can be a millionaire if you will but follow this almost infallible direction.

When you say a woman doesn't invent anything, I ask, Who invented the Jacquard loom that wove every stitch you wear? Mrs. Jacquard. The printer's roller, the printing press, were invented by farmers' wives. Who invented the cotton gin of the South that enriched our country so amazingly? Mrs.

General Greene invented the cotton gin and showed the idea to Mr. Whitney, and he, like a man, seized it. Who was it that invented the sewing machine? If I would go to school tomorrow and ask your children they would say, "Elias Howe."

He was in the Civil War with me, and often in my tent, and I often heard him say that he worked fourteen years to get up that sewing machine. But his wife made up her mind one day that they would starve to death if there wasn't something or other invented pretty soon, and so in two hours she invented the sewing machine. Of course he took out the patent in his name. Men always do that. Who was it that invented the mower and the reaper? According to Mr. McCormick's confidential communication, so recently published, it was a West Virginia woman, who, after his father and he had failed altogether in making a reaper and gave it up, took a lot of shears and nailed them together on the edge of a board, with one shaft of each pair loose, and then wired them so that when she pulled the wire one way it closed them, and when she pulled the wire the other way it opened them, and there she had the principle of the mowing machine. If you look at a mowing machine, you will see it is nothing but a lot of shears. If a woman can invent a mowing machine, if a woman can invent a Jacquard loom, if a woman can invent a cotton gin, if a woman can invent a trolley switch—as she did and made the trolleys possible; if a woman can invent, as Mr. Carnegie said, the great iron squeezers that laid the foundation of all the steel millions of the United States, "we men" can invent anything under the stars! I say that for the encouragement of the men.

Who are the great inventors of the world? Again this lesson comes before us. The great inventor sits next to you, or you are the person yourself. "Oh," but you will say, "I have never invented anything in my life." Neither did the great inventors until they discovered one great secret. Do you think it is a man with a head like a bushel measure or a man like a stroke of lightning? It is neither. The really great man is a plain, straightforward, everyday, common-sense man. You would not dream that he was a great inventor if you did not see something he had actually done. His neighbors do not regard him as so great. You never see anything great over your back fence. You say there is no greatness among your neighbors. It is all away off somewhere else. Their greatness is ever so simple, so plain, so earnest, so practical, that the neighbors and friends never recognize it.

True greatness is often unrecognized. That is sure. You do not know anything about the greatest men and women. I went out to write the life of General Garfield, and a neighbor, knowing I was in a hurry, and as there was a great crowd around the front door, took me around to General Garfield's back door and shouted, "Jim! Jim!" And very soon "Jim" came to the door and let me in, and I wrote the biography of one of the grandest men of the nation, and yet he was just the same old "Jim" to his neighbor. If you know a great man in Philadelphia and you should meet him tomorrow, you would say, "How are you, Sam?" or "Good morning, Jim." Of course you would. That is just what you would do.

One of my soldiers in the Civil War had been sentenced to death, and I went up to the White House in Washington—went there for the first time in my life—to see the President. I went into the waiting room and sat down with a lot of others on the benches, and the secretary asked one after another to tell him what they wanted. After the secretary had been through the line, he went in, and then came back to the door and motioned for me. I went up to that anteroom, and the secretary said: "That is the President's door right over there. Just rap on it and go right in." I never was so taken aback, friends, in all my life, never. The secretary himself made it worse for me, because he had told me how to go in and then went out another door to the left and shut that. There I was, in the hallway by myself before the President of the United States of America's door. I had been on fields of battle, where the shells did sometimes shriek and the bullets did sometimes hit me, but I always wanted to run. I have no sympathy with the old man who says, "I would just as soon march up to the cannon's mouth as eat my dinner." I have no faith in a man who doesn't know enough to be afraid when he is being shot at. I never was so afraid when the shells came around us at Antietam as I was when I went into that room that day; but I finally mustered the courage—I don't know how I ever did—and at arm's length tapped on the door. The man inside did not help me at all, but yelled out, "Come in and sit down!"

Well, I went in and sat down on the edge of a chair, and wished I were in Europe, and the man at the table did not look up. He was one of the world's greatest men, and was made great by one single rule. Oh, that all the young people of Philadelphia were before me now and I could say just this one thing, and that they would remember it. I would give a lifetime for the effect it would have on our city and on civilization. Abraham Lincoln's principle for greatness can be adopted by nearly all. This was his rule: Whatsoever he had to do at all, he put his whole mind into it and held it all there until that was all done. That makes men great almost anywhere. He stuck to those papers at that table and did not look up at me, and I sat there trembling. Finally, when he had put the string around his papers, he pushed them over to one side and looked over to me, and a smile came over his worn face. He said: "I am a very busy man and have only a few minutes to spare, Now tell me in the fewest words what it is you want." I began to tell him, and mentioned the case, and he said: "I have heard all about it and you do not need to say any more. Mr. Stanton was talking to me only a few days ago about that. You can go to the hotel and rest assured that the President never did sign an order to shoot a boy under twenty years of age, and never will. You can say that to his mother anyhow."

Then he said to me, "How is it going in the field?" I said, "We sometimes get discouraged." And he said: "It is all right. We are going to win out now. We are getting very near the light. No man ought to wish to be President of the United States, and I will be glad when I get through; then Tad and I are going out to Springfield, Illinois. I have bought a farm out there and I don't care if I again earn only twenty-five cents a day. Tad has a mule team, and we are going to plant onions."

Then he asked me, "Were you brought up on a farm?" I said, "Yes; in the Berkshire Hills of Massachusetts." He then threw his leg over the corner of the big chair and said, "I have heard many a time, ever since I was young, that up there in those hills you have to sharpen the noses of the sheep in order to get down to the grass between the rocks." He was so familiar, so everyday, so farmer-like, that I felt right at home with him at once.

He then took hold of another roll of paper, and looked up at me, and said, "Good morning." I took the hint then and got up and went out. After I had gotten out I could not realize I had seen the President of the United States at all. But a few days later, when still in the city, I saw the crowd pass through the East Room by the coffin of Abraham Lincoln, and when I looked at the upturned face of the murdered President I felt then that the man I had seen such a short time before, who, so simple a man, so plain a man, was one of the greatest men that God ever raised up to lead a nation on to ultimate liberty. Yet he was only "Old Abe" to his neighbors. When they had the second funeral, I was invited among others, and went out to see that same coffin put back in the tomb at Springfield. Around the tomb stood Lincoln's old neighbors, to whom he was just "Old Abe." Of course that is all they would say.

Did you ever see a man who struts around altogether too large to notice an ordinary working mechanic? Do you think he is great? He is nothing but a puffed-up balloon, held down by his big feet. There is no greatness there.

Who are the great men and women? My attention was called the other day to the history of a very little thing that made the fortune of a very poor man. It was an awful thing, and yet because of that experience—not a great inventor or genius—invented the pin that now is called the safety pin, and out of that safety pin made the fortune of one of the great aristocratic families of this nation.

A poor man in Massachusetts who had worked in the nail-works was injured at thirty-eight, and he could earn but little money. He was employed in the office to rub out the marks on the bills made by pencil memorandums, and he used a rubber until his hand grew tired. He then tied a piece of rubber on the end of a stick and worked it like a plane. His little girl came and said, "Why, you have a patent, haven't you?" The father said afterward, "My daughter told me when I took that stick and put the rubber on the end that there was a patent, and that was the first thought of that." He went to Boston and applied for his patent, and every one of you that has a rubbertipped pencil in your pocket is now paying tribute to the millionaire. No capital, not a penny did he invest in it. All was income, all the way up into the millions.

But let me hasten to one other great thought. "Show me the great men and women who live in Philadelphia." A gentleman over there will get up and say: "We don't have any great men in Philadelphia. They don't live here. They live away off in Rome or St. Petersburg or London or Manayunk, or anywhere else but here in our town." I have come now to the apex of my thought. I have come now to the heart of the whole matter and to the center of my struggle: Why isn't Philadelphia a greater city in its greater wealth? Why does New York excel Philadelphia? People say, "Because of her harbor." Why do many other cities of the United States get ahead of Philadelphia now? There is only one answer, and that is because our own people talk down their own city. If there ever was a community on earth that has to be forced ahead, it is the city of Philadelphia. If we are to have a boulevard, talk it down; if we are going to have better schools, talk them down; if you wish to have wise legislation, talk it down; talk all the proposed improvements down. That is the only great wrong that I can lay at the feet of the magnificent Philadelphia that has been so universally kind to me. I say it is time we turn around in our city and begin to talk up the things that are in our city, and begin to set them before the world as the people of Chicago, New York, St. Louis, and San Francisco do. Oh, if we only could get that spirit out among our people, that we can do things in Philadelphia and do them well!

Arise, ye millions of Philadelphians, trust in God and man and believe in the great opportunities that are right here—not over in New York or Boston, but here—for business, for everything that is worth living for on earth. There was never an opportunity greater. Let us talk up our own city.

But there are two other young men here tonight, and that is all I will venture to say, because it is too late. One over there gets up and says, "There is going to be a great man in Philadelphia, but never was one." "Oh, is that so? When are you going to be great?" "When I am elected to some political office." Young man, won't you learn a lesson in the primer of politics that it is a *prima facie* evidence of littleness to hold office under our form of government? Great men get into office sometimes, but what this country needs is men that will do what we tell them to do. This nation—where the people rule—is governed by the people, for the people, and so long as it is, then the office-holder is but the servant of the people, and the Bible says the servant cannot be greater than the master. The Bible says, "He that is sent cannot be greater than He who sent him." The people rule, or should rule, and if they do, we do not need the greater men in office. If the great men in America took our offices, we would change to an empire in the next ten years.

I know of a great many young women, now that woman's suffrage is coming, who say, "I am going to be President of the United States some day." I believe in woman's suffrage, and there is no doubt but what it is coming, and I am getting out of the way, anyhow. I may want an office by and by myself; but if the ambition for an office influences the women in their desire to vote, I want to say right here what I say to the young men, that if you only get the privilege of casting one vote, you don't get anything that is worth while. Unless you can control more than one vote, you will be unknown, and your influence so dissipated as practically not to be felt. This country is not run by votes. Do you think it is? It is governed by influence. It is governed by the ambitions and the enterprises which control votes. The young woman who thinks she is going to vote for the sake of holding an office is making an awful blunder.

That other young man gets up and says, "There are going to be great men in this country and in Philadelphia." "Is that so? When?" "When there comes a great war, when we get into difficulty through watchful waiting in Mexico; when we get into war with England over some frivolous deed, or with Japan or China or New Jersey or some distant country. Then I will march up to the cannon's mouth; I will sweep up among the glistening bayonets; I will leap into the arena and tear down the flag and bear it away in triumph. I will come home with stars on my shoulder, and hold every office in the gift of the nation, and I will be great." No, you won't. You think you are going to be made great by an office, but remember that if you are not great before you get the office, you won't be great when you secure it. I will only be a burlesque in that shape.

We had a Peace Jubilee here after the Spanish War. Out West they don't believe this, because they said, "Philadelphia would not have heard of any Spanish War until fifty years hence." Some of you saw the procession go up Broad Street. I was away, but the family wrote to me that the tally-ho coach with Lieutenant Hobson upon it stopped right at the front door and the people shouted, "Hurrah for Hobson!" and if I had been there I would have yelled too, because he deserves much more of his country than he has ever received. But suppose I go into school and say, "Who sank the *Merrimac* at Santiago?" and if the boys answer me, "Hobson," they will tell me seven-eights of a lie. There were seven other heroes on that steamer, and they, by virtue of their position, were continually exposed to the Spanish fire, while Hobson, as an officer, might reasonably be behind the smokestack. You have gathered in this house your most intellegent people, and yet, perhaps, not one here can name the other seven men.

We ought not to so teach history. We ought to teach that, however humble a man's station may be, if he does his full duty in that place he is just as much entitled to the American people's honor as is the king upon his throne. But we do not so teach. We are now teaching everywhere that the generals do all the fighting.

I remember that, after the war, I went down to see General Robert E. Lee, that magnificent Christian gentleman of whom both North and South are now proud as one of our great Americans. The general told me about his servant, Rastus, who was an enlisted colored soldier. He called him in one day to make fun of him, and said, "Rastus, I hear that all the rest of your company are killed, and why are you not killed?" Rastus winked at him and said, " 'Cause when there is any fightin' goin' on I stay back with the generals."

I remember another illustration. I would leave it out but for the fact that when you go to the library to read this lecture, you will find this has been printed in it for twenty-five years. I shut my eyes—shut them close—and lo! I see the faces of my youth. Yes, they sometimes say to me, "Your hair is not white; you are working night and day without seeming ever to stop; you can't be old." But when I shut my eyes, like any other man of my years, oh, then come trooping back the faces of the loved and lost of long ago, and I know, whatever men may say, it is evening time.

I shut my eyes now and look back to my native town in Massachusetts, and I see the cattle-show ground on the mountaintop; I can see the horse sheds there. I can see the Congregational Church; see the town hall and mountaineers' cottages; see a great assembly of people turning out, dressed resplendently, and I can see flags flying and handkerchiefs waving and hear bands playing. I can see that company of soldiers that had re-enlisted marching up on the cattle-show ground. I was but a boy, but I was captain of that company and puffed out with pride. A cambric needle would have burst me all to pieces. Then I thought it was the greatest event that ever came to man on earth. If you have ever thought you would like to be a king or queen, you go and be received by the mayor.

The bands played, and all the people turned out to receive us. I marched up that Common so proud at the head of my troops, and we turned down into the town hall. Then they seated my soldiers down the center aisle and I sat down on the front seat. A great assembly of people—a hundred or two—came in to fill the town hall, so that they stood up all around. Then the town officers came in and formed a half circle. The mayor of the town sat in the middle of the platform. He was a man who had never held office before; but he was a good man, and his friends have told me that I might use this without giving them offense. He was a good man, but he thought an office made a man great. He came up and took his seat, adjusted his powerful spectacles, and looked around, when he suddenly spied me sitting there on the front seat. He came right forward on the platform and invited me up to sit with the town officers. No town officer ever took any notice of me before I went to war, except to advise the teacher to thrash me, and now I was invited up on the stand with the town officers. Oh my! The town mayor was then the emperor, the king of our day and our time. As I came up on the platform they gave me a chair about this far, I would say, from the front.

When I had got seated, the chairman of Selectmen arose and came forward to the table, and we all supposed he would introduce the Congregational minister, who was the only orator in town, and that he would give the oration to the returning soldiers. But, friends, you should have seen the surprise which ran over the audience when they discovered that the old fellow was going to deliver that speech himself. He had never made a speech in his life, but he fell into the same error that hundreds of other men have fallen into. It seems so strange that a man won't learn he must speak his piece as a boy if he intends to be an orator when he is grown, but he seems to think all he has to do is to hold an office to be a great orator.

So he came up to the front, and brought with him a speech which he had learned by heart walking up and down the pasture, where he had frightened the cattle. He brought the manuscript with him and spread it out on the table so as to be sure he might see it. He adjusted his spectacles and leaned over it for a moment and marched back on that platform, and then came forward like this—tramp, tramp, tramp. He must have studied the subject a great deal, when you come to think of it, because he assumed an "elocutionary" attitude. He rested heavily upon his left heel, threw back his shoulders, slightly advanced the right foot, opened the organs of speech, and advanced his right foot at an angle of forty-five. As he stood in that elocutionary attitude, friends, this is just the way that speech went. Some people say to me, "Don't you exaggerate?" That would be impossible. But I am here for the lesson and not for the story, and this is the way it went:

"Fellow citizens—" As soon as he heard his voice his fingers began to go like that, his knees began to shake, and then he trembled all over. He choked and swallowed and came around to the table to look at the manuscript. Then he gathered himself up with clenched fists and came back. "Fellow citizens, we are—Fellow citizens, we are—we are—we are—we are—we are—we are very happy—we are very happy—we are very happy—. We are very happy to welcome back to their native town these soldiers who have fought and bled—and come back again to their native town. We are especially—we are especially—we are especially. We are especially pleased to see with us today this young hero" (that meant me)—"this young hero who in imagination" (friends, remember he said that, if he had not said "in imagination" I would not be egotistic enough to refer to it at all)—"this young hero who in imagination we have seen leading—we have seen leading—leading. We have seen leading his troops on to the deadly breach. We have seen his shining—we have seen his shining—his shining—his shining sword—flashing. Flashing in the sunlight, as he shouted to his troops, 'Come on'!"

Oh dear, dear, dear! How little that good man knew about war. If he had known anything about war at all he ought to have known what any of my G.A.R. comrades here tonight will tell you is true, that it is next to a crime for an officer of infantry ever in time of danger to go ahead of his men. "He, with his shining sword flashing in the sunlight, shouting to his troops, 'Come on'!" I never did it. Do you suppose I would get in front of my men to be shot in front by the enemy and in the back by my own men? That is no place for an officer. The place for the officer in actual battle is behind the line. How often, as a staff officer, I rode down the line, when our men were suddenly called to the line of battle, and the Rebel yells were coming out of the woods, and shouted: "Officers to the rear! Officers to rear!" Then every officer gets behind the line of private soldiers, and the higher the officer's rank the farther behind he goes. Not because he is any the less brave, but because the laws of war require that. And yet he shouted, "He, with his shining sword——" In that house there sat the company of my soldiers who had carried that boy across the Carolina rivers that he might not wet his feet. Some of them had gone far out to get a pig or a chicken. Some of them had gone to death under the shell-swept pines in the mountains of Tennessee, yet in the good man's speech they were scarcely known. He did refer to them, but only incidentally. The hero of the hour was this boy. Did the nation owe him anything? No, nothing then and nothing now. Why was he the hero? Simply because that man fell into that same human error— that this boy was great because he was an officer and these were only private soldiers.

Oh, I learned the lesson then that I will never forget so long as the tongue of the bell of time continues to swing for me. Greatness consists not in the holding of some future office, but really consists in doing great deeds with little means and the accomplishment of vast purposes from the private ranks of life. To be great at all one must be great here, now, in Philadelphia. He who can give to this city better streets and better sidewalks, better schools and more colleges, more happiness and more civilization, more of God, he will be great anywhere. Let every man or woman here, if you never hear me again, remember this, that if you wish to be great at all, you must begin where you are and with what you are, in Philadelphia, now. He who can give to his city any blessing, he who can be a good citizen while he lives here, he who can make better homes, he who can be a blessing whether he works in the shops or sits behind the counter or keeps house, whatever be his life, he who would be great anywhere must first be great in his own Philadelphia.

III

AS A
MAN THINKETH

JAMES ALLEN

ABOUT
THE AUTHOR

James Allen (1864-1912) gained fame as a novelist and a poet, yet none of his many books received the lasting fame of *As A Man Thinketh*. Allen did not consider it a major literary effort, but his readers did, passing it from one generation to another with affection and reverence. James Allen was a writer whose thoughts on a positive attitude have helped millions of people realize their full potential.

CONTENTS

Thought and Character...................... 77

Effect of Thought on Circumstances.......... 80

Effect of Thought on Health and the Body..... 88

Thought and Purpose...................... 91

The Thought-factor in Achievement.......... 96

Visions and Ideals......................... 97

Serenity 101

FOREWORD

This little volume (the result of meditation and experience) is not intended as an exhaustive treatise on the much-written-upon subject of the power of thought. It is suggestive rather than explanatory, its object being to stimulate men and women to the discovery and perception of the truth that "They themselves are makers of themselves" by virtue of the thoughts which they choose and encourage; that mind is the master-weaver, both of the inner garment of character and the outer garment of circumstances, and that, as they may have hitherto woven in ignorance and pain they may now weave in enlightenment and happiness.

James Allen

realm of thought as in the world of visible and material things. A noble and Godlike character is not a thing of favor or chance, but is the natural result of continued effort in right thinking, the effect of long-cherished association with Godlike thoughts. An ignoble and bestial character, by the same process, is the result of the continued haboring of groveling thoughts.

Man is made or unmade by himself; in the armory of thought he forges the weapons by which he destroys himself; he also fashions the tools with which he built for himself heavenly mansions of joy and strength and peace. By the right choice and true application of thought, man ascends to the Divine Perfection; by the abuse and wrong application of thought, he descends below the level of the beast. Between these two extremes are all the grades of character, and man is their maker and master.

Of all the beautiful truths pertaining to the soul which have been restored and brought to light in this age, none is more gladdening or fruitful of divine promise and confidence than this—that man is the master of thought, the molder of character, and the maker and shaper of condition, environment, and destiny.

As a being of Power, Intelligence, and Love, and the lord of his own thoughts, man holds the key to every situation, and contains within himself that transforming and regenerative agency by which he may make himself what he wills.

Man is always the master, even in his weakest and most abandoned state; but in his weakness and degradation he is the foolish master who misgoverns his household. When he begins to reflect upon his condition, and to search diligently for the Law upon which his being is established, he then becomes the wise master, directing his energies with intelligence, and fashioning his thoughts to fruitful issues. Such is the *conscious* master, and man can only thus become by discovering *within himself* the laws of thought; which discovery is totally a matter of application, self-analysis, and experience.

Only by much searching and mining are gold and diamonds obtained, and man can find every truth connected with his being if he will dig deep into the mine of his soul; and that he is the maker of his character, the molder of his life, and the builder of his destiny, he may unerringly prove, if he will watch, control, and alter his thoughts, tracing their effect upon himself, upon others, and upon his life and circumstances, linking cause and effect by patient practice and investigation, and utilizing his every experience, even to the most trivial, everyday occurrence, as a means of obtaining that knowledge of himself which is Understanding, Wisdom, Power. In this direction, as in no other, is the law absolute that "He that seeketh findeth; and to him that knocketh it shall be opened"; for only by patience, practice, and ceaseless importunity can a man enter the Door of the Temple of Knowledge.

EFFECT OF THOUGHT
ON
CIRCUMSTANCES

Man's mind may be likened to a garden, which may be intelligently cultivated or allowed to run wild; but whether cultivated or neglected, it must, and will, *bring forth*. If no useful seeds are *put* into it, then an abundance of useless weed seeds will *fall* therein, and will continue to produce their kind.

Just as a gardener cultivates his plot, keeping it free from weeds, and growing the flowers and fruits which he requires, so may a man tend the garden of his mind, weeding out all the wrong, useless and impure thoughts, and cultivating toward perfection the flowers and fruits of right, useful, and pure thoughts. By pursuing this process, a man sooner or later discovers that he is the master-gardener of his soul, the director of his life. He also reveals, within himself, the laws of thought, and understands, with ever-increasing accuracy, how the thought-forces and mind-elements operate in the shaping of his character, circumstances, and destiny.

Thought and character are one, and as character can only manifest and discover itself through environment and circumstance, the outer conditions of a person's life will always be found to be harmoniously related to his inner state. This does not mean that a man's circumstances at any given time are an indication of his *entire* character, but that those circumstances are so intimately connected with some vital thought-element within himself that, for the time being, they are indispensable to his development.

Every man is where he is by the law of his being; the thoughts which he has built into his character have brought him there, and in the arrangement of his life there is no element of chance, but all is the result of a law which cannot err. This is just as true of those who feel "out of harmony" with their surroundings as of those who are contented with them.

As a progressive and evolving being, man is where he is that he may learn that he may grow; and as he learns the spiritual lesson which any circumstance contains for him, it passes away and gives place to other circumstances.

Man is buffeted by circumstances so long as he believes himself to be the creature of outside conditions, but when he realizes that he is a creative power, and that he may command the hidden soil and seeds of his being out of which circumstances grow, he then becomes the rightful master of himself.

That circumstances *grow* out of thought every man knows who has for any length of time practiced self-control and self-purification, for he will have noticed that the alteration in his circumstances has been in exact ratio with his altered mental condition. So true is this that when a man earnestly applies himself to remedy the defects on his character, and makes swift and marked progress, he passes rapidly through a succession of vicissitudes.

The soul attracts that which it secretly harbors; that which it loves, and also that which it fears; it reaches the height of its cherished aspirations; it falls to the level of its unchastened desires, and circumstances are the means by which the soul receives its own.

Every thought-seed sown or allowed to fall into the mind and to take root there, produces its own, blossoming sooner or later into act, and bearing its own fruitage of opportunity and circumstance. Good thoughts bear good fruit, bad thoughts bad fruit.

The outer world of circumstance shapes itself to the inner world of thought, and both pleasant and unpleasant external conditions are factors which make for the ultimate good of the individual. As the reaper of his own harvest, man learns both by suffering and bliss.

Following the inmost desires, aspirations, thoughts, by

which he allows himself to be dominated (pursuing the will-o'-the-wisps of impure imagining or steadfastly walking the highway of strong and high endeavor), a man at last arrives at their fruition and fulfillment in the outer condition of his life.

The laws of growth and adjustment everywhere obtain.

A man does not come to the almshouse or the jail by the tyranny of fate or circumstance, but by the pathway of groveling thoughts and base desires. Nor does a pureminded man fall suddenly into crime by stress of any mere external force; the criminal thought had long been secretly fostered in the heart, and the hour of opportunity revealed its gathered power. Circumstance does not make the man; it reveals him to himself. No such conditions can exist as descending into vice and its attendant sufferings apart from vicious inclinations; or ascending into virtue and its pure happiness without the continued cultivation of virtuous aspirations; and man, therefore, as the lord and master of thought, is the maker of himself, the shaper and author of environment. Even at birth the soul comes to its own, and through every step of its earthly pilgrimage it attracts those combinations of conditions which reveal itself, which are the reflections of its own purity and impurity, its strength and weakness.

Men do not attract that which they *want*, but that which they *are*. Their whims, fancies, and ambitions are thwarted at every step, but their inmost thoughts and desires are fed with their own food, be it foul or clean. The "Divinity that shapes our ends" is in ourselves; it is our very self. Man is manacled only by himself: thought and action are the jailers of Fate—they imprison, being base; they are also the angels of Freedom—they liberate, being noble.

Not what he wishes and prays for does a man get, but what he justly earns. His wishes and prayers are only gratified and answered when they harmonize with his thoughts and actions.

In the light of this truth, what, then, is the meaning of "fighting against circumstances"? It means that a man is continually revolting against an *effect* without, while all the time he is nourishing and preserving its *cause* in his heart.

That cause may take the form of a conscious vice or an unconscious weakness; but whatever it is, it stubbornly retards the efforts of its possessor, and thus calls aloud for remedy.

Men are anxious to improve their circumstances, but are unwilling to improve themselves; they therefore remain bound. The man who does not shrink from self-crucifixion can never fail to accomplish the object upon which his heart is set. This is as true of earthly as of heavenly things. Even the man whose sole object is to acquire wealth must be prepared to make great personal sacrifices before he can accomplish his object; and how much more so he who would realize a strong and well-poised life?

Here is a man who is wretchedly poor. He is extremely anxious that his surroundings and home comforts should be improved, yet all the time he shirks his work, and considers he is justified in trying to deceive his employer on the ground of the insufficiency of his wages. Such a man does not understand the simplest rudiments of those principles which are the basis of true prosperity, and is not only totally unfitted to rise out of his wretchedness, but is actually attracting to himself a still deeper wretchedness by dwelling in, and acting out, indolent, deceptive, and unmanly thoughts.

Here is a rich man who is the victim of a painful and persistent disease as the result of gluttony. He is willing to give large sums of money to get rid of it, but he will not sacrifice his gluttonous desires. He wants to gratify his taste for rich and unnatural viands and have his health as well. Such a man is totally unfit to have health, because he has not yet learned the first principles of a healthy life.

Here is an employer of labor who adopts crooked measures to avoid paying the regulation wage, and, in the hope of making larger profits, reduces the wages of his work-people. Such a man is altogether unfitted for prosperity, and when he finds himself bankrupt, both as regards reputation and riches, he blames circumstances, not knowing that he is the sole author of his condition.

I have introduced these three cases merely as illustrative of the truth that man is the causer (though nearly always unconsciously) of his circumstances, and that, whilst aiming at a good end, he is continually frustrating its accomplishment by encouraging thoughts and desires which cannot possibly harmonize with that end. Such cases could be multiplied and varied almost indefinitely, but this is not necessary, as the reader can, if he so resolves, trace the action of the laws of thought in his own mind and life, and until this is done, mere external facts cannot serve as a ground of reasoning.

Circumstances, however, are so complicated, thought is so deeply rooted, and the conditions of happiness vary so vastly with individuals, that a man's *entire* soul-condition (although it may be known to himself) cannot be judged by another from the external aspect of his life alone. A man may be honest in certain directions, yet suffer privations; a man may be dishonest in certain directions, yet acquire wealth; but the conclusion usually formed that the one man fails *because of his particular honesty*, and that the other prospers *because of his particular dishonesty*, is the result of a superficial judgment, which assumes that the dishonest man is almost totally corrupt, and the honest man almost entirely virtuous. In the light of a deeper knowledge and wider experience, such judgment is found to be erroneous. The dishonest man may have some admirable virtues which the other does not possess; and the honest man obnoxious vices which are absent in the other. The honest man reaps the good results of his honest thoughts and acts; He also brings upon himself the sufferings which his vices produce. The dishonest man likewise garners his own suffering and happiness.

It is pleasing to human vanity to believe that one suffers because of one's virtue; but not until a man has extirpated every sickly, bitter, and impure thought from his mind, and washed every sinful stain from his soul, can he be in a position to know and declare that his sufferings are the result of his good, and not of his bad qualities; and on the way to, yet long before he has reached that supreme perfection, he will have found, working in his mind and life, the Great Law which is absolutely just, and which cannot, therefore, give good for evil, evil for good. Possessed of such knowledge, he will then know, looking back upon his past ignorance and blindness, that his life is, and always was, justly ordered, and that all his past experiences, good and bad, were the equitable outworking of his evolving, yet unevolved self.

Good thoughts and actions can never produce bad results; bad thoughts and actions can never produce good results. This is but saying that nothing can come from corn but corn, nothing from nettles but nettles. Men understand this law in the natural world, and work with it; but few understand it in the mental and moral world (though its operation there is just as simple and undeviating), and they, therefore, do not cooperate with it.

Suffering is *always* the effect of wrong thought in some

direction. It is an indication that the individual is out of harmony with himself, with the Law of his being. The sole and supreme use of suffering is to purify, to burn out all that is useless and impure. Suffering ceases for him who is pure. There could be no object in burning gold after the dross had been removed, and a perfectly pure and enlightened being could not suffer.

The circumstances which a man encounters with suffering are the result of his own mental inharmony. The circumstances which a man encounters with blessedness are the result of his own mental harmony. Blessedness, not material possessions, is the measure of right thought; wretchedness, not lack of material possessions, is the measure of wrong thought. A man may be cursed and rich; he may be blessed and poor. Blessedness and riches are only joined together when the riches are rightly and wisely used; and the poor man only descends into wretchedness when he regards his lot as a burden unjustly imposed.

Indigence and indulgence are the two extremes of wretchedness. They are both equally unnatural and the result of mental disorder. A man is not rightly conditioned until he is a happy, healthy, and prosperous being; and happiness, health and prosperity are the result of a harmonious adjustment of the inner with the outer, of the man with his surroundings.

A man only begins to be a man when he ceases to whine and revile, and commences to search for the hidden justice which regulates his life. And as he adapts his mind to that regulating factor, he ceases to accuse others as the cause of his condition, and builds himself up in strong and noble thoughts; ceases to kick against circumstances, but begins to *use* them as aids to his more rapid progress, and as a means of discovering the hidden powers and possibilities within himself.

Law, not confusion, is the dominating principle in the universe; justice, not injustice, is the soul and substance of life and righteousness, not corruption, is the molding and moving force in the spiritual government of the world. This being so man has but to right himself to find that the universe is right and during the process of putting himself right, he will find that as he alters his thoughts towards things and other people things and other people will alter towards him.

The proof of this truth is in every person, and it therefore admits of easy investigation by systematic introspection and self-analysis. Let a man radically alter his thoughts, and he will be astonished at the rapid transformation it will effect in the material conditions of his life. Men imagine that thought can be kept secret, but it cannot; it rapidly crystallizes into habit, and habit solidifies into circumstances. Bestial thoughts crystallize into habits of drunkenness and sensuality, which solidify into circumstances of destitution and disease: impure thoughts of every kind crystallize into enervating and confusing habits, which solidify into distracting and adverse circumstances: thoughts of fear, doubt, and indecision crystallize into weak, unmanly, and irresolute habits which solidify into circumstances of failure, indigence, and slavish dependence: lazy thoughts crystallize into habits of uncleanliness and dishonesty, which solidify into circumstances of foulness and beggary: hateful and condemnatory thoughts crystallize into habits of accusations and violence, which solidify into circumstances more or less distressing. On the other hand, beautiful thoughts of all kinds crystallize into habits of grace and kindliness, which solidify into genial and sunny circumstances: pure thoughts crystallize into habits of temperance and self-control, which solidify into circumstances of repose and peace: thoughts of courage, self-reliance, and decision crystallize into manly habits, which solidify into circumstances of success, plenty, and freedom: energetic thoughts crystallize into habits of cleanliness and industry, which solidify into circumstances of pleasantness: gentle and forgiving thoughts crystallize into habits of gentleness, which solidify into protective and preservative circumstances: loving and unselfish thoughts crystallize into habits of self-forgetfulness for others, which solidify into circumstances of sure and abiding prosperity and true riches.

A particular train of thought persisted in, be it good or bad, cannot fail to produce its result on the character and circumstances. A man cannot *directly* choose his circumstances, but he can choose his thoughts, and so indirectly, yet surely, shape his circumstances.

Nature helps every man to the gratification of the thoughts which he most encourages, and opportunities are presented which will most speedily bring to the surface both the good and evil thoughts.

Let a man cease from his sinful thoughts, and all the world will soften towards him, and be ready to help him; let him put away his weakly and sickly thoughts, and lo! opportunities will spring upon every hand to aid his strong resolves; let him encourage good thoughts, and no hard fate shall bind him down to wretchedness and shame. The world is your kaleidoscope, and the varying combinations of colors which at every succeeding moment it presents to you are the exquisitely adjusted pictures of your ever-moving thoughts.

You will be what you will be;
　　Let failure find its false content
　　In that poor word, "environment,"
But spirit scorns it, and is free.

It masters time, it conquers space;
　　It cows that boastful trickster, Chance,
　　And bids the tyrant Circumstance
Uncrown, and fill a servant's place.

The human Will, that force unseen,
　　The offspring of a deathless Soul,
　　Can hew a way to any goal,
Though walls of granite intervene.

Be not impatient in delay,
　　But wait as one who understands;
　　When spirit rises and commands,
The gods are ready to obey.

EFFECT OF THOUGHT
ON HEALTH
AND THE BODY

The body is the servant of the mind. It obeys the operations of the mind, whether they be deliberately chosen or automatically expressed. At the bidding of unlawful thoughts the body sinks rapidly into disease and decay; at the command of glad and beautiful thoughts it becomes clothed with youthfulness and beauty.

Disease and health, like circumstances, are rooted in thought. Sickly thoughts will express themselves through a sickly body. Thoughts of fear have been known to kill a man as speedily as a bullet, and they are continually killing thousands of people just as surely though less rapidly. The people who live in fear of disease are the people who get it. Anxiety quickly demoralizes the whole body, and lays it open to the creature of disease; while impure thoughts, even if not physically indulged, will soon shatter the nervous system.

Strong, pure, and happy thoughts build up the body in vigor and grace. The body is a delicate and plastic instrument, which responds readily to the thoughts by which it is impressed, and habits of thought will produce their own effects, good or bad, upon it.

Men will continue to have impure and poisoned blood so long as they propagate unclean thoughts. Out of a clean heart comes a clean life and a clean body. Out of a defiled mind proceeds a defiled life and a corrupt body. Thought is the fount of action, life and manifestations; make the fountain pure, and all will be pure.

Change of diet will not help a man who will not change his thoughts. When a man makes his thoughts pure, he no longer desires impure food.

Clean thoughts make clean habits. The so-called saint who does not wash his body is not a saint. He who has strengthened and purified his thoughts does not need to consider the malevolent microbe.

If you would renew your body, beautify your mind. Thoughts of malice, envy, disappointment, despondency, rob the body of its health and grace. A sour face does not come by chance; it is made by sour thoughts.

Wrinkles that mar are drawn by folly, passion, pride.

I know a woman of ninety-six who has the bright, innocent face of a girl. I know a man well under middle age whose face is drawn into inharmonious contours. The one is the result of a sweet and sunny disposition; the other is the outcome of passion and discontent.

As you cannot have a sweet and wholesome abode unless you admit the air and sunshine freely into your rooms, so a strong body and a bright, happy, or serene countenance can only result from the free admittance into the mind of thoughts of joy and good will and serenity.

On the faces of the aged there are wrinkles made by sympathy; others by strong and pure thoughts; and others are carved by passion: who cannot distinguish them? With those who have lived righteously, age is calm, peaceful, and softly mellowed, like the setting sun. I have recently seen a philosopher on his deathbed. He was not old except in years. He died as sweetly and peacefully as he had lived.

There is no physician like cheerful thought for dissipating the ills of the body; there is no comforter to compare with good will for dispersing the shadows of grief and sorrow. To live continually in thoughts of ill will, cynicism, suspicion, and envy, is to be confined in a self-made prisonhold. But to think well of all, to be cheerful with all, to patiently learn to

THOUGHT
AND PURPOSE

Until thought is linked with purpose there is no intelligent accomplishment. With the majority the baroque of thought is allowed to drift upon the ocean of life. Aimlessness is a vice, and such drifting must not continue for him who would steer clear of catastrophe and destruction.

They who have no central purpose in their life fall an easy prey to petty worries, fears, troubles, and self-pitying, all of which lead, just as surely as deliberately planned sins (though by a different route), to failure, unhappiness, and loss, for weakness cannot persist in a power-evolving universe.

A man should conceive of a legitimate purpose in his heart, and set out to accomplish it. He should make this purpose the centralizing point of his thoughts. It may take the form of spiritual ideal, or it may be a worldly object, according to his nature at the time being; but whichever it is, he should steadily focus his thought-forces upon the object which he has set before him. He should make this purpose his supreme duty, and should devote himself to its attainment, not allowing his thoughts to wander away into ephemeral fancies, longings, and imaginings. This is the royal road to self-control and true concentration of thought. Even if he fails again and again to accomplish his purpose (as he necessarily must until weakness is overcome), the *strength of character gained* will be the measure of his *true* success, and will form a new starting-point for future power and triumph.

Those who are not prepared for the apprehension of a *great* purpose should fix their thoughts upon the faultless performance of their duty, no matter how insignificant their task may appear. Only in this way can the thoughts be gathered and focused, and resolution and energy be developed, which being done, there is nothing which may be accomplished.

The weakest soul, knowing its own weakness, and believing this truth—*that strength can only be developed by effort and practice*, will, thus believing, at once begin to extend itself, and, adding effort to effort, patience to patience, and strength to strength, will never cease to develop, and will at last grow divinely strong.

As the physically weak man can make himself strong by careful and patient training, so the man of weak thoughts can make them strong by exercising himself in right thinking.

To put away aimlessness and weakness, and to begin to think with purpose, is to enter the ranks of those strong ones who only recognize failure as one of the pathways to attainment; who make all conditions serve them, and who think strongly, attempt fearlessly, and accomplish masterfully.

Having conceived of his purpose, a man should mentally mark out a *straight* pathway to its achievement, looking neither to the right nor the left. Doubts and fears should be rigorously excluded; they are disintegrating elements which break up the straight line of effort, rendering it crooked, ineffectual, useless. Thoughts of doubt and fear never accomplish anything, and never can. They always lead to failure. Purpose, energy, power to do, and all strong thoughts cease when doubt and fear creep in.

The will to do springs from the knowledge that we *can* do. Doubt and fear are the great enemies of knowledge, and he who encourages them, who does not slay them, thwarts himself at every step.

He who has conquered doubt and fear has conquered failure. His every thought is allied with power, and all difficulties are bravely met and wisely overcome. His purposes are seasonably planted, and they bloom and bring forth fruit which does not fall prematurely to the ground.

Thought allied fearlessly to purpose becomes creative

force: he who *knows* this is ready to become something higher and stronger than a mere bundle of wavering thoughts and fluctuating sensations; he who *does* this has become the conscious and intelligent wielder of his mental powers.

THE
THOUGHT-FACTOR IN
ACHIEVEMENT

All that a man achieves and all that he fails to achieve is the direct result of his own thoughts. In a justly ordered universe, where loss of equipoise would mean total destruction, individual responsibility must be absolute. A man's weakness and strength, purity and impurity, are his own, and not another man's; they are brought about by himself, and not by another; and they can only be altered by himself, never by another. His condition is also his own, and not another man's. His suffering and his happiness are evolved from within. As he thinks, so he is; as he continues to think, so he remains.

A strong man cannot help a weaker unless that weaker is *willing* to be helped, and even then the weak man must become strong of himself; he must, by his own efforts, develop the strength which he admires in another. None but himself can alter his condition.

It has been usual for men to think and to say, "Many men are slaves because one is an oppressor; let us hate the oppressor." Now, however, there is amongst an increasing few a tendency to reverse this judgment, and to say, "One man is an oppressor because many are slaves; let us depise the slaves." The truth is that oppressor and slave are co-operators in ignorance, and, while seeming to afflict each other, are in reality afflicting themselves. A perfect Knowledge perceives the action of law in the weakness of the oppressed and the misapplied power of the oppressor; a perfect Love, seeing the suffering which both states entail, condemn neither; a perfect Compassion embraces both oppressor and oppressed.

He who has conquered weakness, and has put away all selfish thoughts, belongs neither to oppressor nor oppressed. He is free.

A man can only rise, conquer and achieve by lifting up his thoughts. He can only remain weak, and abject, and miserable, by refusing to lift up his thoughts.

Before a man can achieve anything, even in worldly things, he must lift his thoughts above slavish animal indulgence. He may not, in order to succeed, give up *all* animality and selfishness, by any means; but a portion of it must, at least, be sacrificed. A man whose first thought is bestial indulgence could neither think clearly nor plan methodically; he could not find and develop his latent resources, and would fail in any undertaking. Not having commenced manfully to control his thoughts, he is not in a position to control affairs and to adopt serious responsibilities. He is not fit to act independently and stand alone. But he is limited only by the thoughts which he chooses.

There can be no progress, no achievement without sacrifice, and a man's worldly success will be in the measure that he sacrifices his confused animal thoughts, and fixes his mind on the development of his plans, and the strengthening of his resolution and self-reliance. And the higher he lifts his thoughts, the more manly, upright, and righteous he becomes, the greater will be his success, the more blessed and enduring will be his achievements.

The universe does not favor the greedy, the dishonest, the vicious, although on the mere surface it may sometimes appear to do so; it helps the honest, the magnanimous, the virtuous. All the great teachers of the ages have declared this in varying forms, and to prove and know it a man has but to persist in making himself more and more virtuous by lifting up his thoughts.

Intellectual achievements are the result of thought consecrated to the search for knowledge, or for the beautiful and true in life and nature. Such achievements may be sometimes connected with vanity and ambition, but they are not the outcome of those characteristics; they are the natural outgrowth of long and arduous effort, and of pure and unselfish thoughts.

Spiritual achievements are the consummation of holy aspirations. He who lives constantly in the conception of noble and lofty thoughts, who dwells upon all that is pure and unselfish, will, as surely as the sun reaches its zenith and the moon its full, become wise and noble in character and rise into a position of influence and blessedness.

Achievement, of whatever kind, is the crown of effort, the diadem of thought. By the aid of self-control, resolution, purity, righteousness, and well-directed thought a man ascends; by the aid of animality, indolence, impurity, corruption, and confusion of thoughts a man descends.

A man may rise to high success in the world, and even to lofty altitudes in the spiritual realm, and again descend into weakness and wretchedness by allowing arrogant, selfish, and corrupt thoughts to take possession of him.

Victories attained by right thought can only be maintained by watchfulness. Many give way when success is assured, and rapidly fall back into failure.

All achievements, whether in the business, intellectual, or spiritual world, are the results of definitely directed thought, are governed by the same law and are of the same method; the only difference lies in *the object of attainment*. He who would accomplish little must sacrifice little; he who would achieve much must sacrifice much; he who would attain highly must sacrifice greatly.

VISIONS AND IDEALS

The dreamers are the saviors of the world. As the visible world is sustained by the invisible, so men, through all their trials and sins and sordid vocations, are nourished by the beautiful visions of their solitary dreamers. Humanity cannot forget its dreamers; it cannot let their ideals fade and die; it lives in them; it knows them as the *realities* which it shall one day see and know.

Composer, sculptor, painter, poet, prophet, sage, these are the makers of the after-world, the architects of heaven. The world is beautiful because they have lived; without them laboring humanity would perish.

He who cherishes a beautiful vision, a lofty ideal in his heart will one day realize it. Columbus cherished a vision of another world, and he discovered it; Copernicus fostered the vision of a multiplicity of worlds and a wider universe and he revealed it, Buddha beheld the vision of a spiritual world of stainless beauty and perfect peace, and he entered into it.

Cherish your visions; cherish your ideals; cherish the music that stirs in your heart, the beauty that forms in your mind, the loveliness that drapes your purest thoughts, for out of them will grow all delightful conditions, all heavenly environment; of these, if you but remain true to them, your world will at least be built.

To desire is to obtain; to aspire is to achieve. Shall man's

basest desires receive the fullest measure of gratification, and
his purest aspirations starve for lack of sustenance? Such is
not the law: such a condition of things can never obtain:
"Ask and receive."

Dream lofty dreams, and as you dream, so shall you become. Your Vision is the promise of what you shall one day
be; your Ideal is the prophecy of what you shall at last un-
veil.

The greatest achievement was at first and for a time a
dream. The oak sleeps in the acorn; the bird waits in the egg;
and in the highest vision of the soul a waking angel stirs.
Dreams are the seedlings of realities.

Your circumstances may be uncongenial, but they shall not
long remain so if you but perceive an Ideal and strive to
reach it. You cannot travel *within* and stand still *without*.
Here is a youth hard pressed by poverty and labor; confined
long hours in an unhealthy workshop; unschooled, and lack-
ing all the arts of refinement. But he dreams of better things;
he thinks of intelligence, of refinement, of grace and beauty.
He conceives of, mentally builds up, an ideal condition of
life; the vision of a wider liberty and a larger scope takes
possession of him; unrest urges him to action, and he utilizes
all his spare time and means, small though they are, to the
development of his latent powers and resources. Very soon so
altered has his mind become that the workshop can no longer
hold him. It has become so out of harmony with his mental-
ity that it falls out of his life as a garment is cast aside, and,
with the growth of opportunities which fit the scope of his ex-
panding powers, he passes out of it forever. Years later we
see this youth as a full-grown man. We find him a master of
certain forces of the mind which he wields with world-wide
influence and almost unequaled power. In his hand he holds
the cords of gigantic responsibilities; he speaks, and lo! lives
are changed; men and women hang upon his words and re-
mold their characters, and, sunlike, he becomes the fixed and
luminous center round which innumerable destinies revolve.

He has realized the Vision of his youth. He has become
one with his Ideal.

And you, too, youthful reader, will realize the Vision (not
the ideal wish) of your heart, be it base or beautiful, or a
mixture of both, for you will always gravitate toward that

which you, secretly, most love. Into your hands will be placed
the exact results of your own thoughts; you will receive that
which you earn; no more, no less. Whatever your present environment may be, you will fall, remain, or rise with your
thoughts, your Vision, your Ideal. You will become as small
as your controlling desire; as great as your dominant aspira-
tion: in the beautiful words of Stanton Kirkham Davis, "You
may be keeping accounts, and presently you shall walk out of
the door that for so long has seemed to you the barrier of
your ideals, and shall find yourself before an audience—the
pen still behind your ear, the inkstains on your fingers—and
then and there shall pour out the torrent of your inspiration.
You may be driving sheep, and you shall wander to the
city—bucolic and open-mouthed; shall wander under the in-
trepid guidance of the spirit into the studio of the master, and
after a time he shall say, 'I have nothing more to teach you.'
And now you have become the master, who did so recently
dream of great things while driving sheep. You shall lay
down the saw and the plane to take upon yourself the regeneration of the world."

The thoughtless, the ignorant, and the indolent, seeing only
the apparent effects of things and not the things themselves,
talk of luck, of fortune, and chance. Seeing a man grow rich,
they say, "How lucky he is!" Observing another become intellectual, they exclaim, "How highly favored he is!" And not-
ing the saintly character and wide influence of another, they
remark, "How chance aids him at every turn!" They do not
see the trials and failures and struggles which these men have
voluntarily encountered in order to gain their experience;
have no knowledge of the sacrifices they have made, of the
undaunted efforts they have put forth, of the faith they have
exercised, that they might overcome the apparently unsur-
mountable, and realize the Vision of their heart. They do not
know the darkness and the heartaches; they only see the light
and joy, and call it "Luck"; do not see the long and arduous
journey, but only behold the pleasant goal, and call it "good
fortune"; do not understand the process, but only perceive the
result, and call it "chance."

In all human affairs there are *efforts*, and there are *results*,
and the strength of the effort is the measure of the result.
Chance is not. "Gifts," powers, materials, intellectual, and

SERENITY

Calmness of mind is one of the beautiful jewels of wisdom. It is the result of long and patient effort in self-control. Its presence is an indication of ripened experience, and of a more than ordinary knowledge of the laws and operations of thought.

A man becomes calm in the measure that he understands himself as a thought-evolved being, for such knowledge necessitates the understanding of others as the result of thought, and as he develops a right understanding, and sees more and more clearly the internal relations of things by the action of cause and effect, he ceases to fuss and fume and worry and grieve, and remains poised, steadfast, serene.

The calm man, having learned how to govern himself, knows how to adapt himself to others; and they, in turn reverence his spiritual strength, and feel that they can learn of him and rely upon him. The more tranquil a man becomes, the greater is his success, his influence, his power for good. Even the ordinary trader will find his business prosperity increase as he develops a greater self-control and equanimity, for people will always prefer to deal with a man whose demeanor is strongly equable.

The strong, calm man is always loved and revered. He is like a shade-giving tree in a thirsty land, or a sheltering rock in a storm. "Who does not love a tranquil heart, a sweet-tempered, balanced life? It does not matter whether it rains or shines, or what changes come to those possessing these blessings, for they are always sweet, serene, and calm. That exquisite poise of character which we call serenity is the last lesson of culture; it is the flowering of life, the fruitage of the soul. It is precious as wisdom, more to be desired than gold—yea, than even fine gold. How insignificant mere money-seeking looks in comparison with a serene life—a life that dwells in the oceans of Truth, beneath the waves, beyond the reach of tempests, in the Eternal Calm!

"How many people we know who sour their lives, who ruin all that is sweet and beautiful by explosive tempers, who destroy their poise of character, and make bad blood! It is a question whether the great majority of people do not ruin their lives and mar their happiness by lack of self-control. How few people we meet in life who are well-balanced, who have that exquisite poise which is characteristic of the finished character!"

Yes, humanity surges with uncontrolled passion, is tumultuous with ungoverned grief, is blown about by anxiety and doubt. Only the wise man, only he whose thoughts are controlled and purified, make the winds and the storms of the soul obey him.

Tempest-tossed souls, wherever ye may be, under whatsoever conditions ye may live, know this—in the ocean of life, the isles of Blessedness are smiling, and the sunny shore of your ideal awaits your coming. Keep your hand firmly upon the helm of thought. In the barque of your soul reclines the commanding Master; He does but sleep; wake Him. Self-control is strength; Right Thought is mastery; Calmness is power. Say unto your heart, "Peace, be still!"

IV

THE PRACTICE OF THE PRESENCE OF GOD

BROTHER LAWRENCE

ABOUT
THE AUTHOR

Brother Lawrence (1611-1691) was born Nicholas Herman in French Lorraine. His formal education was believed meager and his family background undistinguished. At age 18, he experienced a religious conversion, and from that time forth sought to serve the Lord. Though there are few details of his wanderings between the time he committed his life to Christ and his entrance into a monastery in 1666, it is known that he worked as a soldier and later a footman prior to becoming a lay brother at age 55 with the Carmelites, an order of monks, in Paris.

His assignment: The monastery kitchen where he was in his own words, "lord of all pots and pans and things." It was in that setting, among the clamor and clatter of dirty dishes, that Brother Lawrence cheerfully worked and quietly prayed—at the same time. "The time of business," he said, "does not with me differ from time of prayer." His example caused those about him to inquire of his secret, and at their urging he reluctantly set down his thoughts on practicing the continual presence of God.

CONTENTS

CONVERSATIONS

First Conversation 109
Second Conversation 110
Third Conversation 113
Fourth Conversation 115

LETTERS

First Letter 119
Second Letter 120
Third Letter 123
Fourth Letter 124
Fifth Letter 126
Sixth Letter 127
Seventh Letter 128
Eighth Letter 129
Ninth Letter 130
Tenth Letter 131
Eleventh Letter 132
Twelfth Letter 133
Thirteenth Letter 134
Fourteenth Letter 134
Fifteenth Letter 135

CONVERSATIONS

FIRST CONVERSATION

The first time I saw Brother Lawrence was upon the third of August, 1666. He told me that God had done him a singular favor in his conversion at the age of eighteen.

That in the winter, seeing a tree stripped of its leaves, and considering that within a little time the leaves would be renewed, and after that the flowers and fruit appear, he received a high view of the providence and power of God, which has never since been effaced from his soul. That this view had perfectly set him loose from the world, and kindled in him such a love for God that he could not tell whether it had increased during the more than forty years he had lived since.

That he had been footman to M. Fieubert, the treasurer, and that he was a great awkward fellow who broke everything.

That he had desired to be received into a monastery, thinking that he would there be made to smart for his awkwardness and the faults he should commit, and so he should sacrifice to God his life, with its pleasures; but that God had disappointed him, he having met with nothing but satisfaction in that state.

That we should establish ourselves in a sense of God's

presence by continually conversing with Him. That it was a shameful thing to quit His conversation to think of trifles and fooleries.

That we should feel and nourish our souls with high notions of God; which would yield us great joy in being devoted to Him.

That we ought to quicken—i.e. to enliven—our faith. That it was lamentable we had so little; and that instead of taking *faith* for the rule of their conduct, men amused themselves with trivial devotions, which changed daily. That the way of faith was the spirit of the church, and that it was sufficient to bring us to a high degree of perfection.

That we ought to give ourselves up to God, with regard both to things temporal and spiritual, and seek our satisfaction only in the fulfilling of His will, whether He lead us by suffering or by consolation, for all would be equal to a soul truly resigned. That there needed fidelity in those drynesses or insensibilities and irksomenesses in prayer by which God tries our love to Him; that *then* was the time for us to make good and effectual acts of resignation, whereof one alone would oftentimes very much promote our spiritual advancement.

That as for the miseries and sins he heard of daily in the world, he was so far from wondering at them that, on the contrary, he was surprised that there were not more, considering the malice sinners were capable of; that, for his part, he prayed for them; but knowing that God could remedy the mischiefs they did when He pleased, he gave himself no further trouble.

That to arrive at such resignation as God requires, we should watch attentively over all the passions which mingle as well in spiritual things as in those of a grosser nature; that God would give light concerning those passions to those who truly desire to serve Him. That if this was my design, sincerely to serve God, I might come to him (Brother Lawrence) as often as I pleased, without any fear of being troublesome; but if not, that I ought no more to visit him.

SECOND CONVERSATION

That he had always been governed by love, without selfish views; and that having resolved to make the love of God the *end* of all his actions, he had found reasons to be well satisfied with his method. That he was pleased when he could take up a straw from the ground for the love of God, seeking Him only, and nothing else, not even His gifts.

That he had been long troubled in mind from a certain belief that he should be damned; that all the men in the world could not have persuaded him to the contrary; but that he had thus reasoned with himself about it: *I engaged in a religious life only for the love of God, and I have endeavored to act only for Him; whatever becomes of me, whether I be lost or saved, I will always continue to act purely for the love of God. I shall have this good at least that till death I shall have done all that is in me to love Him.* That this trouble of mind had lasted four years, during which time he had suffered much; but that at last he had seen that this trouble arose from want of faith, and that since he had passed his life in perfect liberty and continual joy. That he had placed his sins betwixt him and God, as it were, to tell Him that he did not deserve His favors, but that God still continued to bestow them in abundance.

That in order to form a habit of conversing with God continually, and referring all we do to Him, we must first apply to Him with some diligence; but that after a little care we should find His love inwardly excite us to it without any difficulty.

That he expected, after the pleasant days God had given him, he should have his turn of pain and suffering; but that he was not uneasy about it, knowing very well that as he could do nothing of himself, God would not fail to give Him the strength to bear it.

That when an occasion of practicing some virtue offered, he addressed himself to God, *saying, Lord, I cannot do this unless Thou enablest me;* and that then he received strength more than sufficient.

That when he had failed in his duty, he only confessed his fault, saying to God, *I shall never do otherwise if You leave me to myself; it is You who must hinder my falling, and mend what is amiss.* That after this he gave himself no further uneasiness about it.

That we ought to act with God in the greatest simplicity, speaking to Him frankly and plainly, and imploring His assistance in our affairs, just as they happen. That God never failed to grant it, as he had often experienced.

That he had been lately sent into Burgundy, to buy the provision of wine for the society, which was a very unwelcome task for him, because he had no turn for business, and because he was lame and could not go about the boat but by rolling himself over the casks. That, however, he gave himself no uneasiness about it, nor about the purchase of the wine. That he said to God it was His business he was about, and that he afterward found it very well performed. That he had been sent into Auvergne, the year before, upon the same account; that he could not tell how the matter passed, but that it proved very well.

So, likewise, in his business in the kitchen (to which he had naturally a great aversion), having accustomed himself to do everything there for the love of God, and with prayer, upon all occasions, for His grace to do his work well, he had found everything easy, during fifteen years that he had been employed there.

That he was very well pleased with the post he was now in; but that he was as ready to quit that as the former, since he was always pleasing himself in every condition by doing little things for the love of God.

That with him the set times of prayer were not different from other times; that he retired to pray, according to the directions of his superior, but that he did not want such retirement, nor ask for it, because his greatest business did not divert him from God.

That as he knew his obligation to love God in all things, and as he endeavored so to do, he had no need of a director to advise him, but that he needed much a confessor to absolve him. That he was very sensible of his faults, but not discouraged by them; that he confessed them to God, but did not plead against Him to excuse them. When he had so done, he peaceably resumed his usual practice of love and adoration.

That in his trouble of mind he had consulted nobody, but knowing only by the light of faith that God was present, he contented himself with directing all his actions to Him, i.e., doing them with a desire to please Him, let what would come of it.

That useless thoughts spoil all; that the mischief began there; but that we ought to reject them as soon as we perceived their impertinence to the matter in hand, or our salvation, and return to our communion with God.

That at the beginning he had often passed his time appointed for prayer in rejecting wandering throughts and falling back into them. That he could never regulate his devotion by certain methods as some do. That, nevertheless, at first he had *meditated* for some time, but afterwards that went off, in a manner he could give no account of.

That all bodily mortifications and other exercises are useless, except as they serve to arrive at the union with God by love; that he had well considered this, and found it the shortest way to go straight to Him by a continual exercise of love and doing all things for His sake.

That we ought to make a difference between the acts of the understanding and those of the will; that the first were comparatively of little value, and the others, all. That our only business was to love and delight ourselves in God.

That all possible kinds of mortification, if they were void of the love of God, could not efface a single sin. That we ought, without anxiety, to expect the pardon of our sins from the blood of Jesus Christ, only endeavoring to love Him with all our hearts. That God seemed to have granted the greatest favors to the greatest sinners, as more signal monuments of His mercy.

That the greatest pains or pleasures of this world were not to be compared with what he had experienced of both kinds in a spiritual state; so that he was careful for nothing and feared nothing, desiring only one thing of God, viz., that he might not offend Him.

That he had no scruples; for, said he, when I fail in my duty, I readily acknowledge it, saying, *I am used to do so; I shall never do otherwise if I am left to myself.* If I fail not, then I give God thanks, acknowledging that the strength comes from Him.

THIRD CONVERSATION

He told me that the foundation of the spiritual life in him had been a high notion and esteem of God in faith; which when he had once well conceived, he had no other care at first but faithfully to reject every other thought, *that he might perform all his actions for the love of God.* That when sometimes he had not thought of God for a good while, he did not disquiet himself for it; but, after having acknowledged his wretchedness to God, he returned to Him with so much the greater trust in Him as he had found himself wretched through forgetting Him.

That the trust we put in God honors Him much and draws down great graces.

That it was impossible not only that God should deceive, but also that He should long let a soul suffer which is perfectly resigned to Him, and resolved to endure everything for His sake.

That he had so often experienced the ready succors of divine grace upon all occasions, that from the same experience, when he had business to do, he did not think of it beforehand; but when it was time to do it, he found in God, as in a clear mirror, all that was fit for him to do. That of late he had acted thus, without anticipating care; but before the experience above mentioned, he had used it in his affairs.

When outward business diverted him a little from the thought of God, a fresh remembrance coming from God invested his soul, and so inflamed and transported him that it was difficult for him to contain himself.

That he was more united to God in his outward employments than when he left them for devotion and retirement.

That he expected hereafter some great pain of body or mind; that the worst that could happen to him was to lose that sense of God which he had enjoyed so long; but that the goodness of God assured him He would not forsake him utterly, and that He would give him strength to bear whatever evil He permitted to happen to him; and therefore that he feared nothing, and had no occasion to consult with anybody about his state. That when he had attempted to do it, he had always come away more perplexed; and that as he was conscious of his readiness to lay down his life for the love of God, he had no apprehension of danger. That perfect resignation to God was a sure way to heaven, a way in which we had always sufficient light for our conduct.

That in the beginning of the spiritual life we ought to be faithful in doing our duty and denying ourselves; but after that, unspeakable pleasures followed. That in difficulties we need only have recourse to Jesus Christ, and beg His grace; with that everything became easy.

That many do not advance in the Christian progress because they stick in penances and particular exercises, while they neglect the love of God, which is the *end*. That this appeared plainly by their works, and was the reason why we see so little solid virtue.

That there needed neither art nor science for going to God, but only a heart resolutely determined to apply itself to nothing but Him, or for His sake, and to love Him only.

FOURTH CONVERSATION

He discoursed with me frequently, and with great openness of heart, concerning his manner of *going* to God, whereof some part is related already.

He told me that all consists in one hearty renunciation of everything which we are sensible does not lead to God. That we might accustom ourselves to a continual conversation with Him, with freedom and in simplicity. That we need only to recognize God intimately present with us, to address ourselves to Him every moment, that we beg His assistance for knowing His will in things doubtful, and for rightly performing those which we plainly see He requires of us, offering them to Him before we do them, and giving Him thanks when we have done.

That in this conversation with God we are also employed in praising, adoring, and loving Him incessantly, for His infinite goodness and perfection.

That, without being discouraged on account of our sins, we should pray for His grace with a perfect confidence, as relying upon the infinite merits of our Lord Jesus Christ. That God never failed offering us His grace at each action; that he distinctly perceived it, and never failed of it, unless when his thoughts had wandered from a sense of God's presence, or he had forgotten to ask His assistance.

That God always gave us light in our doubts when we had no other design but to please Him.

That our sanctification did not depend upon *changing* our works, but in doing that for God's sake which we commonly do for our own. That it was lamentable to see how many people mistook the means for the end, addicting themselves to certain works, which they performed very imperfectly, by reason of their human or selfish regards.

That the most excellent method he had found of going to

God was that of doing our common business without any view of pleasing men, and (as far as we are capable) purely for the love of God.

That it was a great delusion to think that the times of prayer ought to differ from other times; that we are as strictly obliged to adhere to God by action in the time of action as by prayer in the season of prayer.

That his prayer was nothing else but a sense of the presence of God, his soul being at that time insensible to everything but divine love; and that when the appointed times of prayer were past, he found no difference, because he still continued with God, praising and blessing Him with all his might, so that he passed his life in continual joy; yet hoped that God would give him somewhat to suffer when he should grow stronger.

That we ought, once for all, heartily to put our whole trust in God, and make a total surrender of ourselves to Him, secure that He would not deceive us.

That we ought not to be weary of doing little things for the love of God, who regards not the greatness of the work, but the love with which it is performed. That we should not wonder if, in the beginning, we often failed in our endeavors, but that at last we should gain a habit, which will naturally produce its acts in us, without our care, and to our exceeding great delight.

That the whole substance of religion was faith, hope, and charity, by the practice of which we become united to the will of God; that all besides is indifferent, and to be used as a means that we may arrive at our end, and be swallowed up therein, by faith and charity.

That all things are possible to him who *believes;* that they are less difficult to him who *hopes;* that they are more easy to him who *loves;* and still more easy to him who perseveres in the practice of these three virtues.

That the end we ought to propose to ourselves is to become, in this life, the most perfect worshipers of God we can possibly be, as we hope to be through all eternity.

That when we enter upon the spiritual life, we should consider and examine to the bottom what we are. And then we should find ourselves worthy of all contempt, and not deserving indeed the name of Christians; subject to all kinds of misery and numberless accidents, which trouble us and cause perpetual vicissitudes in our health, in our humors, in our internal and external dispositions; in fine, persons whom God would humble by many pains and labors, as well within as without. After this we should not wonder that troubles, temptation, oppositions, and contradictions happen to us from men. We ought, on the contrary, to submit ourselves to them, and bear them as long as God pleases, as things highly advantageous to us.

That the greater perfection a soul aspires after, the more dependent it is upon divine grace.

Being questioned by one of his own society (to whom he was obliged to open himself) by what means he had attained such an habitual sense of God, he told them that, since his first coming to the monastery, he had considered God as the end of all his thoughts and desires, as the mark to which they should tend, and in which they should terminate.

That in the beginning of his novitiate he spent the hours appointed for private prayer in thinking of God, so as to convince his mind of, and to impress deeply upon his heart, the divine existence, rather by devout sentiments, and submission to the lights of faith, than by studied reasonings and elaborate meditations. That by this short and sure method he exercised himself in the knowledge and love of God, resolving to use his utmost endeavor to live in a continual sense of His presence, and, if possible never to forget Him more.

That when he had thus in prayer filled his mind with great sentiments of that infinite Being, he went to his work appointed in the kitchen (for he was cook to the society). There having first considered severally the things his office required, and when and how each thing was to be done, he spent all the intervals of his time, as well before as after his work, in prayer.

That when he began his business, he said to God, with a filial trust in Him: *O my God, since Thou art with me, and I must now, in obedience to Thy commands, apply my mind to these outward things, I beseech Thee to grant me the grace to continue in Thy presence; and to this end do Thou prosper me with Thy assistance, receive all my works, and possess all my affections.*

As he proceeded in his work he continued his familiar conversation with his Maker, imploring His grace, and offering to Him all his actions.

When he had finished he examined himself how he had discharged his duty; if he found *well,* he returned thanks to

God; if otherwise, he asked pardon, and, without being discouraged, he set his mind right again, and continued his exercise of the *presence* of God as if he had never deviated from it. "Thus," said he, "by rising after my falls, and by frequently renewed acts of faith and love, I am come to a state wherein it would be as difficult for me not to think of God as it was at first to accustom myself to it."

As Brother Lawrence had found such an advantage in walking in the presence of God, it was natural for him to recommend it earnestly to others; but his example was a stronger inducement than any arguments he could propose. His very countenance was edifying, such a sweet and calm devotion appearing in it as could not but affect the beholders. And it was observed that in the greatest hurry of business in the kitchen he still preserved his recollection and heavenly-mindedness. He was never hasty nor loitering, but did each thing in its season, with an even, uninterrupted composure and tranquillity of spirit. "The time of business," said he, "does not with me differ from the time of prayer; and in the noise and clatter of my kitchen, while several persons are at the same time calling for different things, I possess God in as great tranquillity as if I were upon my knees at the blessed sacrament."

LETTERS

FIRST LETTER

Since you desire so earnestly that I should communicate to you the method by which I arrived at that *habitual sense of God's presence*, which our Lord, of His mercy, has been pleased to vouchsafe to me, I must tell you that it is with great difficulty that I am prevailed on by your importunities and now I do it only upon the terms that you show my letter to nobody. If I knew that you would let it be seen, all the desire that I have for your advancement would not be able to determine me to it. The account I can give you is:

Having found in many books different methods of going to God, and divers practices of the spiritual life, I thought this would serve rather to puzzle me than facilitate what I sought after, which was nothing but how to become wholly God's. This made me resolve to give the all for the all; so after having given myself wholly to God, that He might take away my sin, I renounced, for the love of Him, everything that was not He and I began to live as if there was none but He and I in the world. Sometimes I considered myself before Him as a poor criminal at the feet of his judge; at other times I beheld Him in my heart as my Father, as my God. I worshipped Him the oftenest that I could, keeping my mind in His holy presence and recalling it as often as I found it wandered from Him. I found no small pain in this exercise, and yet I continued it, notwithstanding all the difficulties that occurred, without troubling or disquieting myself when my mind had wandered involuntarily. I made this my business as much all the day long as at the appointed times of prayer; for at all times, every hour, every minute, even in the height of my business, I drove away from my mind everything that was capable of interrupting my thought of God.

Such has been my common practice ever since I entered in religion; and though I have done it very imperfectly, yet I have found great advantages by it. These, I well know, are to be imputed to the mere mercy and goodness of God, because we can do nothing without Him, and I still less than any. But when we are faithful to keep ourselves in His holy presence, and set Him always before us, this not only hinders our offending Him and doing anything that may displease Him, at least wilfully, but it also begets in us a holy freedom, and, if I may so speak, a familiarity with God, wherewith we ask, and that successfully, the graces we stand in need of. In time, by often repeating these acts, they become habitual, and the presence of God rendered as it were natural to us. Give Him thanks, if you please, with me, for His great goodness toward me, which I can never sufficiently admire, for the many favors He has done to so miserable a sinner as I am. May all things praise Him. Amen.

I am, in our Lord,

Yours . . .

SECOND LETTER

To the Reverend—

Not finding my manner of life in books, although I have no difficulty about it, yet for greater security, I shall be glad to know your thoughts concerning it.

In a conversation some days since with a person of piety, he told me the spiritual life was a life of grace, which begins with servile fear, which is increased by hope for eternal life, and which is consummated by pure love; that each of these states had its different stages, by which one arrives at last at that blessed consummation.

I have not followed all these methods. On the contrary,

from I know not what instincts, I found they discouraged me. This was the reason why, at my entrance into religion, I took a resolution to give myself up to God, as the best return I could make for His love, and for the love of Him, to renounce all besides.

For the first year I commonly employed myself during the time set apart for devotion with the thought of death, judgment, heaven, hell, and my sins. Thus I continued some years, applying my mind carefully the rest of the day, and even in the midst of my business, *to the presence of God*, whom I considered always as *with* me, often as *in* me.

At length I came insensibly to do the same thing during my set time of prayer, which caused in me great delight and consolation. This practice produced in me so high an esteem for God that faith alone was capable to satisfy me in that point.*

Such was my beginning, and yet I must tell you that for the first ten years I suffered much. The apprehension that I was not devoted to God as I wished to be, my past sins always present to my mind, and the great unmerited favors which God did me, were the matter and source of my sufferings. During this time I fell often, and rose again presently. It seemed to me that all creatures, reason, and God Himself were against me, and faith alone for me. I was troubled sometimes with thoughts that to believe I had received such favors was an effect of my presumption, which pretended to be at once where others arrive with difficulty; at other times, that it was a wilful delusion, and that there was no salvation for me.

When I thought of nothing but to end my days in these troubles (which did not at all diminish the trust I had in God, and which served only to increase my faith), I found myself changed all at once; and my soul, which till that time was in trouble, felt a profound inward peace, as if she were in her center and place of rest.

Ever since that time I walk before God simply, in faith, with humility and with love, and I apply myself diligently to do nothing and think nothing which may displease Him. I

---

* I suppose he means that all distinct notions he could form of God were unsatisfactory, because he perceived them to be unworthy of God; and therefore his mind was not to be satisfied but by the views of faith, which apprehend God as infinite and incomprehensible, as He is in Himself, and not as He can be conceived by human ideas.

hope that when I have done what I can, He will do with me what He pleases.

As for what passes in me at present, I cannot express it. I have no pain or difficulty about my state, because I have no will but that God, which I endeavor to accomplish in all things, and to which I am so resigned that I would not take up a straw from the ground against His order, or from any other motive than purely that of love to Him.

I have quitted all forms of devotion and set prayers but those to which my state obliges me. And I make it my business only to persevere in His holy presence, wherein I keep myself by a simple attention, and a general fond regard to God, which I may call an *actual presence* of God; or, to speak better, an habitual, silent, and secret conversation of the soul with God, which often causes me joys and raptures inwardly, and sometimes also outwardly, so great that I am forced to use means to moderate them and prevent their appearance to others.

In short, I am assured beyond all doubt that my soul has been with God above these thirty years. I pass over many things that I may not be tedious to you, yet I think it proper to inform you after what manner I consider myself before God, whom I behold as my King.

I consider myself as the most wretched of men, full of sores and corruption, and who has committed all sorts of crimes against his King. Touched with a sensible regret, I confess to Him all my wickedness, I ask His forgiveness, I abandon myself in His hands that He may do what He pleases with me. The King, full of mercy and goodness, very far from chastising me, embraces me with love, makes me eat at His table, serves me with His own hands, gives me the key of His treasures; He converses and delights Himself with me incessantly, in a thousand and a thousand ways, and treats me in all respects as His favorite. It is thus I consider myself from time to time in His holy presence.

My most useful method is this simple attention, and such a general passionate regard to God, to whom I find myself often attached with greater sweetness and delight than that of an infant at the mother's breast; so that, if I dare use the expression, I should choose to call this state the bosom of God, for the inexpressible sweetness which I taste and experience there.

If sometimes my thoughts wander from it by necessity or

infirmity, I am presently recalled by inward motions so charming and delicious that I am ashamed to mention them. I desire your reverence to reflect rather upon my great wretchedness, of which you are fully informed, than upon the great favors which God does me, all unworthy and ungrateful as I am.

As for my set hours of prayer, they are only a continuation of the same exercise. Sometimes I consider myself there as a stone before a carver, whereof he is to make a statue; presently myself thus before God, I desire Him to form His perfect image in my soul, and make me entirely like Himself.

At other times, when I apply myself to prayer, I feel all my spirit and all my soul lift itself up without any care or effort of mine, and it continues as it were suspended and firmly fixed in God, as in its center and place of rest.

I know that some charge this state with inactivity, delusion, and self-love. I confess that it is a holy inactivity, and would be a happy self-love if the soul in that state were capable of it, because, in effect, while she is in this repose, she cannot be disturbed by such acts as she was formerly accustomed to, and which were then her support which would now rather hinder than assist her.

Yet I cannot bear that this should be called delusion, because the soul which thus enjoys God desires herein nothing but Him. If this be delusion in me, it belongs to God to remedy it. Let Him do what He pleases with me; I desire only Him, and to be wholly devoted to Him. You will, however, oblige me in sending me your opinion, to which I always pay a great deference, for I have a singular esteem for your reverence, and am, in our Lord.

Yours . . .

THIRD LETTER

We have a God who is infinitely gracious and knows all about our wants. I always thought that He would reduce you to extremity. He will come in His own time, and when you least expect it. Hope in Him more than ever; thank Him with me for the favors He does you, particularly for the fortitude and patience which He gives you in your afflictions. It is a plain mark of the care He takes of you. Comfort yourself, then, with Him, and give thanks for all.

I admire also the fortitude and bravery of Mr.——. God has given him a good disposition and a good will; but there is in him still a little of the world and a great deal of youth. I hope the affliction which God has sent him will prove a wholesome remedy to him, and make him enter into himself. It is an accident which should engage him to put all trust in *Him* who accompanies him everywhere. Let him think of Him as often as he can, especially in the greatest dangers. A little lifting up of the heart suffices. A little remembrance of God, one act of inward worship, though upon a march, and a sword in hand, are prayers, which, however short, are nevertheless very acceptable to God; and far from lessening a soldier's courage in occasions of danger, they best serve to fortify it.

Let him then think of God the most he can. Let him accustom himself, by degrees to this small but holy exercise. No one will notice it, and nothing is easier than to repeat often in the day these little internal adorations. Recommend to him, if you please, that he think of God the most he can, in the manner here directed. It is very fit and most necessary for a soldier who is daily exposed to the dangers of life. I hope that God will assist him and all the family, to whom I present my service, being theirs and

Yours . . .

FOURTH LETTER

I have taken this opportunity to communicate to you the sentiments of one of our society, concerning the admirable effects and continual assistances which he receives from *the presence of God*. Let you and me both profit by them.

You must know his continual care has been, for about forty years past that he has spent in religion, to be always with God, and to do nothing, say nothing, and think nothing which may displease Him, and this without any other view than purely for the love of Him, and because He deserves infinitely more.

He is now so accustomed to that divine presence that he receives from it continual succors upon all occasions. For about thirty years his soul has been filled with joys so continual, and sometimes so great, that he is forced to use means to moderate them, and to hinder their appearing outwardly.

If sometimes he is a little too much absent from that divine presence, God presently makes Himself to be felt in his soul to recall him, which oftens happens when he is most engaged in his outward business. He answers with exact fidelity to these inward drawings, either by an elevation of his heart toward God, or by a meek and fond regard to Him; or by such words as love forms upon these occasions, as, for instance, *My God, here I am all devoted to Thee. Lord, make me according to Thy heart.* And then it seems to him (as in effect he feels it) that this God of love, satisfied with such few words, reposes again, and rests in the fund and center of his soul. The experience of these things gives him such an assurance that God is always in the fund or bottom of his soul that it renders him incapable of doubting it upon any account whatever.

Judge by this what content and satisfaction he enjoys while he continually finds in himself so great a treasure. He is no longer in an anxious search after it, but has it open before him, and may take what he pleases of it.

He complains much of our blindness, and cries often that we are to be pitied who content ourselves with so little. *God,* saith he, *has infinite treasure to bestow, and we take up with a little sensible devotion, which passes in a moment. Blind as we are, we hinder God and stop the current of His graces. But when He finds a soul penetrated with a lively faith, He pours into it His graces and favors plentifully; there they flow like a torrent which, after being forcibly stopped against its ordinary course, when it has found a passage, spreads itself with impetuosity and abundance.*

Yes, we often stop this torrent by the little value we set upon it. But let us stop it no more; let us enter into ourselves and break down the bank which hinders it. Let us make way for grace; let us redeem the lost time, for perhaps we have but little left. Death follows us close; let us be well prepared for it; for we die but once, and a miscarriage there is irretrievable.

I say again, let us enter into ourselves. The time presses, there is no room for delay; our souls are at stake. I believe you have taken such effectual measures that you will not be surprised. I commend you for it; it is the one thing necessary.

We must, nevertheless, always work at it, because not to advance in the spiritual life is to go back. But those who have the gale of the Holy Spirit go forward even in sleep. If the vessel of our soul is still tossed with winds and storms, let us awake the Lord, who reposes in it, and He will quickly calm the sea.

I have taken the liberty to impart to you these good sentiments, that you may compare them with your own. It will serve again to kindle and inflame them, if by misfortune (which God forbid, for it would be indeed a great misfortune) they should be, though never so little, cooled. Let us then both recall our first fervors. Let us profit by the example and the sentiments of this brother, who is little known of the world, but known of God, and extremely caressed by Him. I will pray for you; do you pray instantly for me, who am, in our Lord,

Yours . . .

FIFTH LETTER

I received this day two books and a letter from Sister—, who is preparing to make her profession, and upon that account desires the prayers of your holy society, and yours in particular. I perceive that she reckons much upon them; pray do not disappoint her. Beg of God that she may make her sacrifice in the view of His love alone, and with a firm resolution to be wholly devoted to Him. I will send you one of these books, which treat of the presence of God, a subject which, in my opinion contains the whole spiritual life; and it seems to me that whoever duly practices it will soon become spiritual.

I know that for the right practice of it the heart must be empty of all other things, because God will possess the heart *alone;* and as He cannot possess it alone without emptying it of all besides, so neither can He act there, and do in it what He pleases, unless it be left vacant to Him.

There is not in the world a kind of life more sweet and delightful than that of a continual conversation with God. Those only can comprehend it who practice and experience it; yet I do not advise you to do it from that motive. It is not pleasure which we ought to seek in this exercise; but let us do it from a principle of love, and because God would have us.

Were I a preacher, I should above all other things, preach the practice of the presence of God; and were I a director, I should advise all the world to do it, so necessary do I think it, and so easy, too.

Ah, knew we but the want of the grace and assistance of God, we should never lose sight of Him—no, not for a moment. Believe me; make immediately a holy and firm resolution nevermore wilfully to forget Him, and to spend the rest of your days in His sacred presence, deprived, for the love of Him, if He thinks fit, of all consolations.

Set heartily about this work, and if you do it as you ought, be assured that you will soon find the effects of it. I will assist you with my prayers, poor as they are. I recommend myself earnestly to yours and those of your holy society, being theirs, and more particularly

Yours . . .

SIXTH LETTER

(To the same)

I have received from Mrs.— the things which you gave her for me. I wonder that you have not given me your thoughts of the little book I sent to you, and which you must have received. Pray set heartily about the practice of it in your old age; it is better late than never.

I cannot imagine how religious persons can live satisfied without the practice of the presence of God. For my part, I keep myself retired with Him in the fund or center of my soul as much as I can; and while I am so with Him I fear nothing; but the least turning from Him insupportable.

This exercise does not much fatigue the body; it is, however, proper to deprive it sometimes, nay, often, of many little pleasures which are innocent and lawful, for God will not permit that a soul which desires to be devoted entirely to Him should take other pleasures than with Him: that is more than reasonable.

I do not say that therefore we must put any violent constraint upon ourselves. No, we must serve God in a holy freedom; we must do our business faithfully, without trouble or disquiet, recalling our mind to God mildly, and with tranquillity, as often as we find it wandering from Him.

It is, however, necessary to put our whole trust in God, laying aside all other cases, and even some particular forms of devotion, though very good in themselves, yet such as one often engages in unreasonably, because these devotions are only means to attain to the end. So when by this exercise of the presence of God we are *with Him* who is our end, it is then useless to return to the means; but we may continue with Him our commerce of love, persevering in His holy presence, one while by an act of praise, or adoration, or of desire; one while by an act of resignation or thanksgiving; and in all the ways which our spirit can invent.

Be not discouraged by the repugnance which you may find in it from nature; you must do yourself violence. At the first one often thinks it lost time, but you must go on, and resolve to persevere in it to death, notwithstanding all the difficulties that may occur. I recommend myself to the prayers of your holy society, and yours in particular. I am, in our Lord,

Yours ...

SEVENTH LETTER

I pity you much. It will be of great importance if you can leave the care of your affairs to—, and spend the remainder of your life only in worshiping God. He requires no great matters of us: a little remembrance of Him from time to time; a little adoration; sometimes to pray for His grace, sometimes to offer Him your sufferings, and sometimes to return Him thanks for the favors He has given you, and still gives you, in the midst of your troubles, and to console yourself with Him the oftenest you can. Lift up your heart to Him, sometimes even at your meals, and when you are in company; the least little remembrance will always be acceptable to Him. You need not cry very loud; He is nearer to us than we are aware of.

It is not necessary for being with God to be always at church. We may make an oratory of our heart wherein to retire from time to time to converse with Him in meekness, humility, and love. Every one is capable of such familiar conversation with God some more, some less. He knows what we can do. Let us begin, then. Perhaps He expects but one generous resolution on our part. Have courage. We have but little time to live; you are near sixty-four, and I am almost eighty. Let us live and die with God. Sufferings will be sweet and pleasant to us while we are with Him; and the greatest pleasures will be, without Him, a cruel punishment to us. May He be blessed for all. Amen.

Accustom yourself, then, by degrees thus to worship Him, to beg His grace, to offer Him your heart from time to time in the midst of your business, even every moment, if you can. Do not always scrupulously confine yourself to certain rules, or particular forms of devotion, but act with a general confidence in God, with love and humility. You may assure—of my poor prayers, and that I am their servant, and particularly

Yours in our Lord . . .

EIGHTH LETTER
(Concerning Wandering Thoughts in Prayer)

You tell me nothing new; you are not the only one that is troubled with wandering thoughts. Our mind is extremely roving; but, as the will is mistress of all our facilities, she must recall them, and carry them to God as their last end.

When the mind, for want of being sufficiently reduced by recollection at our first engaging in devotion, has contracted certain bad habits of wandering and dissipation, they are difficult to overcome, and commonly draw us, even against our wills, to the things of the earth.

I believe one remedy for this is to confess our faults and to humble ourselves before God. I do not advise you to use multiplicity of words in prayer, many words and long discourses being often the occasions of wandering. Hold yourself in prayer before God like a dumb or paralytic beggar at a rich man's gate. Let it be your business to keep your mind in the presence of the Lord. If it sometimes wander and withdraw itself from Him, do not much disquiet yourself for that: trouble and disquiet serve rather to distract the mind than to recollect it; the will must bring it back in tranquillity. If you persevere in this manner, God will have pity on you.

One way to recollect the mind easily in the time of prayer, and preserve it more in tranquillity, is *not to let it wander too far at other times.* You should keep it strictly in the presence of God; and being accustomed to think of Him often, you will find it easy to keep your mind calm in the time of prayer, or at least to recall it from its wanderings.

I have told you already at large, in my former letters, of the advantages we may draw from this practice of the presence of God. Let us set about it seriously, and pray for one another.

Yours . . .

NINTH LETTER

The enclosed is an answer to that which I received from—; pray deliver it to her. She seems to me full of good will, but she would go faster than grace. One does not become holy all at once. I recommend her to you; we ought to help one another by our advice, and yet more by our good examples. You will oblige me to let me hear of her from time to time, and whether she be very fervent and very obedient.

Let us thus think often that our only business in this life is to please God, and that all besides is but folly and vanity. You and I have lived about forty years in religion (i.e., a monastic life). Have we employed them in loving and serving God, who by His mercy has called us to this state, and for that every end? I am filled with shame and confusion when I reflect, on one hand, upon the great favors which God has done, and incessantly continues to do me; and on the other, upon the ill use I have made of them, and my small advancement in the way of perfection.

Since by His mercy He gives us still a little time, let us begin in earnest; let us repair the lost time; let us return with a full assurance to that Father of mercies, who is always ready to receive us affectionately. Let us renounce, let us generously renounce, for the love of Him, all that is not Himself; He deserves infinitely more. Let us think of Him perpetually. Let us put all our trust in Him. I doubt not but we shall soon find the effects of it in receiving the abundance of His grace, with which we can do all things, and without which we can do nothing but sin.

We cannot escape the dangers which abound in life without the actual and *continual* help of God. Let us, then, pray

to Him for it continually. How can ~~we~~
thinking of Him often? And how can ~~we~~
but by a holy habit which we should fo
me that I am always saying the same thi
is the best and easiest method I know; a
I advise all the world to do it. We must know ~~before~~ we can
love. In order to know God, we must often think of Him;
and when we come to love Him, we shall also think of Him
often, for our heart will be with our treasure. This is an argument which well deserves your consideration.

I am,

Yours . . .

TENTH LETTER

I have had a good deal of difficulty to bring myself to
write to Mr.—, and I do it now purely because you and
Madam— desire me. Pray write the directions and send it to
him. I am very pleased with the trust which you have in God;
I wish that He may increase it in you more and more. We
cannot have too much in so good and faithful a Friend, who
will never fail us in this world nor in the next.

If Mr.— makes his advantage of the loss he has had, and
puts all his confidence in God, He will soon give him another
friend, more powerful and more inclined to serve him. He
disposes of hearts as He pleases. Perhaps Mr.— was too
much attached to him he has lost. We ought to love our
friends, but without encroaching upon the love due to God,
which must be the principle.

Pray remember what I have recommended to you, which
is, to think often on God, by day, by night, in your business,
and even in your diversions. He is always near you and with
you; leave Him not alone. You would think it rude to leave a
friend alone who came to visit you; why, then, must God be
neglected: Do not, then, forget Him, but think on Him often,
adore Him continually, live and die with Him; this is the glorious employment of a Christian. In a word, this is our profession; if we do not know it, we must learn it. I will
endeavor to help you with my prayers, and am, in our Lord,

Yours . . .

ELEVENTH LETTER

I do not pray that you may be delivered from your pains, but I pray God earnestly that He would give you strength and patience to bear them as long as He pleases. Comfort yourself with Him who holds you fastened to the cross. He will loose you when He thinks fit. Happy those who suffer with Him. Accustom yourself to suffer in that manner, and seek from Him the strength to endure as much, and as long, as He shall judge to be necessary for you. The men of the world do not comprehend these truths, nor is it to be wondered at, since they suffer like what they are, and not like Christians. They consider sickness as a pain to nature, and not as a favor from God; and seeing it only in that light, they find nothing in it but grief and distress. But those who consider sickness as coming from the hand of God, as the effect of His mercy, and the means which He employs for their salvation—such commonly find in it great sweetness and sensible consolation.

I wish you could convince yourself that God is often (in some sense) nearer to us, and more effectually present with us, in sickness than in health. Rely upon no other physician; for, according to my apprehension, He reserves your cure to Himself. Put, then, all your trust in Him, and you will soon find the effects of it in your recovery, which we often retard by putting greater confidence in physic than in God.

Whatever remedies you make use of, they will succeed only so far as He permits. When pains come from God, He only can cure them. He often sends diseases of the body to cure those of the soul. Comfort yourself with the sovereign Physician both of the soul and body.

Be satisfied with the condition in which God places you; however happy you may think me, I envy you. Pains and suffering would be a paradise to me while I should suffer with my God, and the greatest pleasures would be hell to me if I could relish them without Him. All my consolation would be to suffer something for His sake.

I must, in a little time, go to God. What comforts me in this life is that I now see Him by faith; and I see Him in such a manner as might make me say sometimes, *I believe no more, but I see.* I feel what faith teaches us, and in that assurance and that practice of faith I will live and die with Him.

Continue, then, always with God; it is the only support and comfort for your affliction. I shall beseech Him to be with you. I present my service.

Yours . . .

TWELFTH LETTER

If we were well accustomed to the exercise of the presence of God, all bodily diseases would be much alleviated thereby. God often permits that we should suffer a little to purify our souls and oblige us to continue *with* Him.

Take courage; offer Him your pains incessantly; pray to Him for strength to endure them. Above all, get a habit of entertaining yourself often with God, and forget Him the least you can. Adore Him in your infirmities, offer yourself to Him from time to time, and in the height of your sufferings beseech Him humbly and affectionately (as a child his father) to make you comfortable to His holy will. I shall endeavor to assist you with my poor prayers.

God has many ways of drawing us to Himself. He sometimes hides Himself from us; but *faith* alone, which will not fail us in time of need, ought to be our support, and the foundation of our confidence, which must be all in God.

I know not how God will dispose of me. I am always happy. All the world suffer; and I, who deserve the severest discipline, feel joys so continual and so great that I can scarce contain them.

I would willingly ask of God a part of your sufferings, but that I know my weakness, which is so great that if He left me one moment to myself I should be the most wretched man alive. And yet I know not how He can leave me alone, because faith gives me as strong a conviction as sense can do that He never forsakes us until we have first forsaken Him. Let us fear to leave Him. Let us be always with Him. Let us live and die in His presence. Do you pray for me as I for you.

I am,

Yours . . .

THIRTEENTH LETTER

(To the Same)

I am in pain to see you suffer so long. What gives me ease and sweetens the feelings I have for your griefs is that they are proofs of God's love toward you. See them in that view and you will bear them more easily. As your case is, it is my opinion that you should leave off human remedies, and resign yourself entirely to the providence of God. Perhaps He stays only for that resignation and a perfect trust in Him to cure you. Since, notwithstanding all your cares, physic has hitherto proved unsuccessful, and your malady still increases, it will not be tempting God to abandon yourself in His hands and expect all from Him.

I told you in my last that He sometimes permits bodily diseases to cure the distempers of the soul. Have courage, then; make a virtue of necessity. Ask of God, not deliverance from your pains, but strength to bear resolutely, for the love of Him, all that He should please, and as long as He shall please.

Such prayers, indeed, are a little hard to nature, but most acceptable to God, and sweet to those that love Him. Love sweetens pains; and when one loves God, one suffers for His sake with joy and courage. Do you so, I beseech you; comfort yourself with Him, who is the only Physician of all our maladies. He is the Father of the afflicted, always ready to help us. He loves us infinitely, more than we imagine. Love Him, then, and seek no consolation elsewhere. I hope you will soon receive it. Adieu. I will help you with my prayers, poor as they are, and shall always be, in our Lord,

Yours . . .

FOURTEENTH LETTER

(To the Same)

I render thanks to our Lord for having relieved you a little, according to your desire. I have been often near expiring, but I never was so much satisfied as then. Accordingly, I did not pray for any relief, but I prayed for strength to suffer with courage, humility, and love. Ah, how sweet it is to suffer with God! However great the sufferings may be, receive them with love. It is paradise to suffer and be with Him; so that if in this life we would enjoy the peace of paradise we must accustom ourselves to a familiar, humble, affectionate conversation with Him. We must hinder our spirits' wandering from Him upon any occasion. We must make our heart a spiritual temple, wherein to adore Him incessantly. We must watch continually over ourselves, that we may not do nor say nor think anything that may displease Him. When our minds are thus employed about God, suffering will become full of unction and consolation.

I know that to arrive at this state the beginning is very difficult, for we must act purely in faith. But though it is difficult, we know also that we can do all things with the grace of God, which He never refuses to them who ask it earnestly. Knock, persevere in knocking, and I answer for it that He will open to you in His due time, and grant you all at once what He has deferred during many years. Adieu. Pray to Him for me as I pray to Him for you. I hope to see Him quickly.

> I am,
>
> Yours . . .

FIFTEENTH LETTER

(To the Same)

God knoweth best what is needful for us, and all that He does is for our good. If we knew how much He loves us, we should always be ready to receive equally and with indifference from His hand the sweet and the bitter. All would please that came from Him. The sorest afflictions never appear intolerable, except when we see them in the wrong light. When we see them as dispensed by the hand of God, when we know that it is our loving Father who abases and distresses us, our sufferings will lose their bitterness and become even matter of consolation.

Let us our employment be to *know* God; the more one knows Him, the more one desires to know Him. And as knowledge is commonly the measure of love, the deeper and more extensive our knowledge shall be, the greater will be our love; and if our love of God were great, we should love Him equally in pains and pleasures.

Let us not content ourselves with loving God for the mere sensible favors, how elevated soever, which He has done or may do us. Such favors, though never so great, cannot bring us so near to Him as faith does in one simple act. Let us seek Him often by faith. He is within us; seek Him not elsewhere. If we do love Him alone, are we not rude, and do we not deserve blame, if we busy ourselves about trifles which do not please and perhaps offend Him? It is to be feared these trifles will one day cost us dear.

Let us begin to be devoted to Him in good earnest. Let us cast everything besides out of our hearts. He would possess them alone. Beg this favor of Him. If we do what we can in our parts, we shall soon see that change wrought in us which we aspire after. I cannot thank Him sufficiently for the relaxation He has vouchsafed you. I hope from His mercy the favor to see Him within a few days.* Let us pray for one another.

I am, in our Lord.

Yours . . .

* He took to his bed two days after, and died within the week.

V

THE
IMITATION OF
CHRIST

THOMAS à KEMPIS

ABOUT
THE AUTHOR

Thomas à Kempis (1380-1471) was born and lived the first 12 years of his life in Kempen, Germany, a few miles northwest of Dusseldorf. He was the son of John and Gertrude Haemerken (the family name means "little hammer"). At age 12 he entered a school in Deventer where Latin and the copying and illustrating of manuscripts were taught. Seven years later he followed his older brother to the monastery of Mount St. Agnes at Agnetenberg, taking the vows of religion—poverty, chastity and obedience. He was ordained a priest in 1413 at age 33. Though Thomas served in various posts (treasurer of the order and subprior) he eventually turned to the quiet life of counselor, copyist and writer.

He was remarkably prolific, writing two biographies, several devotionals and many sermons, but only *The Imitation of Christ*, completed in 1427, was to gain lasting fame. It has been hailed as the widest read, most influential religious book in the world with the exception of the Bible.

CONTENTS

THE FIRST BOOK
Admonitions Useful for a Spiritual Life.

CHAPTER   PAGE

1. Of the Imitation of Christ and contempt of all the vanities of the world, ... 147
2. Of thinking humbly of ourselves, ... 148
3. Of the doctrine of Truth, ... 150
4. Of wisdom and forethought in our action, ... 152
5. Of reading the Holy Scriptures, ... 152
6. Of inordinate affections, ... 153
7. Of avoiding vain hope and pride, ... 154
8. That too much familiarity is to be shunned, ... 155
9. Of obedience and subjection, ... 155
10. Of avoiding many words, ... 156
11. Of the obtaining of peace, and of zealous desire for growth in grace, ... 157
12. Of the profit of adversity, ... 158
13. Of resisting temptation, ... 159
14. Of avoiding rash judgment, ... 161
15. Of works done out of charity, ... 162
16. Of bearing with the faults of others, ... 163
17. Of life in a religious community, ... 164

CHAPTER   PAGE

18. Of the examples of the Holy Fathers, ... 165
19. Of the exercises of a good religious person, ... 167
20. Of the love of solitude and silence, ... 169
21. Of compunction of heart, ... 172
22. Of the consideration of human misery, ... 173
23. Of meditation on death, ... 176
24. Of judgment, and the punishment of sinners, ... 179
25. Of the zealous amendment of our whole life, ... 181

THE SECOND BOOK
Admonitions Concerning Inward Things

CHAPTER   PAGE

1. Of the inward life, ... 185
2. Of humble submission, ... 188
3. Of a good and peaceable man, ... 189
4. Of a pure mind, and a simple intention, ... 190
5. Of the consideration of one's self, ... 191
6. Of the joy of a good conscience, ... 192
7. Of the love of Jesus above all things, ... 193
8. Of familiar friendship with Jesus, ... 194
9. Of the want of all comfort, ... 196
10. Of gratitude for the grace of God, ... 199
11. That the lovers of the Cross of Jesus are few, ... 201
12. Of the royal way of the holy Cross, ... 202

THE THIRD BOOK
Of Internal Consolation.

CHAPTER   PAGE

1. Of Christ's speaking inwardly to the faithful soul, ... 207
2. That the truth speaketh inwardly without noise of words, 208

THE THIRD BOOK

CHAPTER   PAGE

3. That the words of God are to be heard with humility,
   and that many weigh them not, ... 209
4. That we ought to live in truth and humility before God, 211
5. Of the wonderful effect of divine love, ... 213
6. Of the proving of a true lover, ... 215
7. That grace is to be guarded by humility, ... 217
8. Of a mean conceit of ourselves in the sight of God, ... 219
9. That all things are to be referred unto God,
   as their last end, ... 220
10. That to despise the world and serve God, is sweet, ... 221
11. That the longings and desires of our hearts are to be
    examined and moderated, ... 223
12. Of the growth of patience in the soul, and of striving
    against concupiscence, ... 224
13. Of humble obedience after the example of Jesus Christ, . 225
14. Of considering the secret judgments of God, that so
    we be not lifted up for anything good in us, ... 226
15. In everything which we desire, how we ought to feel,
    and what we ought to say, ... 228
16. That true comfort is to be sought in God alone, ... 229
17. That all our anxieties are to be rested on God, ...:... 230
18. That temporal sufferings must be borne patiently,
    after the example of Christ, ... 231
19. Of the endurance of injuries, and of the proof of
    true patience, ... 232
20. Of the acknowledging of our own infirmities;
    and of the sufferings of this life, ... 234
21. That we are to rest in God above all his gifts
    and benefits, ... 235
22. Of the remembrance of God's manifold benefits, ... 237
23. Of four things that bring great inward peace, ... 239
24. Of avoiding curious enquiry into the lives of others, ... 241
25. Wherein firm peace of heart and true spiritual
    progress existeth, ... 242
26. Of the excellency of a free mind, which is sooner
    gained by humble prayer than by study, ... 243

THE THIRD BOOK

CHAPTER   **PAGE**

27. That it is love of self which most hindereth from the chiefest good, ... 244
28. Against the tongues of slanderers, ... 246
29. How that we ought to call upon God, and to bless him, when tribulation is upon us, ... 246
30. Of craving the divine aid, and of confidence of recovering grace, ... 247
31. Of the contempt of all creatures, in order to find out the Creator, ... 249
32. Of self-denial, and renouncing every evil appetite, ... 251
33. Of inconstancy of heart, and having our final intent directed unto God, ... 252
34. That God is precious above all things and in all things to him that loveth him, ... 253
35. That there is no security from temptation in this life, ... 254
36. Against the vain judgments of men, ... 255
37. Of pure and entire resignation for the obtaining freedom of heart, ... 256
38. Of good government of ourselves in things outward, and of recourse to God in dangers, ... 258
39. That a man should not be over-careful in matters of business, ... 259
40. That man hath of himself no good thing, nor any thing whereof he can glory, ... 259
41. Of the contempt of all temporal honor, ... 261
42. That our peace is not to be set on men, ... 261
43. Against vain and secular knowledge, ... 262
44. Of not attracting to ourselves outward things, ... 264
45. That credit is not to be given to all; and that man is prone to offend in words, ... 264
46. Of putting our trust in God when evil words arise, ... 266
47. That all grievous things are to be endured for the sake of eternal life, ... 268
48. Of the day of eternity, and this life's straitnesses, ... 269
49. Of the desire of everlasting life, and how great rewards are promised to those that strive resolutely, ... 272

THE THIRD BOOK

CHAPTER   PAGE

50. How the desolate ought to give up himself into the
     hands of God, ... 274
51. That a man ought to employ himself in works of humility,
     when strength is wanting for higher employment, ... 277
52. That a man ought not to account himself as worthy of
     comfort, but rather as deserving of chastisement, ... 278
53. That the grace of God is not given to those who relish
     earthly things, ... 279
54. Of the different stirrings of nature and grace, ... 281
55. Of the corruption of nature, and the efficiency
     of divine grace, ... 284
56. That we ought to deny ourselves and imitate
     Christ by the Cross, ... 286
57. That a man should not be too much dejected, even
     when he falleth into some defects, ... 287
58. That high matters and God's secret judgments are not
     to be narrowly inquired into, ... 289
59. That all our hope and trust are to be fixed in God alone, 292

THE FOURTH BOOK
Concerning the Communion

CHAPTER   PAGE

A devout exhortation to the Holy Communion, ... 294
1. With how great reverence Christ ought to be received, .. 295
2. That the great goodness and love of God is exhibited
    to man in this sacrament, ... 299
3. That it is profitable to communicate often, ... 301
4. That many benefits are bestowed upon those that
    communicate devoutly, ... 303
5. Of the dignity of this sacrament, and of the
    ministerial function, ... 305
6. An Enquiry concerning spiritual exercise
    before communion, ... 306

THE FOURTH BOOK

7. Of thoroughly searching our own conscience, and of holy purposes of amendment, ... 307

8. Of the oblation of Christ on the cross, and of resignation of ourselves, ... 308

9. That we ought to offer up ourselves and all that is ours unto God, and to pray for all, ... 309

10. That the holy communion is not lightly to be forborne, .. 311

11. That the body and blood of Christ and the Holy Scriptures are most necessary unto a faithful soul, ... 314

12. That he who is about to communicate with Christ ought·to prepare himself with great diligence, ... 316

13. That the devout soul ought with the whole heart to seek union with Christ in this sacrament, ... 318

14. Of the fervent desire of some devout persons to receive the body and blood of Christ, ... 319

15. That the grace of devotion is obtained by humility and denial of ourselves, ... 321

16. That we ought to lay open our necessities to Christ, and to crave his grace, ... 322

17. Of fervent love, and vehement desire to receive Christ, .. 323

18. That a man should not be a curious searcher into the holy sacrament, but an humble follower of Christ, submitting his sense to divine faith, ... 325

THE FIRST BOOK

ADMONITIONS USEFUL FOR
A SPIRITUAL LIFE

1.

*Of the Imitation of Christ, and Contempt of
all the Vanities of the World.*

He that followeth Me, walketh not in darkness," saith the
Lord. These are the words of Christ, by which we are taught
to imitate His life and manners, if we would be truly enlightened, and be delivered from all blindness of heart. Let
therefore our chief endeavor be to meditate upon the life of
Jesus Christ.

2. The doctrine of Christ exceedeth all the doctrines of
holy men; and he that hath the Spirit, will find therein the
hidden manna.

But it falleth out, that many, albeit they often hear the
Gospel of Christ, are yet but little affected, because they have
not the Spirit of Christ.

Whosoever then would fully and feelingly understand the
words of Christ, must endeavor to conform his life wholly to
the life of Christ.

3. What will it avail thee to be engaged in profound reasonings concerning the Trinity, if thou be void of humility, and art thereby displeasing to the Trinity?

Surely great words do not make a man holy and just; but a virtuous life maketh him dear to God.

I had rather FEEL compunction, than know the definition thereof.

If thou knewest the whole Bible by heart, and the sayings of all the philosophers, what would it profit thee without the love of God and without grace?

Vanity of vanities, all is vanity, except to love God, and Him only to serve.

This is the highest wisdom, by contempt of the world to tend towards the kingdom of Heaven.

4. It is therefore vanity to seek after perishing riches and to trust in them.

It is also vanity to strive after honors, and to climb to high degree.

It is vanity to follow the desires of the flesh, and to labor for that for which thou must afterwards suffer grievous punishment.

It is vanity to desire to live long, and not to care to live well.

It is vanity to mind only this present life, and not to make provision for those things which are to come.

It is vanity to love that which speedily passeth away, and not to hasten thither where everlasting joy awaiteth thee.

5. Call often to mind that proverb, "The eye is not satisfied with seeing, nor the ear filled with hearing."

Endeavor therefore to withdraw thy heart from the love of visible things, and to turn thyself to the invisible.

For they that follow their lusts stain their own consciences, and lose the grace of God.

2.
Of Thinking Humbly of Ourselves.

All men naturally desire knowledge; but what availeth knowledge without the fear of God?

Surely, an humble husbandman that serveth God, is better

than a proud philosopher who, neglecting himself, is occupied in studying the course of the heavens.

Whoso knoweth himself, is lowly in his own eyes, and delighteth not in the praises of men.

If I understood all things in the world, and had not charity, what would it avail me in the sight of God, who will judge me according to my deeds?

2. Cease from an inordinate desire of knowledge, for therein is much distraction and deceit.

Learned men are anxious to seem learned to others, and to be called wise.

There be many things to know which doth little or nothing profit the soul: And he is very unwise who minds other things more than those that tend to his salvation.

Many words do not satisfy the soul; but a good life comforteth the mind, and a pure conscience giveth great confidence toward God.

3. The more thou knowest, and the better thou understandest, the more strictly shalt thou be judged, unless thy life be also the more holy.

Be not therefore elated in thine own mind because of any art of science, but rather let the knowledge given thee make thee afraid.

If thou thinkest that thou understandest and knowest much; yet know that there be many more things which thou knowest not.

Affect not to be overwise, but rather acknowledge thine own ignorance.

Why wilt thou prefer thyself before others, seeing there be many more learned, and more skillful in the Scripture than thou?

If thou wilt know or learn anything profitably, desire to be unknown, and to be little esteemed.

4. The highest and most profitable lesson is the true knowledge and lowly esteem of ourselves.

It is great wisdom and perfection to think nothing of ourselves, and to think always well and highly of others.

If thou shouldest see another openly sin, or commit some heinous offence, yet oughtest thou not to think the better of thyself; for thou knowest not how long thou shalt be able to stand.

We are all frail, but do thou esteem none more frail than thyself.

3.
Of the Doctrine of Truth.

Happy is he whom truth by itself doth teach, not by figures and words that pass away, but as it is in itself.

Our own opinion and our own sense do often deceive us, and they discern but little.

What availeth it to cavil and dispute much about dark and hidden things, for ignorance of which we shall not be reproved at the day of judgment?

It is a great folly to neglect the things that are profitable and necessary, and to choose to dwell upon that which is curious and hurtful. We have eyes and see not.

2. And what have we to do with *genera* and *species*? He to whom the Eternal Word speaketh, is delivered from many an opinion.

From one Word are all things, and all things utter one Word; and this is the *Beginning*, which also speaketh unto us.

No man without that Word understandeth or judgeth rightly.

He to whom all things are one, he who reduceth all things to one, and seeth all things in one; may enjoy a quiet mind, and remain at peace in God.

O God, who art the truth, make me one with thee in everlasting love.

It wearieth me often to read and hear many things: In Thee is all that I would have and can desire.

Let all doctors hold their peace; let all creatures be silent in Thy sight; speak Thou alone unto me.

3. The more a man is at one within himself, and becometh of single heart, so much the more and higher things doth he understand without labor; for that he receiveth the light of wisdom from above.

A pure, single, and stable spirit is not distracted, though it be employed in many works; for that it doeth all to the honor of God, and being at rest within, seeketh not itself in anything it doth.

Who hinder and trouble thee more than the unmortified affections of thine own heart?

A good and devout man arrangeth within himself beforehand those things which he ought to do.

Neither do they draw him to the desires of an inordinate inclination, but he ordereth them according to the direction of right reason.

Who hath a greater combat than he that laboreth to overcome himself?

This ought to be our endeavor, to conquer ourselves, and daily to wax stronger, and to grow in holiness.

4. All perfection in this life hath some imperfection mixed with it; and no knowledge of ours is without some darkness.

A humble knowledge of thyself is a surer way to God than a deep search after learning.

Yet learning is not to be blamed, nor the mere knowledge of anything whatsoever, for that is good in itself, and ordained by God; but a good conscience and a virtuous life are always to be preferred before it.

But because many endeavor rather to get knowledge than to live well; therefore they are often deceived, and reap either none or but little fruit.

5. O, if men bestowed as much labor in the rooting out of vices, and the planting of virtues, as they do in the moving of questions, neither would so many evils be done, nor so great scandal be given in the world.

Truly, at the day of judgment we shall not be examined as to what we have read, but as to what we have done; not as to how well we have spoken, but as to how religiously we have lived.

Tell me, where are all those Doctors and Masters, with whom thou wast well acquainted, whilst they lived and flourished in learning?

Others occupy their places, and perhaps do scarce ever think of those who went before them. In their lifetime they seemed something, but now they are not spoken of.

6. O, how quickly doth the glory of the world pass away! Would that their life had been answerable to their learning! Then had their study and reading been to good purpose.

How many perish by reason of vain learning of this world, who take little care of the serving of God.

And because they rather choose to be great than humble, therefore they become vain in their imaginations.

He is truly great who hath great love.

He is truly great that is little in himself, and that maketh no account of any height of honor.

He is truly wise, that accounteth all earthly things as dung, that he may win Christ.

And he is truly learned, that doeth the will of God, and forsaketh his own will.

4.
Of Wisdom and Forethought in our Actions.

We must not trust every saying or suggestion, but warily and patiently ponder things according to the will of God.

Yet, alas, such is our weakness, that we often rather believe and speak evil of others than good.

But perfect men do not easily credit every one who speaks to them; for they know that human frailty is prone to evil, and very subject to error in words.

2. It is great wisdom not to be rash in thy doings, nor to stand stiffly in thine own conceits;

As also not to believe every thing which thou hearest, nor immediately to relate again to others what thou hast heard or dost believe.

Consult with him that is wise and of sound judgment, and seek to be instructed by one better than thyself, rather than to follow thine own inventions.

A good life maketh a man wise according to God, and giveth him experience in many things.

The more humble a man is in himself, and the more subject unto God, the more wise and peaceful shall he be in all things.

5.
Of Reading the Holy Scriptures.

Truth, not eloquence, is to be sought for in Holy Scripture.

Each part of the scripture is to be read with the same Spirit wherewith it was written.

We should rather search after profit in the Scriptures, than after subtle arguments.

We ought to read plain and devout books as willingly as those high and profound.

Let not the authority of the writer be a stumbling-block, whether he be of great or small learning; but let the love of pure truth draw thee to read. Enquire not who spoke this or that, but mark what is spoken.

2. Men pass away, but the truth of the Lord remaineth for ever. God speaks unto us in sundry ways without respect of persons.

Our own curiosity often hindereth us in reading of the Scriptures, when we will examine and discuss that which we should rather pass over without more ado.

If thou desire to profit, read with humility, simplicity, and faithfulness; nor ever desire the repute of learning.

Enquire willingly, and hear with silence the words of holy men. Let not the parables of the Elders displease thee, for they are not given without cause.

6.
Of Inordinate Affections.

Whensoever a man desireth any thing inordinately, he becometh presently disquieted in himself.

The proud and covetous can never rest. The poor and humble in spirit dwell in the multitude of peace.

The man that is not yet perfectly dead to himself, is quickly tempted and overcome in small and trifling things.

The weak in spirit, and he that is yet in manner carnal and prone to the things of sense, can hardly withdraw himself altogether from earthly desires.

And therefore he is often afflicted when he goeth about to withdraw himself from them; and is easily angered when any opposeth him.

2. And if he hath followed his appetite, he is presently disquieted with remorse of conscience; for that he hath yielded to his passion which profiteth him nothing to the obtaining of the peace which he sought.

True quietness of heart therefore is gotten by resisting our passions, not by obeying them.

There is then no peace in the heart of a carnal man, nor in

him that is given to outward things, but in the spiritual and devout man.

7.
Of Avoiding Vain Hope and Pride.

He is vain that putteth his trust in man, or in creatures. Be not ashamed to serve others for the love of Jesus Christ: nor to be esteemed poor in this world.

Presume not upon thyself, but place thy hope in God.

Do what lieth in thy power, and God will assist thy good will.

Trust not in thine own knowledge, nor in the skill of any living creature; but rather in the grace of God, who helpeth the humble, and humbleth those that are proud.

2. Glory not in wealth if thou have it, nor in friends because they are powerful; but in God who giveth all things, and who desireth to give thee Himself above all things.

Esteem not thyself for the height of thy stature nor for the beauty of thy person, which may be disfigured and destroyed by a little sickness.

Please not thyself in thy natural gifts or wit, lest thereby thou displease God, to whom appertaineth all the good whatsoever thou hast by nature.

3. Esteem not thyself better than others, lest perhaps in the sight of God, who knoweth what is in man, thou be accounted worse than they.

Be not proud of well-doing; for the judgment of God is far different from the judgment of men, and that often offendeth Him which pleaseth them.

If there be any good in thee, believe that there is much more in others, that so thou mayest preserve humility.

It hurteth thee not to submit to all men: but it hurteth thee most of all to prefer thyself even to one.

The humble enjoy continual peace, but in the heart of the proud is envy, and frequent indignation.

8.
That too much Familiarity is to be Shunned.

Lay not thy heart open to every one; but treat of thy affairs with the wise, and such as fear God.

Converse not much with the young, nor with strangers.

Flatter not the rich: neither do thou appear willingly before the great.

Keep company with the humble and singlehearted, with the devout and virtuous; and confer with them of those things that may edify. Be not familiar with any woman; but commend all good women in general to God.

Desire to be familiar with God alone and His Angels, and avoid the acquaintance of men.

2. We must have love towards all, but familiarity with all is not expedient.

Sometimes it falleth out, that a person unknown to us is much esteemed of, from the good report given him by others; whose presence notwithstanding is not grateful to the eyes of those who see him.

We think sometimes to please others by our society, and we rather displease them with those bad qualities which they discover in us.

9.
Of Obedience and Subjection.

It is a great matter to live in obedience, to be under a superior and not to be at our own disposing.

It is much safer to obey than to govern.

Many live under obedience, rather for necessity than for love; such are discontented, and do easily repine. Neither can they attain to freedom of mind, unless they willingly and heartily put themselves under obedience for the love of God.

Go whither thou wilt, thou shalt find no rest, but in humble subjection under the government of a superior. Many have deceived themselves, imagining to find happiness in change.

2. True it is, that every one willingly doeth that which agreeth with his own liking, and inclineth most to those that are of his own mind.

But if God be amongst us, we must sometimes cease for the sake of peace to adhere to our own opinion.

Who is so wise that he can fully know all things?

Be not therefore too confident in thine own opinion; but be willing to hear the judgment of others.

If thy thought be good, and yet thou partest with it for God, and followest the opinion of another, this shall turn to thy good.

3. I have often heard, that it is safer to hear and to take counsel, than to give it.

It may also fall out, that a man's opinion may be good; but to refuse to yield to others when reason or a special cause requireth it, is a mark of pride and stiffness.

10.
Of Avoiding Many Words.

Fly the tumult of the world as much as thou canst; for the treating of worldly affairs is a great hindrance, although it be done with sincere intention;

For we are quickly defiled, and enthralled by vanity.

Oftentimes I could wish that I had held my peace when I have spoken; and that I had not been in company.

Why do we so willingly speak and talk one with another, when notwithstanding we seldom cease our converse before we have hurt our conscience?

The cause why we so willingly talk, is for that by discoursing one with another, we seek to receive comfort one of another, and desire to ease our mind wearied with many thoughts:

And we very willingly talk and think of those things which we most love or desire; or of those things which we feel to be against us.

2. But, alas, oftentimes in vain, and to no end; for this outward comfort is the cause of no small loss of inward and divine consolation.

Therefore we must watch and pray, lest our time pass away idly.

If it be lawful and expedient for thee to speak, speak those things that may edify.

Evil habit and neglect of our own growth in grace do give too much liberty to inconsiderate speech.

Yet discourse of spiritual things doth greatly further our spiritual growth, especially when persons of one mind and spirit associate together in God.

11.

Of the Obtaining of Peace, and of Zealous Desire for Growth in Grace.

We might enjoy much peace, if we would not busy ourselves with the words and deeds of other men, and things which appertain nothing with to our charge.

How can he abide long in peace, who thrusteth himself into the cares of others, who seeketh occasions abroad, who little or seldom cometh to himself?

Blessed are the single-hearted; for they shall enjoy much peace.

2. Why were some of the Saints so perfect and contemplative? Because they labored to mortify themselves wholly to all earthly desires; and therefore they could with their whole heart fix themselves upon God, and be free for holy retirement.

We are too much led by our passions, and too solicitous for transitory things.

We also seldom overcome any one vice perfectly, and are not inflamed with a fervent desire to grow better every day and therefore we remain cold and lukewarm.

3. If we are perfectly intent upon our own hearts, and not entangled with outward things, then should we be able to relish divine things, and to have some experience of heavenly contemplation.

The greatest, and indeed the whole impediment is that we are not free from passions and lusts, neither do we endeavor to walk in the perfect way of the Saints; and when but a small adversity befalleth us, we are too quickly dejected, and turn ourselves to human consolations.

4. If we would endeavor like brave men to stand in the

battle, surely we should feel the assistance of God from Heaven.

For He who giveth us occasion to fight, to the end we may get the victory, is ready to succor those that fight, and that trust in His grace.

If we esteem our progress in religious life to consist only in some outward observances, our devotion will quickly be at an end.

But let us lay the axe to the root, that being freed from passions, we may find rest to our souls.

5. If every year we would root out one vice, we should sooner become perfect men.

But now oftentimes we perceive, on the contrary, that we were better and purer at the beginning of our conversion, than after many years of our profession.

Our fervor and profiting should increase daily: but now it is accounted a great matter, if a man can retain but some part of his first zeal.

If we would do but a little violence to ourselves at the beginning, then should we be able to perform all things afterwards with ease and delight.

6. It is a hard matter to forego that to which we are accustomed, but it is harder to go against our own will.

But if thou dost not overcome small and easy things, when wilt thou overcome harder things?

Resist thy inclination in the very beginning, and unlearn evil habits, lest perhaps by little and little they draw thee to greater difficulty.

O if thou didst but consider how much inward peace unto thyself, and joy unto others, thou wouldest procure by demeaning thyself well, I think that thou wouldest be more careful of thy spiritual progress.

12.
Of the Profit of Adversity.

It is good that we have sometimes some troubles and crosses; for they often make a man enter into himself, and consider that he is here in banishment, and ought not to place his trust in any wordly thing.

It is good that we be sometimes contradicted, and that men

think ill or inadequately; and this, although we do and intend well.

These things help often to the attaining of humility, and defend us from vainglory: for then we are more inclined to seek God for our inward witness, when outwardly we be contemned by men, and when there is no credit given unto us.

2. And therefore a man should settle himself so fully in God, that he need not to seek many comforts of men.

When a good man is afflicted, tempted, or troubled with evil thought; then he understandeth better the great need he hath of God, without whom he perceiveth he can do nothing that is good.

Then also he sorroweth, lamenteth, and prayeth, by reason of the miseries he suffereth.

Then he is weary of living longer, and wisheth that death would come, that he might depart and be with Christ.

Then also he well perceiveth, that perfect security and full peace cannot be had in this world.

13.
Of Resisting Temptation.

So long as we live in this world we cannot be without tribulation and temptation.

Hence it is written in Job, "The life of man upon earth is a life of temptation."

Every one therefore ought to be careful about his temptations, and to watch in prayer, lest the devil find an advantage to deceive him; for he never sleepeth, but goeth about, seeking whom he may devour.

No man is so perfect and holy, but he hath sometimes temptations, and we cannot be altogether without them.

2. Nevertheless temptations are often very profitable to us, though they be troublesome and grievous; for in them a man is humbled, purified, and instructed.

All the Saints passed through man's tribulations and temptations, and profited thereby.

And they that could not bear temptations became reprobate, and fell away.

There is no order so holy, nor place so secret, as that there be not temptations or adversities in it.

3. There is no man that is altogether free from temptations whilst he liveth on earth: for the root thereof is in ourselves, who are born with inclination to evil.

When one temptation or tribulation goeth away, another cometh; and we shall ever have something to suffer, because we are fallen from the state of our felicity.

Many seek to fly temptations, and fall more grievously into them.

By flight alone we cannot overcome, but by patience and true humility we become stronger than all our enemies.

4. He that only avoideth them outwardly, and doth not pluck them up by the roots, shall profit little; yea, temptations will the sooner return unto him, and will be more violent than before.

By little and little, and by patience with long-suffering, through God's help, thou shalt more easily overcome, than by violence and thine own disquietude.

Often take counsel in temptations, and deal not roughly with him that is tempted; but give him comfort, as thou wouldest wish to be done to thyself.

5. The beginning of all evil temptations is inconstancy of mind, and small confidence in God.

For as a ship without a helm is tossed to and fro by the waves, so the man who is careless and forsaketh his purpose, is many ways tempted.

Fire trieth iron, and temptation a just man.

We know not oftentimes what we are able to do, but temptation shows us what we are.

Yet we must be watchful, especially in the beginning of the temptation; for the enemy is then more easily overcome, if he be not suffered to enter the door of our hearts, but be resisted at the very gate, on his first knocking.

Wherefore one said, "Withstand the beginnings: the remedy is applied too late, when the evil has grown strong through long delay."

For first there cometh to the mind a bare thought of evil, then a strong imagination thereof, afterwards delight, and evil motion, and then consent.

And so by little and little our wicked enemy getteth complete entrance, for that he is not resisted in the beginning.

And the longer a man is negligent in resisting, the weaker does he become daily in himself, and the stronger the enemy against him.

6. Some suffer great temptations in the beginning of their conversion; others in the latter end. Others again are much troubled almost through the whole of their life.

Some are but slightly tempted, according to the wisdom and equity of the Divine appointment, which weigheth the states and deserts of men, and ordaineth all things for the welfare of His own chosen ones.

7. We ought not therefore to despair when we are tempted, but so much the more fervently to pray unto God, that He will vouchsafe to help us in all tribulations; for He will surely, according to the words of St. Paul, make with the temptation a way to escape, that we may be able to bear it.

Let us therefore humble our souls under the hand of God in all temptations and tribulations; for He will save and exalt the humble in spirit.

8. In temptations and afflictions a man is proved, how much he hath profited; and his reward is thereby the greater, and his graces do more eminently shine forth.

Neither is it any such great thing if a man be devout and fervent, when he feeleth no affliction; but if in time of adversity he bear himself patiently, there is hope then of great growth in grace.

Some are kept from great temptations, and in small ones which do daily occur are often overcome; to the end that, being humbled, they may never presume on themselves in great matters, while they are worsted in so small things.

14.
Of Avoiding Rash Judgment.

Turn thine eyes unto thyself, and beware thou judge not the deeds of other men. In judging of others, a man laboreth in vain, often erreth and easily sinneth; but in judging and examining himself, he always laboreth fruitfully.

We often judge of things according as we fancy them; for private affection bereaves us easily of a right judgment.

If God were always the pure object of our desire, we should not be easily troubled, through the repugnance of our carnal mind.

2. But oftentimes something lurketh within, or else occurreth from without, which draweth us after it.

Many secretly seek themselves in what they do, and know it not.

They seem also to live in good peace of mind, when things are done according to their will and opinion; but if things happen otherwise than they desire, they are straightway moved and much vexed.

The diversities of judgments and opinions cause often times dissensions between friends and countrymen, between religious and devout persons.

3. An old custom is hardly broken, and no man is willing to be led farther than himself can see.

If thou dost more rely upon thine own reason or industry, than upon that power which brings thee under the obedience of Jesus Christ, it will be long before thou become illuminated; for God will have us perfectly subject unto Him, that, being inflamed with His love, we may transcend the narrow limits of human reason.

15.
Of Works done out of Charity.

Nor no worldly thing, nor for the love of any man, is any evil to be done; but yet, for the welfare of one that standeth in need, a good work is sometimes to be intermitted without any scruple, or even to be changed for a better.

For by doing this, a good work is not lost, but changed into better.

Without charity the outward work profiteth nothing; but whatsoever is done of charity, be it never so little and contemptible in the sight of the world, it becomes wholly fruitful.

For God weigheth more with how much love a man worketh, than how much he doeth. He doeth much that loveth much.

2. He doeth much that doeth a thing well. He doeth well that rather serveth the common weal than his own will.

Oftentimes a work seemeth to be of charity, and it is rather a work of the flesh; because natural inclination, self-will, hope of reward, and desire of our own interest are motives seldom absent.

3. He that hath true and perfect charity seeketh himself in nothing; but only desireth in all things that the glory of God should be exalted.

He also envieth none, because he seeketh no private good; neither doth he will to rejoice in himself, but wisheth above all things to be made happy in the enjoyment of God.

He attributeth nothing that is good to any man, but wholly referreth it unto God, from whom as from their fountain all things proceed; in whom finally all the Saints do rest as in their highest fruition.

If a man had but one spark of true charity, he would certainly discern that all earthly things are full of vanity.

16.
Of Bearing with the Faults of Others.

Those things that a man cannot amend in himself or in others, he ought to suffer patiently, until God order them otherwise.

Think that perhaps it is better so for thy trial and patience, without which all our good deeds are not much to be esteemed.

Thou oughtest to pray notwithstanding when thou hast such impediments, that God would vouchsafe to help thee, and that thou mayest bear them rightly.

2. If one that is once or twice warned will not give over, contend not with him: but commit all to God, that His will may be done, and His name honored in all His servants, who well knoweth how to turn evil into good.

Endeavor to be patient in bearing with the defects and infirmities of others, of what sort soever they be: for that thyself also hast many failings which must be borne with by others.

If thou canst not make thyself such an one as thou wouldest, how canst thou expect to have another in all things to thy liking?

We would willingly have others perfect, and yet we amend not our own faults.

3. We will have others severely corrected, and will not be corrected ourselves.

The large liberty of others displeaseth us; and yet we will not have our own desires denied us.

We will have others kept under by strict laws; but in no sort will ourselves be restrained.

And thus it appeareth, how seldom we weigh our neighbor in the same balance with ourselves.

If all men were perfect, what should we have to suffer of our neighbor for the sake of God?

4. But now God hath thus ordered it, that we may learn to bear one another's burdens; for no man is without fault; no man but hath his burden; no man is sufficient of himself; no man is wise enough of himself; but we ought to bear with one another, comfort one another, help, instruct, and admonish one another.

Occasions of adversity best discover how great virtue or strength each one hath.

For occasions do not make a man frail, but they show what he is.

17.
Of Life in a Religious Community.

Thou must learn to break thine own will in many things, if thou wilt have peace and concord with others.

It is no small matter to dwell in a religious community, or monastery, to hold thy place there without giving offence, and to continue faithful even unto death.

Blessed is he that hath there lived well, and ended happily.

If thou wilt stand firm and grow as thou oughtest, esteem thyself as a pilgrim and stranger upon earth.

Thou must be contented for Christ's sake to be esteemed as a fool in this world, if thou desire to lead the life of a monk.

2. Dress and tonsure profit little; but change of heart and perfect mortification of the passions make a true monk.

He that seeketh anything else but merely God, and the salvation of his soul, shall find nothing but tribulation and sorrows.

Neither can he remain long in peace, that laboreth not to be the least, and subject unto all.

3. Thou camest to serve, not to rule. Know that thou wast

called to suffer and to labor, and not to be idle, nor to spend thy time in talk.

Here therefore men are proved as gold in the furnace.

Here no man can stand, unless he humble himself with his whole heart for the love of God.

18.
Of the Examples of the Holy Fathers.

Consider the lively examples of the holy Fathers, in whom true perfection and religion shone; and thou shalt see how little it is, and almost nothing, which we do now in these days.

Alas! What is our life, if we be compared to them!

The Saints and friends of Christ served the Lord in hunger and thirst, in cold and nakedness, in labor and weariness, in watchings and fastings, in prayer and holy meditations, in many persecutions and reproaches.

2. O how many and grievous tribulations suffered the Apostles, Martyrs, Confessors, Virgins, and all the rest that endeavored to follow the steps of Christ! For they hated their lives in this world, that they might keep them unto life eternal.

O how strict and self-renouncing a life led those holy Fathers in the wilderness! How long and grievous temptations suffered they! How often were they assaulted by the enemy! What frequent and fervent prayers offered they to God! What rigorous abstinences did they use! How great zeal and care had they of their spiritual advancement! How strong a combat had they for the overcoming of their lusts! What pure and upright intentions kept they towards God!

In the day they labored; and in the night they attended to continual prayer: although even while they labored, they never ceased from mental prayer.

3. They spent all their time with profit; every hour seemed but short for the service of God. And by reason of the great sweetness they felt in contemplation, they forgot the necessity of refreshment for the body.

They renounced all riches, dignities, honors, friends, and kinsfolk; they desired to have nothing which appertained to the world; they scarce took the necessaries of life; they grudged even the necessary care of the body.

Therefore they were poor in earthly things, but very rich in grace and virtues.

Outwardly they were destitute, but inwardly they were refreshed with grace and divine consolation.

4. They were strangers to the world, but near and familiar friends to God.

They seemed to themselves as nothing, and to this present world despicable; but were precious and beloved in the eyes of God.

They were grounded in true humility, they lived in simple obedience, they walked in love and patience: and therefore they grew daily in the Spirit, and obtained great grace in God's sight.

They were given for an example to all Religious persons; and they should more provoke us to endeavor after spiritual advancement, than the number of the lukewarm livers should prevail to make us remiss.

5. O how great was the fervor of all Religious persons in the beginning of their holy institution!

How great was their devotion to prayer! What ambition to excel others in virtue! What exact discipline then flourished! How great reverence and obedience, under the rule of their superiors, observed they in all things!

Their footsteps yet remaining testify that they were indeed holy and perfect men; who fighting so valiantly trod the world under their feet.

Among us he is greatly accounted of, who is not a transgressor, and who can with patience endure that which he hath received.

6. O the lukewarmness and negligence of our times! that we so quickly decline from the ancient fervor, and are come to that pass, that very sloth and lukewarmness of spirit make our life tedious unto us.

Would to God the desire to grow in virtues did not wholly sleep in thee, who hast often seen the many examples of religious persons!

19.
Of the Exercises of a Good Religious Person.

The life of a good Religious person ought to excel in all virtues; that he may inwardly be such as outwardly he seemeth to me.

And rightly there ought to be much more within than is perceived without. For God beholdeth us; whom we are bound most highly to reverence wheresoever we are, and to walk in purity like angels in His sight.

Daily ought we to renew our purposes, and to stir up ourselves to greater fervor, as though this were the first day of our conversion, and to say,

"Help me, my God, in this my good purpose, and in Thy holy service; and grant that I may now this day begin perfectly; for that which I have done hitherto is as nothing."

2. According to our purpose shall be the success of our spiritual profiting; and much diligence is necessary to him that will profit much.

And if he that firmly purposeth often faileth, what shall he do that seldom or but weakly purposeth anything?

Yet in various ways it happens that we forsake our purpose, and a slight omission of our spiritual exercises is not without loss to our souls.

The purpose of just men depends not upon their own wisdom, but upon God's grace; on whom they always rely for whatsoever they take in hand.

For man proposes, but God disposes; neither is the way of man in himself.

3. If an accustomed exercise he sometimes omitted, either for some act of piety, or profit to our brother; it may easily afterwards be recovered again.

But if, out of weariness of carelessness, we lightly omit it, it is very blameworthy, and will be felt to be hurtful. Do the best we can, we shall still too easily fail in many things.

Yet must we always have some fixed purpose, and especially against those sins which do most of all hinder us.

We must diligently search into, and set in order both our outward and inward things, because both of them are of importance to our progress in godliness.

4. If thou canst not continually collect thyself, yet do it sometimes, at the least twice a day, namely, in the morning and at night.

In the morning fix thy good purpose; and at night examine thyself what thou hast done, how thou hast behaved thyself in word, deed, and thought; for in these perhaps thou hast oftentimes offended both God and thy neighbor.

Gird up thy loins like a man against the vile assaults of the devil; bridle thy riotous appetite, and thou shalt be the better able to keep under all the unruly motions of the flesh.

Never be entirely idle; but either be reading, or writing, or praying, or meditating, or endeavoring something for the public good.

As for bodily exercises they must be used with discretion, neither are they to be practised of all men alike.

5. Those devotions which belong not to the community ought not to be exposed to public view; for private devotions are practised most safely in secret.

Nevertheless thou must beware thou neglect not those which are public, being more ready for what is private. But having fully and faithfully accomplished all which thou art bound and enjoined to do, if thou hast any spare time, betake thee to thyself, as thy devotion calleth thee.

All cannot use one kind of spiritual exercise, but one is more useful for this person, another for that.

According to the seasonableness of times also, divers exercises are fitting; some suit better with us on working days, others on holy days.

In the time of temptation, we have need of some, and of others in time of peace and quietness.

Some suit us when we are pensive, and others when we rejoice in the Lord.

6. About the time of the chief festivals, good exercises are to be renewed, and the prayers of godly saints more fervently to be implored.

From festival to festival we should purpose, as though we were then to depart out of this world, and to come to the everlasting festival.

Therefore ought we carefully to prepare ourselves at holy times, and to live more devoutly, and to keep more exactly all things that we are to observe, as though we were shortly at God's hands to receive the reward of our labors.

7. But if that reward be deferred, let us think with our-

selves that we are not sufficiently prepared, and unworthy yet of so great glory which shall be revealed in us in due time; and let us endeavor to prepare ourselves better for our departure.

"Blessed is that servant (saith the Evangelist St. Luke) whom his Lord when He cometh shall find watching: Verily, I say unto you, He shall make him ruler over all His goods."

20.
Of the Love of Solitude and Silence.

Seek a convenient time of leisure for thyself, and meditate often upon God's loving-kindness.

Meddle not with things too high for thee; but read such things as may rather yield compunction to thy heart and occupation to thy head.

If thou wilt withdraw thyself from speaking vainly, and from gadding idly, as also from hearkening after novelties and rumors, thou shalt find leisure enough and suitable for meditation on good things.

The greatest Saints avoided the society of men, when they could conveniently; and did rather choose to live to God in secret.

2. One said, "As oft as I have been among men, I returned home less a man than I was before."

And this we find true, when we talk long together. It is easier not to speak at all, than not to exceed in speech.

It is easier for me to lie hid at home, than to be able sufficiently to watch over himself abroad.

He therefore that intends to attain to the more inward and spiritual things of religion, must with JESUS depart from the multitude and press of people!

No man doth safely appear abroad, but he who can abide at home.

No man doth safely speak, but he that is glad to hold his peace.

No man doth safely rule, but he that is glad to be ruled.

No man doth safely rule, but he that hath learned gladly to obey.

3. No man rejoiceth safely, unless he hath within him the testimony of a good conscience.

And yet always the security of the Saints was full of the fear of God.

Neither were they the less anxious and humble in themselves, for that they shone outwardly with grace and great virtues.

But the security of bad men ariseth from pride and presumption, and in the end it deceiveth them.

Although thou seem to be a good Religious person, or a devout solitary, yet never promise thyself security in this life.

4. Oftentimes those who have been in the greatest esteem and account amongst men have fallen into the greatest danger, by overmuch self-confidence.

Wherefore to many it is more profitable not to be altogether free from temptations, but to be often assaulted, lest they should feel too safe, and so perhaps be puffed up with pride; or else should too freely give themselves to worldly comforts.

O how good a conscience would he keep, that would never seek after transitory joy, nor ever entangle himself with the world!

O what great peace and quietness would he possess, that would cut off all vain anxiety, and think only upon divine things, and such as are profitable for his soul, and would place all his confidence in God!

5. No man is worthy of heavenly comfort, unless he have diligently exercised himself in holy compunction.

If thou desirest true contrition of heart, enter into thy secret chamber, and shut out the tumults of the world, as it is written, "Commune with your own heart, and in your chamber, and be still." In thy chamber thou shalt find what abroad thou shalt too often lose.

The more thou visitest thy chamber, the more thou wilt enjoy it; the less thou comest thereunto, the more thou wilt loathe it. If in the beginning of thy conversion thou art content to remain in it, and keep to it well, it will afterwards be to thee a dear friend, and a most pleasant comfort.

6. In silence and in stillness a religious soul advantageth itself, and learneth the mysteries of Holy Scripture.

There it findeth rivers of tears, wherein it may every night wash and cleanse itself; that it may be so much the more familiar with its Creator, by how much the farther off it liveth from all worldly disquiet.

Whoso therefore withdraweth himself from his acquaintance and friends, God will draw near unto him with His holy angels.

It is better for a man to live privately, and to have regard to himself, than to neglect his soul, though he could work wonders in the world.

It is commendable in a Religious person seldom to go abroad, to be unwilling to see or to be seen.

7. Why art thou desirous to see that which it is unlawful for thee to have? The world passeth away and the lust thereof.

The lusts of the flesh draw us to rove abroad; but when the time is past, what carriest thou home with thee but a burdened conscience and a distracted heart?

A merry going forth bringeth often a mournful return; and a joyful night maketh often a sad morning.

So all carnal joy enters gently, but in the end it bites and stings to death.

What canst thou see elsewhere, which thou canst not see here? Behold the Heaven and the earth and all the elements; for of these are all things created.

8. What canst thou see anywhere that can long continue under the sun?

Thou thinkest perchance to satisfy thyself, but thou canst never attain it.

Couldst thou see all things persent before thine eyes, what were it but a vain sight?

Lift up thine eyes to God in the highest, and pray Him to pardon thy sins and negligences.

Leave vain things to the vain; but be thou intent upon those things which God hath commanded thee.

Shut thy door upon thee, and call unto thee JESUS, thy Beloved.

Stay with him in thy closet; for thou shalt not find so great peace anywhere else.

If thou hadst not gone abroad and hearkened to idle rumors, thou wouldst the better have preserved a happy peace of mind. But since thou delightest sometimes to hear new things, it is but fit thou suffer for it some disquietude of heart.

21.
Of Compunction of Heart.

If thou wilt make any progress in godliness, keep thyself in the fear of God, and affect not too much liberty. Restrain all thy senses under discipline, and give not thyself over to foolish mirth.

Give thyself to compunction of heart, and thou shalt gain much devotion thereby.

Compunction layeth open much good, which dissoluteness is wont quickly to destroy.

It is a wonder that any man can ever perfectly rejoice in this life if he duly consider, and thoroughly weigh his state of banishment, and the many perils wherewith his soul is environed.

2. Through levity of heart, and small care for our failings, we feel not the real sorrows of our souls; and so oftentimes we vainly laugh, when we have just cause to weep.

There is no true liberty nor right joy but in the fear of God accompanied with a good conscience.

Happy is he who can cast off all distracting impediments, and bring himself to the one single purpose of holy compunction.

Happy is he who can abandon all that may defile his conscience or burden it.

Contend manfully; one habit overcometh another.

If thou canst let others alone in their matters, they likewise will not hinder thee in thine.

3. Busy not thyself in matters which appertain to others; neither do thou entangle thyself with the affairs of thy betters.

Still have an eye to thyself first, and be sure more especially to admonish thyself before all thy friends.

If thou hast not the favor of men, be not grieved at it; but take this to heart, that thou dost not behave thyself so warily and circumspectly as it becometh the servant of God, and a devout, religious man.

It is better oftentimes and safer that a man should not have many consolations in this life, especially such as are according to the flesh.

' But that we have not divine consolations at all, or do very seldom taste them, the fault is ours, because we seek not after compunction of heart, nor do altogether forsake the vain and outward comforts of this world.

4. Know that thou art unworthy of divine consolation, and that thou hast rather deserved much tribulation.

When a man hath perfect compunction, then is the whole world grievous and bitter unto him.

A good man findeth always sufficient cause for mourning and weeping.

For whether he consider his own or his neighbor's estate, he knoweth that none liveth here without tribulation.

And the more narrowly a man looketh into himself, so much the more he sorroweth.

Our sins and wickedness wherein we lie so enwrapt, that we can seldom apply ourselves to heavenly contemplations, do minister unto us matter of just sorrow and inward compunction.

5. Didst thou oftener think of thy death than of length of life, there is no question but thou wouldst be more zealous to amend.

If also thou didst but consider within thyself the infernal pains in the other world, I believe thou wouldst willingly undergo any labor or sorrow in this world, and not be afraid of the greatest austerity.

But because these things enter not the heart, and we still love those things only that delight us, therefore it is we remain cold and very dull in religion.

6. It is often our want of spirituality which maketh our miserable body so easily to complain.

Pray therefore unto the Lord with all humility, that he will vouchsafe to give thee the spirit of compunction. And say with the Prophet, "Feed me, O Lord, with the bread of tears, and give me plenteousness of tears to drink."

22.
Of the Consideration of Human Misery.

Miserable thou art, wheresoever thou be, or whithersoever thou turnest, unless thou turn thyself unto God.

Why art thou troubled when things succeed not as thou

wouldst or desirest? For who is he that hath all things according to his mind? Neither I, nor thou, nor any man upon earth.

There is none in this world, even though he be king or bishop, without some tribulation or perplexity.

Who is then in the best càse? Even he who is able to suffer something for God.

2. Many weak and infirm persons say, Behold, what a happy life súch an one leads; how wealthy, how great he is, in what power and dignity!

But lift up thine eyes to the riches of Heaven, and thou shalt see that all the goods of this life and nothing to be accounted of. They are very uncertain, and rather burdensome than otherwise, because they are never possessed without anxiety and fear.

Man's happiness consisteth not in having abundance of temporal goods, but a moderate portion is sufficient for him.

Truly it is misery even to live upon the earth.

The more spiritual a man desires to be, the more bitter does this present life become to him; because he sees more clearly and perceives more sensibly the defects of human corruption.

For to eat and to drink, to sleep and to watch, to labor and to rest, and to be subject to other necessities of nature, is doubtless a great misery and affliction to a religious man, who would gladly be set loose, and freed from all sin.

3. For the inward man is much weighed down in this world by the needs of the body.

Therefore the Prophet prayeth with great devotion to be enabled to be free from them, saying "Bring thou me out of my distresses."

But woe be to them that know not their own misery; and a greater woe to them that love this miserable and corruptible life!

For some there be who so much dote upon it, that although by labor or by begging they can scarce get mere necessaries, yet if they might be able to live here always they would care nothing at all for the kingdom of God.

4. O how senseless are these men and unbelieving in heart, who lie so deeply sunk in the earth, that they can relish nothing but carnal things!

But miserable as they are, they shall in the end feel to their cost how vile and how nothing that was which they loved.

Whereas the saints of God and all the devout friends of Christ regarded not those things which pleased the flesh, nor those which were in repute in this life, but longed after the everlasting riches with their whole hope and earnest effort.

Their whole desire was carried upward to things durable and invisible, that the desire of things visible might not draw them to things below.

5. O my brother, cast not away thy confidence of making progress in godliness; there is yet time, the hour is not yet past.

Why wilt thou defer thy good purpose from day to day? Arise and begin in this very instant, and say, Now is the time to be doing, now is the time to be striving, now is the fit time to amend myself.

When thou art ill at ease and much troubled, then is the time of earning thy reward.

Thou must pass through fire and water before thou come to a wealthy place.

Unless thou doest violence to thyself, thou shalt never get the victory over sin.

So long as we carry about us this frail body of ours, we can never be without sin, nor live without weariness and pain.

We would gladly have rest from all misery, but seeing that by sin we have lost our innocency, we have together with that lost also the true felicity.

Therefore it becomes us to have patience, and to wait for the mercy of God, till this tyranny be overpast, and mortality be swallowed up of life.

6. O how great is human frailty, which is always prone to evil!

To-day thou confessest thy sins, and to-morrow thou committest the very same which thou hast confessed.

Now, thou art purposed to look well unto thy ways, and within a while thou so behavest thyself, as though thou hadst never any such purpose at all.

Good cause have we therefore to humble ourselves, and never to have any great conceit of ourselves: since we are so frail and so inconstant.

That also may quickly be lost by our own negligence, which, by the grace of God, with much labor we have scarce at length obtained.

7. What will become of us in the end, who begin so early to wax lukewarm?

Woe be unto us, if we will so give ourselves unto ease as if all were now peace and safety, when as yet there appeareth no sign of true holiness in our conversation!

We have much need like young novices to be newly instructed again to good life, if haply there be some hope of future amendment, and greater proficiency in things spiritual.

23.
Of Meditation on Death.

Very quickly there will be an end of thee here; see therefore to thy state: to-day man is; to-morrow he is gone.

And when he is out of sight, quickly also is he out of mind.

O the stupidity and hardness of man's heart, which thinketh only upon the present, and doth not rather care for what is to come!

Thou oughtest so to order thyself in all thy thoughts and actions, as if to-day thou wert to die.

If thou hadst a good conscience, thou wouldst not greatly fear death.

It were better to avoid sin, than to escape death.

If to-day thou art not prepared, how wilt thou be so tomorrow?

Tomorrow is uncertain, and how knowest thou that thou shalt live till tomorrow?

2. What availeth it to live long, when there is so small amendment in us?

Alas, length of days doth not always better us, but often rather increaseth our sin.

O that we had spent but one day in this world thoroughly well!

Many there are who reckon years of conversion; and yet full slender oftentimes is the fruit of amendment.

If to die be accounted dreadful, to live long may perhaps prove more dangerous.

Happy is he that always hath the hour of his death before his eyes, and daily prepareth himself to die.

If at any time thou hast seen another man die, make account that thou must also pass the same way.

3. When it is morning, think that thou mayest die before night;

And when evening comes, dare not to promise thyself the next morning.

Be thou therefore always in readiness, and so lead thy life that death may never take thee unprepared.

Many die suddenly and when they look not for it; for the Son of Man will come in an hour when we think not.

When that last hour shall come, thou wilt begin to have a far different opinion of thy whole life that is past, and be exceeding sorry that thou hast been so careless and remiss.

4. O how wise and happy is he that now laboreth to be such an one in his life, as he will desire to be found at the hour of death!

A perfect contempt to the world, a fervent desire to go forward in all virtue, a love of discipline, a laborious repentance, a ready obedience, a denying of ourselves, and an endurance of any affliction whatsoever for the love of Christ, will give us great confidence that we shall die happily.

Whilst thou art in health thou mayest do much good: but when thou art sick, I see not what thou wilt be able to do.

Few by sickness grow better and more reformed; so also they who wander much abroad, seldom thereby become holy.

5. Trust not to friends and kindred, neither do thou put off the care of thy soul's welfare till hereafter; for men will forget thee, sooner than thou art aware of.

It is better to look to it betime, and to send some good before thee, than to trust to other men's help.

If thou be not careful for thyself now, who will be careful for thee hereafter?

Time now is very precious: now is the day of salvation; now is the accepted time.

But alas! That thou shouldst spend time so idly here, in which thou mightest purchase life eternal.

The time will come, when thou shalt desire one day or hour to amend in, and I know not that it will be granted thee.

6. O beloved, from how great danger mightest thou deliver thyself, from how great fear free thyself, if thou wouldst be ever fearful and mindful of death!

Labor now so to live, that at the hour of death thou mayest rather rejoice than fear.

Learn now to die to the world, that thou mayest then begin to live with Christ.

Learn now to contemn all things, that thou mayest then freely go to Christ.

Chastise thy body now by repentance, that thou mayest then have assured confidence.

7. Ah! fool, why dost thou think to live long, when thou canst not promise to thyself one day.

How many have been deceived and suddenly snatched away!

How often dost thou hear these reports, Such a man is slain, another man is drowned, a third has broken his neck with a fall from some high place, this man died eating, and that man playing! One perished by fire, another by the sword, another of the plague, another was slain by thieves. Thus death is the end of all, and man's life suddenly passeth away like a shadow.

8. Who shall remember thee when thou art dead? And who shall pray for thee?

Do now, even now, my beloved, whatsoever thou art able to do; for thou knowest not when thou shalt die, nor yet what shall befall thee after thy death.

Now, whilst thou hast time, heap unto thyself everlasting riches.

Think on nothing but the salvation of thy soul, care for nothing but the things of God.

Make now friends to thyself by honoring the saints of God, and imitating their actions, that when thou failest, they may receive thee into everlasting habitations.

9. Keep thyself as a stranger and pilgrim upon the earth, who hath nothing to do with the affairs of this world.

Keep thy heart free, and lifted up to God, because thou hast here no abiding city.

Send thither thy daily prayers and sighs together with thy tears that after death thy spirit may be found worthy to pass in felicity to the Lord. *Amen.*

24.
Of Judgment, and the Punishment of Sinners.

On all things look to the end, and see how thou wilt be able to stand before that severe Judge from whom nothing is hid, who is not pacified with gifts, nor admitteth any excuses, but will judge according to right.

O wretched and foolish sinner, who sometimes fearest the countenance of an angry man, what answer wilt thou make to God who knoweth all thy wickedness!

Why dost thou not provide for thyself against that great day of judgment, when no man can excuse or answer for another, but every one shall have enough to answer for himself!

Now may thy pains profit, thy tears be accepted, thy groans be heard, thy grief may bring thee peace, and purge thy soul.

2. The patient man hath a great and wholesome purgatory, who though he receive injuries, yet grieveth more for the malice of another, than for his own suffering; who prayeth willingly for his adversaries, and from his heart forgiveth their offences. He delayeth not to ask forgiveness of whomsoever he hath offended; he is sooner moved to compassion than to anger; he often offereth violence to himself, and laboreth to bring his body wholly into subjection to the spirit.

It is better to purge out our sins, and cut off our vices here, than to keep them to be punished hereafter.

Verily we do but deceive ourselves through an inordinate love of the flesh.

3. What is there that the fire of hell shall feed upon, but thy sins?

The more thou sparest thyself now and followest the flesh, the more severe hereafter shall be thy punishment, and thou storest up greater fuel for that flame.

In what things a man hath sinned, in the same shall he be the more grievously punished.

There shall the slothful be pricked forward with burning goads, and the gluttons be tormented with extreme hunger and thirst.

There shall the luxurious and lovers of pleasure be bathed

in burning pitch and stinking brimstone, and envious, like mad dogs, shall howl for very grief.

4. There is no sin but shall have its own proper torment.

There the proud shall be filled with all confusion; the covetous shall be pinched with miserable penury.

One hour of pain there shall be more bitter than a thousand years of the sharpest penance here!

There is no quiet, no comfort for the damned there; yet here we have some intermission of our labors, and enjoy the comfort of our friends.

Be now solicitous and sorrowful because of thy sins, that at the day of judgment thou mayest be secure with the blessed.

For then shall the righteous with great boldness stand against such as have vexed and oppressed them.

Then shall he stand to judge them, who doth now humbly submit himself to the censures of men.

Then shall the poor and humble have great confidence, but the proud man shall be compassed with fear on every side.

5. Then will it appear that he was wise in this world, who had learned to be a fool and despised for Christ's sake.

Then shall every affliction patiently undergone delight us, when the mouth of all iniquity shall be stopped.

Then shall all the devout rejoice, and all the profane mourn.

Then shall the mortified flesh more rejoice than that which hath been pampered with all pleasures.

Then shall the poor attire shine gloriously, and the precious robes seem vile and contemptible.

Then the poor cottage shall be more commended than the gilded palace.

Then shall constant patience more avail us than all earthly power.

Then simple obedience shall be exalted above all worldly wisdom.

6. Then shall a good and clear conscience more rejoice a man than all the learning of philosophy.

Then shall the contempt of riches weigh more than all the worldling's treasure.

Then shalt thou be more comforted that thou hast prayed devoutly than that thou hast fared daintily.

Then shalt thou be more glad that thou hast kept silence than that thou hast spoken much.

Then shall good works avail more than many goodly words.

Then a strict life and severe repentance shall be more pleasing than all earthly delights.

Accustom thyself now to suffer a little, that thou mayest then be delivered from more grievous pains.

Prove first here what thou canst endure hereafter.

If now thou canst endure so little, how wilt thou then be able to support eternal torments?

If now a little suffering make thee so impatient, what will hell-fire do hereafter?

Assure thyself thou canst not have two joys; it is impossible to take thy pleasure here in this world, and after that to reign with Christ.

7. Suppose that thou hadst up to this day lived always in honors and delights, what would it all avail thee if thou wert doomed to die at this instant?

All therefore is vanity, except to love God and serve Him only.

For he that loveth God with all his heart is neither afraid of death, nor of punishment, nor of judgment, nor of hell; for perfect love gives secure access to God.

But he that takes delight in sin, what marvel is it if he be afraid both of death and judgment?

Yet it is good, although love be not yet of force to withhold thee from sin, that at least the fear of hell should restrain thee.

But he that layeth aside the fear of God, can never continue long in good estate, but falleth quickly into the snares of the devil.

25.
Of the Zealous Amendment of our Whole Life.

Be watchful and diligent in the service of God; and often bethink thyself wherefore thou camest hither, and why thou hast left the world. Was it not that thou mightest live to God, and become a spiritual man?

Be fervent then in going forward, for shortly thou shalt receive the reward of thy labors; there shall not be then any more fear or sorrow in thy coasts.

Labor but a little now, and thou shalt find great rest, yea, perpetual joy.

If thou continuest faithful and fervent in thy work, no doubt but that God will be faithful and liberal in rewarding thee.

Thou oughtest to have a good hope of getting the victory; but thou must not be secure, lest thou wax either negligent or proud.

2. When one that was in anxiety of mind, often wavering between fear and hope, did once, being oppressed with grief, humbly prostrate himself in a church before the altar, in prayer, and said within himself, O if I knew that I should yet persevere! He presently heard within him an answer from God, which said, If thou didst know it, what wouldst thou do? Do now what thou wouldst do then, and thou shalt be secure.

And being herewith comforted and strengthened, he committed himself wholly to the will of God, and his anxious wavering ceased.

Neither had he the mind to search curiously any farther, to know what should befall him, but rather labored to understand what was the perfect and acceptable will of God for the beginning and accomplishing of every good work.

3. "Trust in the Lord, and do good," saith the Prophet, "so shalt thou dwell in the land, and verily thou shalt be fed."

One thing there is that draweth many back from a spiritual progress, and the diligent amendment of their lives: the fear of the difficulty, or the labor of the combat.

But they especially exceed others in all virtue, who make the greatest effort to overcome those things which are most grievous and contrary unto them.

For there a man improveth most and obtaineth greatest grace, where he most overcometh himself and mortifieth himself in spirit.

4. But all men have not equally much to overcome and mortify.

Yet he that is zealous and diligent, though he have more passions, shall profit more than another that is of a more temperate natural disposition, if he be less fervent in the pursuit of all virtue.

Two things especially much further our amendment, to wit, To withdraw ourselves violently from those vices to which our nature is most inclined, and to labor earnestly for that good which we most lack.

Be careful also to avoid with great diligence those things in thyself, which do commonly displease thee in others.

5. Gather some profit to thy soul wheresoever thou art; so that if thou seest or hearest of any good examples, thou stir up thyself to the imitation thereof.

But if thou observe anything worthy of reproof, beware thou do not the same. And if at any time thou hast done it, labor quickly to amend thyself.

As thine eye observeth others, so art thou also noted again by others.

O how sweet and pleasant a thing it is, to see brethren fervent and devout, well-mannered and well-disciplined!

And on the contrary how sad and grievous a thing it is to see them live in a dissolute and disordered sort, not applying themselves to that for which they are called!

How hurtful a thing is it, when they neglect the good purposes of their vocation, and busy themselves in that which is not committed to their care!

6. Be mindful of the profession which thou hast made, and have always before the eyes of thy soul the remembrance of thy Saviour crucified.

Thou hast good cause to be ashamed in looking upon the life of JESUS Christ, seeing thou hast not as yet endeavored to conform thyself more unto Him, though thou hast been a long time in the way of God.

A Religious person that exerciseth himself seriously and devoutly in the most holy life and passion of our Lord, shall there abundantly find whatsoever is necessary and profitable for him; neither shall he need to seek any better thing *out* of JESUS.

O If JESUS crucified would come into our hearts, how quickly and fully should we be taught!

7. A fervent Religious person taketh and beareth well all that is commanded him.

But he that is negligent and lukewarm hath tribulation upon tribulation, and on all sides is afflicted; for he is void of inward consolation, and is forbidden to seek outward comforts.

A Religious person that liveth not according to discipline, lieth open to great mischief, to the ruin of his soul.

He that seeketh liberty and ease, shall ever live in disquiet; for one thing or other will displease him.

8. O that we had nothing else to do, but always with our mouth and whole heart to praise our Lord God!

O that thou mightest never have need to eat, or drink, or sleep; but mightest always praise God, and only employ thyself in spiritual exercises. Thou shouldst then be much more happy than now thou art, when for so many necessities thou art constrained to serve thy body!

Would God there were not these necessities, but only the spiritual refreshments of the soul, which, alas, we taste too seldom!

9. When a man cometh to that estate, that he seeketh not his comfort from any creature, then doth he begin perfectly to relish God. Then shall he be contented with whatsoever doth befall him.

Then shall he neither rejoice in having much, nor be sorrowful for having little; but entirely and confidently commit himself to God, who shall be unto him all in all; to whom nothing doth perish nor die, but all things do live unto Him, and serve Him at his command without delay.

10. Remember always thine end, and that time lost never returns. Without care and diligence thou shalt never get virtue.

If thou begin to wax lukewarm, it will begin to be evil with thee.

But if thou give thyself to fervor of spirit thou shalt find much peace, and feel less labor, by reason of the assistance of God's grace, and the love of virtue.

The fervent and diligent man is prepared for all things.

It is harder work to resist vices and passions, than to toil in bodily labors.

He that avoideth not small faults, by little and little falleth into greater.

Thou wilt always rejoice in the evening, if thou have spent the day profitably.

Be watchful over thyself, stir up thyself, admonish thyself, and whatever becomes of others, neglect not thyself.

The more violence thou usest against thyself, the greater shall be thy profiting. *Amen.*

THE SECOND BOOK

ADMONITIONS CONCERNING
INWARD THINGS.

1.
Of the Inward Life.

The kingdom of God is within you," saith the Lord. Turn thee with thy whole heart unto the Lord, and forsake this wretched world, and thy soul shall find rest.

Learn to despise outward things, and to give thyself to things inward, and thou shalt perceive the kingdom of God to be come in thee.

"For the kingdom of God is peace and joy in the Holy Ghost," which is not given to the unholy.

Christ will come unto thee, and show thee His own consolation, if thou prepare for Him a worthy mansion within thee.

All His glory and beauty is from within, and there He delighteth Himself.

The inward man he often visiteth; and hath with him sweet-discourses, pleasant solace, much peace, familiarity exceeding wonderful.

2. O faithful soul, make ready thy heart for this Bridegroom, that He may vouchsafe to come unto thee, and to dwell within thee.

For thus saith He, "If any man love me, he will keep my words, and we will come unto him and will make our abode with him."

Give therefore admittance unto Christ, and deny entrance to all others.

When thou hast Christ, thou art rich, and hast enough. He will be thy faithful and provident helper in all things, so that thou shalt not need to trust in men.

For men soon change, and quickly fail; but Christ remaineth for ever, and standeth by us firmly unto the end.

3. There is no great trust to be put in a frail and mortal man, even though he be profitable and dear unto us: neither ought we to be much grieved, if sometimes he cross and contradict us.

They that to-day take thy part, to-morrow may be against thee; and often do men turn like the wind.

Put all thy trust in God, let Him be thy fear and thy love: He shall answer for thee, and will do all things well, and as is best for thee.

Thou hast not here an abiding city; and wheresoever thou mayest be, thou art a stranger and pilgrim: neither shalt thou ever have rest, unless thou be inwardly united unto Christ.

4. Why dost thou here gaze about, since this is not the place of thy rest? In heaven ought to be thy home, and all earthly things are to be looked upon as it were by the way.

All things pass away, and thou together with them.

Beware thou cleave not unto them, lest thou be caught, and so perish. Let thy thoughts be on the Highest, and thy prayers for mercy directed unto Christ without ceasing.

If thou canst not contemplate high and heavenly things, rest thyself in the passion of Christ, and dwell willingly on His sacred wounds.

For if thou fly devoutly unto the wounds and precious marks of the Lord JESUS, thou shalt feel great comfort in tribulation: neither wilt thou much care for the slights of men, and wilt easily bear the words of those that reproach thee.

5. Christ was also in the world, despised of men, and His greatest necessity forsaken by His acquaintance and friends in the midst of reproaches.

Christ was willing to suffer and be despised; and darest thou complain of anything?

Christ had adversaries and backbiters; and dost thou wish to have all men thy friends and benefactors?

Whence shall thy patience attain her crown, if no adversity befall thee?

If thou art willing to suffer no contradiction, how wilt thou be the friend of Christ?

Suffer with Christ, and for Christ, if thou desire to reign with Christ.

6. If thou hadst but once perfectly entered into the secrets of the Lord JESUS, and tasted a little of His ardent love; then wouldst thou not regard thine own convenience or inconvenience, but rather wouldst rejoice in reproaches, if they should be cast upon thee; for the love of JESUS maketh a man despise himself.

A lover of JESUS and of the truth, and a true inward Christian, and one free from inordinate affections, can freely turn himself unto God, and lift himself above himself in spirit, and rest in full enjoyment.

7. He that judgeth of all things as they are, and not as they are said or esteemed to be, is truly wise, and taught rather of God than of men.

He that knoweth how to live inwardly, and to make small reckoning of things without, neither requireth places, nor awaiteth times for performing of religious exercises.

A spiritual man quickly recollecteth himself, because he never poureth out himself wholly to outward things.

He is not hindered by outward labor or business, which may be necessary for the time: but as things fall out, so he suits himself to them.

He that is well ordered and disposed within himself, careth not for the strange and perverse behavior of men.

A man is hindered and distracted in proportion as he draweth outward things unto himself.

8. If it were well with thee, and thou wert thoroughly purified from sin, all things would fall out to thee for good, and to thy progress.

But many things displease and often trouble thee, because thou art not yet perfectly dead unto thyself, nor separated from all earthly things.

Nothing so defileth and entangleth the heart of man, as the impure love of things created.

If thou refuse outward comfort, thou wilt be able to contemplate the things of Heaven, and often to receive internal joy.

2.
Of Humble Submission.

Regard not much who is for thee, or who against thee: but give all thy thought and care to this, that God be with thee in everything thou doest.

Have a good conscience, and God will defend thee.

For whom God will help, no malice of man shall be able to hurt.

If thou canst be silent and suffer, without doubt thou shalt see that the Lord will help thee.

He knoweth the time and the manner to deliver thee, and therefore thou oughtest to resign thyself unto Him.

It belongeth to God to help, and to deliver from all confusion.

It is often very profitable, to keep us more humble, that others know and rebuke our faults.

2. When a man humbleth himself for his failings, then he easily pacifieth others, and quickly satisfieth those that are offended with him.

God protecteth the humble and delivereth him; the humble he loveth and comforteth unto the humble man He inclineth Himself; unto the humble He giveth great grace; and after his humiliation He raiseth him to glory.

Unto the humble He revealeth His secrets, and sweetly draweth and inviteth him unto Himself.

The humble man, though he suffer confusion, hath yet much peace; for that he resteth on God, and not on the world.

Do not think that thou hast made any progress, unless thou esteem thyself inferior to all.

3.
Of a Good and Peaceable Man.

First keep thyself in peace, and then shalt thou be able to make peace among others.

A peaceable man doth more good than he that is well learned.

A passionate man draweth even good into evil, and easily believeth the worst.

A good and peaceable man turneth all things to good.

He that is in peace, is not suspicious of any. But he that is discontented and troubled, is tossed with divers suspicions: he is neither quiet himself, nor suffereth others to be quiet.

He often speaketh that which he ought not to speak; and leaveth undone that which it were more expedient for him to do.

He considereth what others are bound to do, and neglecteth that which he is bound to do himself.

First, therefore, have a careful zeal over thyself, and then thou mayest justly show thyself zealous also of thy neighbor's good.

2. Thou knowest well how to excuse and color thine own deeds, but thou art not willing to receive the excuses of others.

It were more just that thou shouldst accuse thyself, and excuse thy brother.

If thou wilt thyself be borne with, bear also with another.

Behold, how far off thou art yet from true charity and humility; for that knows not how to be angry with any, or to be moved with indignation, but only against a man's self.

It is no great matter to associate with the good and gentle; for this is naturally pleasing to all, and every one willingly enjoyeth peace, and loveth those best that agree with him.

But to be able to live peaceably with hard and perverse persons, or with the disorderly, or with such as go contrary to us, is a great grace, and a most commendable and manly thing.

3. Some there are that keep themselves in peace, and are in peace also with others.

And there are some that neither are in peace themselves,

nor suffer others to be in peace: They are troublesome to others, but always more troublesome to themselves.

And others there are that keep themselves in peace, and study to bring back others unto peace.

Nevertheless, our whole peace in this miserable life consisteth rather in humble endurance, than in not suffering things that are contrary to us.

He that knowest best how to suffer, will best keep himself in peace. That man is conqueror of himself, and lord of the world, the friend of Christ, and an heir of heaven.

4.
Of a Pure Mind, and a Simple Intention.

By two wings a man is lifted up from things earthly, namely, by Simplicity and Purity.

Simplicity ought to be in our intention; purity in our affections. Simplicity doth tend towards God; purity doth apprehend and taste Him.

No good action will hinder thee, if thou be in thy heart free from inordinate affection.

If thou intend and seek nothing else but the will of God and the good of thy neighbor, thou shalt thoroughly enjoy inward liberty.

If thy heart were sincere and upright, then every creature would be unto thee a living mirror, and a book of holy doctrine.

There is no creature so small and abject, that it representeth not the goodness of God.

2. If thou wert inwardly good and pure, then wouldst thou be able to see and understand all things well without impediment.

A pure heart penetrateth heaven and hell.

Such as every one is inwardly, so he judgeth outwardly,

If there be joy in the world, surely a man of a pure heart possesseth it.

And if there be anywhere tribulation and affliction, an evil conscience best knoweth it.

As iron put into the fire loseth its rust, and becometh clearly red-hot, so he that wholly turneth himself unto God, putteth off all slothfulness, and is transformed into a new man.

3. When a man beginneth to grow lukewarm, then he is afraid of a little labor, and willingly receiveth comfort from outward things.

But when he once beginneth to overcome himself perfectly, and to walk manfully in the way of God; then he esteemeth those things to be light, which before seemed grievous unto him.

5.
Of the Consideration of One's Self.

We cannot trust much to ourselves, because grace oftentimes is wanting to us, and understanding also.

There is but little light in us, and that which we have we quickly lose by our negligence.

Oftentimes too we do not perceive our own inward blindness how great it is.

We often do a bad act, and make a worse excuse.

We are sometimes moved with passion, and we think it to be zeal.

We reprehend small things in others, and pass over greater matters in ourselves.

We quickly enough feel and weigh what we suffer at the hands of others; but we mind not what others suffer from us.

He that well and rightly considereth his own works, will find little cause to judge hardly of another.

2. He who is a Christian at heart preferreth the care of himself before all other cares. And he that diligently attendeth unto himself, can easily keep silence concerning others.

Thou wilt never be thus in heart religious, unless thou pass over other men's matters with silence, and look especially to thyself.

If thou attend wholly unto God and thyself, thou wilt be but little moved with whatsoever thou seest abroad.

Where art thou, when thou art not with thyself? And when thou hast run over all, what hast thou then profited, if thou hast neglected thyself?

If thou desirest peace of mind and true unity of purpose,

thou must still put all other things behind thee, and look only upon thyself.

3. Thou shalt profit much, if thou keep thyself free from all temporal care.

Thou shalt greatly lose if thou take thought for any temporal thing.

Let nothing be great unto thee, nothing high, nothing pleasing, nothing acceptable, but only God Himself, or that which is of God.

Esteem all comfort vain, which thou receivest from any creature.

A soul that loveth God, despiseth all things that are inferior unto God.

God alone is everlasting, and of infinite greatness, filling all creatures; the comfort of the soul, and the true joy of the heart.

6.
Of the Joy of a Good Conscience.

The glory of a good man, is the testimony of a good conscience.

Have a good conscience, and thou shalt ever have joy.

A good conscience is able to bear very much, and is very cheerful in adversities.

An evil conscience is always fearful and unquiet.

Thou shalt rest sweetly, if thy heart condemn thee not.

Never rejoice, but when thou hast done well.

Sinners have never true joy, nor feel inward peace; because "There is no peace to the wicked," saith the Lord.

And if they should say, "We are in peace, no evil shall fall upon us, and who shall dare to hurt us?" Believe them not; for upon a sudden will arise the wrath of God, and their deeds shall be brought to naught, and their thoughts shall perish.

2. To glory in tribulation, is no hard thing for him that loveth; for so to glory, is to glory in the Cross of the Lord.

That glory is short, which is given and received from men.

Sorrow always accompanieth the glory of the world.

The glory of the good is in their consciences, and not in

the tongues of men. The gladness of the just is of God, and in God; and their joy is of the truth.

He that desireth true and everlasting glory, careth not for that which is temporal.

And he that seeketh temporal glory, or despiseth it not from his soul, showeth himself to have but little esteem of the glory of heaven.

He enjoyeth great tranquillity of heart, that careth neither for the praise, nor dispraise of men.

3. He will easily be content and at peace, whose conscience is pure.

Thou art not the more holy for being praised; nor the more worthless for being dispraised.

What thou art, that thou art; neither by words canst thou be made greater than what thou art in the sight of God.

If thou consider what thou art in thyself, thou wilt not care what men say of thee.

Man looketh on the countenance, but God on the heart. Man considereth the deeds, but God weigheth the intentions.

To be always doing good, and to esteem little of one's self, is the sign of an humble soul.

To be unwilling to have any created being for our comforter, is a sign of great purity and inward confidence.

4. He that seeketh no testimony on his behalf from without, doth show that he hath wholly committed himself unto God.

"For not he that commendeth himself is approved (saith St. Paul), but whom God commendeth."

To walk in the heart with God, and not to be held in bondage by any outward affection, is the state of a spiritual man.

7.
Of the Love of Jesus above all Things.

Blessed is he that understandeth what it is to love JESUS, and to despise himself for JESUS' sake.

Thou oughtest to leave thy beloved for the Beloved; for JESUS will be loved alone above all things.

The love of things created is deceitful and inconstant; the love of JESUS is faithful and constant.

He that cleaveth unto creatures, shall fall with that which is subject to fall; he that embraceth JESUS shall stand firmly for ever.

Love Him, and keep Him for thy friend, who, when all go away, will not forsake thee, nor suffer thee to perish in the end.

Sometime or other thou must be separated from all, whether thou wilt or no.

2. Keep close to JESUS both in life and in death, and commit thyself unto His faithfulness, who, when all fail, can alone help thee.

Thy Beloved is of such a nature, that He will admit of no rival; but will have thy heart alone, and sit on His own Throne as King.

If thou couldst empty thyself perfectly of all created things, JESUS would willingly dwell with thee.

Whatsoever trust thou reposeth in men, out of JESUS, is all little better than lost.

Trust not nor lean upon a reed shaken by the wind; for that all flesh is grass, and all the glory thereof shall wither away as the flower of the field.

3. Thou wilt soon be deceived, if thou only look to the outward appearance of men.

For, if thou seekest thy comfort and thy profit in others, thou shalt often feel loss.

If thou seekest JESUS in all things, thou shalt surely find JESUS.

But if thou seekest thyself, thou shalt also find thyself, but to thine own destruction.

For if a man do not seek JESUS, he is more hurtful to himself, than the whole world and all his enemies could be.

8.
Of Familiar Friendship with Jesus.

When JESUS is present, all is well, and nothing seems difficult; but when JESUS is not present, everything is hard.

When JESUS speaks not inwardly to us, all other comfort is nothing worth; but if JESUS speak but one word, we feel great consolation.

Did not Mary Magdalene rise immediately from the place

where she wept, when Martha said to her, "The Master is come, and calleth for thee"?

Happy hour! When JESUS calleth from tears to spiritual joy.

How dry and hard art thou without JESUS! How foolish and vain, if thou desire anything out of JESUS!

Is not this a greater loss, than if thou shouldst lose the whole world?

2. What can the world profit thee without JESUS?

To be without JESUS is a grievous hell; and to be with JESUS, a sweet paradise.

If JESUS be with thee no enemy shall be able to hurt thee.

He that findeth JESUS findeth a good treasure, yea, a good above all good.

And he that loseth JESUS loseth overmuch, yea more than the whole world!

Most poor is he who liveth without JESUS; and he most rich who is dear to JESUS.

3. It asketh great skill to know how to hold converse with JESUS; and to know how to retain JESUS, is great wisdom.

Be thou humble and peaceable, and JESUS will be with thee.

Be devout and quiet and JESUS will stay with thee.

Thou mayest soon drive away JESUS, and lose his favor, if thou wilt turn aside to outward things.

And if thou shouldst drive Him from thee and lose Him, unto whom wilt thou flee, and whom wilt thou then seek for thy friend?

Without a friend thou canst not well live; and if JESUS be not above all friends to thee, thou shalt be indeed sad and desolate.

Therefore thou doest not wisely, if thou trust or rejoice in any other.

It is preferable to have all the world against us rather than to have JESUS offended with us.

Amongst all therefore that be dear unto us, let JESUS alone be specially beloved.

4. Love all for JESUS, but JESUS for Himself.

JESUS Christ alone is singularly to be loved; and He alone is found Good and Faithful above all friends.

For Him, and in Him, let friends as well as foes be dear unto thee; and all these are to be prayed for, that He would make them all to know and to love Him.

Never desire to be singularly commended or beloved, for that appertaineth only unto God, who hath none like unto Himself.

Neither do thou desire that the heart of any should be set on thee, nor do thou set thy heart on the love of any; but let JESUS be in thee, and in every good man.

5. Be pure and free within, and entangle not thy heart with any creature.

Thou oughtest to be naked and open before God, ever carrying thy heart pure towards Him, if thou wouldest be free to consider and see how sweet the Lord is.

And truly, unless thou be prevented and drawn by His grace, thou shalt never attain to that happiness of forsaking and taking leave of all, in order that thou alone mayest be united to Him alone.

For when the grace of God cometh unto a man, then he is made able for all things. And when it goeth away, then is he poor and weak, and as it were left only for affliction.

In this case thou oughtest not to be cast down, nor to despair but to resign thyself calmly to the will of God, and whatever comes upon thee, to endure it for the glory of JESUS Christ; for after winter followeth summer, after night the day returneth, and after a tempest a great calm.

9.

Of the Want of all Comfort.

It is no hard matter to despise human comfort, when we have that which is divine.

It is much, and very much, to be able to lack both human and divine comfort; and, for God's honor, to be willing cheerfully to endure desolation of heart; and to seek one's self in nothing, nor to regard one's own merit.

What great matter is it, if at the coming of grace thou be cheerful and devout? This hour is wished for of all men.

He rideth easily enough, whom the grace of God carrieth.

And what marvel if he feel not his burden, who is borne up by the Almighty, and led by the Sovereign Guide?

2. We are always willing to have something for our com-

fort; and a man doth not without difficulty strip himself of self.

The holy martyr Laurence and his priest overcame the world, because whatsoever seemed delightsome in the world he despised; and for the love of Christ he patiently suffered God's chief priest Sixtus, whom he most dearly loved, to be even taken away from him.

He therefore overcame the love of man by the love of the Creator; and he rather chose what pleased God, than human comfort.

So also do thou learn to part even with a near and dear friend for the love of God.

Nor do thou think it hard, when thou art deserted by a friend, as knowing that we all at last must be separated one from another.

3. A man must strive long and mightily within himself, before he can learn fully to master himself and to draw his whole heart unto God.

When a man trusteth in himself, he easily slideth unto human comforts.

But a true lover of Christ, and a diligent follower of all virtue, does not fall back on comforts, nor seek such sensible sweetnesses; but rather prefers hard exercises, and to sustain severe labors for Christ.

4. When therefore spiritual comfort is given thee from God, receive it with thankfulness; but understand that it is the gift of God, not thy desert.

Be not puffed up, be not too joyful, nor vainly presumptuous; but rather be the more humble for that gift, more wary too and fearful in all thine actions; for that hour will pass away, and temptation will follow.

When consolation is taken from thee, do not immediately despair; but with humility and patience wait for the heavenly visitation; for God is able to give thee back again more ample consolation.

This is nothing new nor strange unto them that have experience in the way of God; for the great saints and ancient prophets had oftentimes experience of such kind of vicissitudes.

5. For which cause, one, while he was basking in divine grace, said, "I said in my prosperity, I shall never be moved."

But in the absence of it, he adds this experience of what he was in himself, "Thou didst turn Thy face from me, and I was troubled."

Yet in the midst of all this he doth not by any means despair, but more earnestly beseecheth the Lord, and saith, "Unto Thee, O Lord, will I cry, and I will pray unto my God."

At length, he receiveth the fruit of his prayer, and testifieth that he was heard, saying, "The Lord hath heard me, and taken pity on me; the Lord is become my helper."

But wherein? "Thou hast turned," saith he, "my sorrow into joy, and thou hast compassed me about with gladness."

If great saints were so dealt with, we that are weak and poor ought not to despair, if we be sometimes hot and sometimes cold; for the Spirit cometh and goeth according to the good pleasure of his own will. For which cause holy Job saith, "Thou visitest him early in the morning, and suddenly Thou provest him."

6. Whereupon then can I hope, or wherein ought I to trust, save in the great mercy of God alone, and in the only hope of heavenly grace?

For whether I have with me good men, either religious brethren, or faithful friends; whether holy books, or beautiful treatises, or sweet psalms and hymns; all these help but little, and have but little savor, when grace forsaketh me, and I am left in mine own poverty.

At such time there is no better remedy than patience, and the denying of myself according to the will of God.

7. I never found any so religious and devout, that he had not sometimes a withdrawing of grace, or felt not some decrease of zeal.

There was never saint so highly rapt and illuminated, who first or last was not tempted.

For he is not worthy of the high contemplation of God, who hath not been exercised with some tribulation for God's sake.

For temptation going before is wont to be a sign of comfort to follow.

For unto those that are proved by temptations heavenly comfort is promised. "To him that overcometh," saith He, "I will give to eat of the tree of life."

8. But divine consolation is given, that a man may be stronger to bear adversities.

There followeth also temptation, lest he should wax proud of any good.

The devil sleepeth not, neither is the flesh as yet dead; therefore cease not to prepare thyself to the battle; for on thy right hand and on thy left are enemies who never rest.

10.
Of Gratitude for the Grace of God.

Why seekest thou rest, since thou art born to labor?

Dispose thyself to patience rather than to comfort, and to the bearing of the cross rather than to gladness.

What worldly man is there that would not willingly receive spiritual joy and comfort if he could always have it?

For spiritual comforts exceed all the delights of the world, and the pleasures of the flesh.

For all worldly delights are either vain or unclean; but spiritual delights alone are pleasant and honest, being sprung from virtue, and infused by God into pure minds.

But no man can always enjoy these divine comforts according to his desire; for the time of temptation is never far away.

2. But false freedom of mind and great confidence in ourselves are very contrary to heavenly visitations.

God doeth well for us in giving the grace of comfort; but man doeth evil in not returning all again unto God with thanksgiving.

And therefore the gifts of grace flow in us, because we are unthankful to the giver, and return them not wholly to the source and fountain.

For grace ever attendeth him that is duly thankful; and from the proud shall be taken that which is wont to be given to the humble.

3. I desire not that consolation that taketh from me compunction; nor do I affect that contemplation which leadeth to a high mind.

For all that is high is not holy; nor all that is sweet, good; nor every desire, pure; nor is every thing that is dear unto us pleasing to God.

Willingly do I accept of that grace, whereby I may ever be

found more humble, and more affected with fear, and may become more ready to renounce myself.

He that is taught by the gift of grace, and schooled by the withdrawing thereof, will not dare to attribute any good to himself, but will rather acknowledge himself to be poor and naked. Give unto God that which is God's, and ascribe unto thyself that which is thine own; that is, give thanks to God for His grace; and acknowledge that to thyself alone is to be attributed sin, and the punishment due to sin.

4. Set thyself always in the lowest place and the highest shall be given thee; for the highest is not without the lowest.

The chiefest Saints before God are the least in their own judgments; and the more glorious they are, so much the humbler within themselves.

Those that are full of truth and heavenly glory, are not desirous of empty glory.

Those that are firmly settled and grounded in God, can in no way be proud.

And they that ascribe all good unto God, whatsoever they have received, seek not glory one of another, but desire that glory which is from God alone; and above all things that God may be praised in Himself, and in all His saints; and are always pressing on for this very thing.

5. Be therefore thankful for the least gift, so shalt thou be meet to receive greater.

Let the least be unto thee even as the greatest, yea, the most contemptible gift as of especial value.

If thou consider the worth of the giver, no gift will seem little, or of too mean esteem. For that cannot be little which is given by the most High God.

Yea, if He should give punishment and stripes, it ought to be a matter of thankfulness; because He doeth always for our welfare, whatsoever He permitted to happen unto us.

He that desireth to keep the grace of God, let him be thankful for grace given, and patient for the taking away thereof: let him pray that it may return; let him be cautious and humble, lest he lose it.

11.
That the Lovers of the Cross of JESUS are Few.

JESUS hath now many lovers of His heavenly kingdom, but few bearers of His cross.

He hath many desirous of consolation, but few of tribulation.

He findeth many companions of His table, but few of His abstinence.

All desire to rejoice with Him, few are willing to endure anything for Him.

Many follow JESUS unto the breaking of bread; but few to the drinking of the cup of His passion.

Many reverence His miracles, few follow the ignominy of His cross.

Many love JESUS so long as no adversities befall them.

Many praise and bless Him so long as they receive any consolation from Him.

But if Jesus hide Himself, and leave them but a little while, they fall either into complaining, or into too much dejection of mind.

2. But they who love JESUS for His own sake, and not for some special comfort which they receive, bless Him in all tribulation and anguish of heart, as well as in the state of highest comfort.

Yea although He should never be willing to give them comfort, they notwithstanding would ever praise Him, and wish to be always giving thanks.

3. O how powerful is the pure love of JESUS, which is mixed with no self-interest, nor self-love!

Are not all those to be called mercenary, who are ever seeking consolations?

Do they not show themselves to be rather lovers of themselves than of Christ, who are always thinking of their own profit and advantage?

Where shall one be found who is willing to serve God for naught?

4. Rarely is any one found so spiritual as to have suffered the loss of all things.

For where is any man to be found that is indeed poor in spirit, and thoroughly void of all leaning on created things? "From afar, yea from the ends of the earth, is his value."

If a man should give all his substance, it is as yet nothing.

And if he should practise great repentance, still it is little.

And if he should attain to all knowledge, he is still afar off.

And if he should be of great virtue, and of very fervent devotion, yet there is much wanting: especially one thing, which is most necessary for him.

What is that? That leaving all, he forsake himself, and go wholly from himself, and retain nothing of self-love.

And when he hath done all that is to be done, so far as he knoweth, let him think that he hath done nothing.

5. Let him not think that of great weight which might be esteemed great; but let him in truth pronounce himself to be an unprofitable servant, as the Truth Himself saith, "When you shall have done all things that are commanded you, say, we are unprofitable servants."

Then may he be truly poor and naked in spirit, and say with the Prophet, "I am desolate and afflicted."

Yet none is richer than that man, none more powerful, none more free; for he knoweth how to leave himself and all things, and to set himself in the lowest place.

12.
Of the Royal Way of the Holy Cross.

Unto many this seemeth an hard speech, "Deny thyself, take up thy cross, and follow JESUS."

But much harder will it be to hear that last word, "Depart from me, ye cursed, into everlasting fire."

For they who now willingly hear and follow the word of the cross, shall not then fear to hear the sentence of everlasting damnation.

This sign of the cross shall be in the heaven, when the Lord shall come to judgment.

Then all the servants of the cross, who in their life-time conformed themselves unto Christ crucified, shall draw near unto Christ the judge with great confidence.

2. Why therefore fearest thou to take up the cross which leadeth thee to a kingdom?

In the cross is salvation, in the cross is life, in the cross is protection against our enemies, in the cross is infusion of heavenly sweetness, in the cross is strength of mind, in the cross joy of spirit, in the cross the height of virtue, in the cross the perfection of sanctity.

There is no salvation of the soul, nor hope of everlasting life, but in the cross.

Take up therefore thy cross and follow JESUS, and thou shalt go into life everlasting. He went before, bearing His cross, and died for thee on the cross; that thou mightest also bear thy cross and desire to die on the cross with Him.

For if thou be dead with Him, thou shalt also live with Him. And if thou be His companion in punishment, thou shalt be partaker with Him also in glory.

3. Behold! In the cross all doth consist, and all lieth in our dying thereon; for there is no other way unto life, and unto true inward peace, but the way of the holy cross, and of daily mortification.

Go where thou wilt, seek whatsoever thou wilt, thou shalt not find a higher way above, nor safer way below, than the way of the holy cross.

Dispose and order all things according to thy will and judgment; yet thou shalt ever find, that of necessity thou must suffer somewhat, either willingly or against thy will and so thou shalt ever find the cross.

For either thou shalt feel pain in thy body, or in thy soul thou shalt suffer tribulation.

4. Sometimes thou shalt be forsaken of God, sometimes thou shalt be troubled by thy neighbors; and, what is more, oftentimes thou shalt be wearisome to thyself.

Neither canst thou be delivered or eased by any remedy or comfort; but so long as it pleaseth God, thou must bear it.

For God will have thee learn to suffer tribulation without comfort; and that thou subject thyself wholly to Him, and by tribulation become more humble.

No man hath so in his heart a sympathy with the passion of Christ, as he who hath suffered the like himself.

The cross therefore is always ready and everywhere waits for thee.

Thou canst not escape it whithersoever thou runnest; for wheresoever thou goest, thou carriest thyself with thee, and shalt ever find thyself.

Both above and below, without and within, which way soever thou dost turn thee, everywhere of thou shalt find the cross; and everywhere of necessity thou must hold fast patience, if thou wilt have inward peace, and enjoy an everlasting crown.

5. If thou bear the cross cheerfully, it will bear thee, and lead thee to the desired end, namely, where there shall be an end of suffering, though here there shall not be.

If thou bear it unwillingly, thou makest for thyself a burden and increasest thy load, which yet notwithstanding thou must bear.

If thou cast away one cross, without doubt thou shalt find another, and that perhaps more heavy.

6. Thinkest thou to escape that which no mortal man could ever avoid? Which of the saints in the world was without crosses, and tribulations?

For not even our Lord JESUS Christ was ever one hour without the anguish of His Passion, so long as He lived. "Christ" (saith He) "must needs suffer, and rise again from the dead, and so enter into His glory." And how dost thou seek any other way than this royal way, which is the way of the holy cross?

7. Christ's whole life was a cross and martyrdom: and dost thou seek rest and joy for thyself?

Thou art deceived, thou art deceived if thou seek any other thing than to suffer tribulations; for this whole mortal life is full of miseries, and marked on every side with crosses.

And the higher a person hath advanced in the Spirit, so much the heavier crosses he oftentimes findeth; because the grief of his banishment increaseth with his love to God.

8. Nevertheless this man, though so many ways afflicted, is not without refreshing comfort, for that he perceiveth very much benefit to accrue unto him by the bearing of his own cross.

For whilst he willingly putteth himself under it, all the burden of tribulation is turned into the confidence of divine comfort.

And the more the flesh is wasted by affliction, so much the more is the spirit strengthened by inward grace.

And sometimes he is so comforted with the desire of tribulation and adversity, for the love of conformity to the cross of Christ, that he would not wish to be without grief and tribulation; because he believes that he shall be unto God so much the more acceptable, the more and more grievous things he is permitted to suffer for Him.

This is not the power of man, but it is the grace of Christ, which can and doth so much in frail flesh; so that what naturally it always abhors and flees from, that through fervor of spirit it encounters and loves.

9. It is not according to man's inclination to bear the cross, to love the cross, to chastise the body and bring it into subjection, to flee honors, willingly to suffer contumelies, to despise one's self and to which to be despised, to endure all adversities and losses, and to desire no prosperity in this world.

If thou look to thyself, thou shalt be able of thyself to accomplish nothing of this kind.

But if thou trust in the Lord, strength shall be given thee from heaven, and the world and the flesh shall be made subject to thy command.

Neither shalt thou fear thine enemy the devil, if thou be armed with faith, and signed with the cross of Christ.

10. Set thyself therefore, like a good and faithful servant of Christ, to bear manfully the cross of thy Lord, who out of love was crucified for thee.

Prepare thyself to bear many adversities and divers kinds of troubles in this miserable life; for so it will be with thee, wheresoever thou art, and so surely thou shalt find it, wheresoever thou hide thyself.

So it must be; nor is there any remedy nor means to escape from tribulation and sorrow, but only to endure them.

Drink of Lord's cup with hearty affection, if thou desire to be His friend, and to have part with Him.

As for comforts, leave them to God; let Him do therein as shall best please Him.

But do thou set thyself to suffer tribulations, and account them the greatest comforts; for the sufferings of this present time, although thou alone couldst suffer them all, cannot worthily deserve the glory which is to come.

11. When thou shalt come to this estate, that tribulation shall seem sweet, and thou shalt relish it for Christ's sake; then think it to be well with thee, for thou hast found a paradise upon earth.

As long as it is grievous to thee to suffer, and thou desirest to escape, so long shalt thou be ill at ease, and the desire of escaping tribulation shall follow thee everywhere.

12. If thou dost set thyself to that thou oughtest, namely, to suffering and to death, it will quickly be better with thee, and thou shalt find peace.

Although thou shouldst have been rapt even unto the third heaven with Paul, thou art not by this secured that thou shalt suffer no adversity. "I will show him" (saith JESUS) "how great things he must suffer for my name."

It remaineth therefore, that thou suffer, if it please thee to love JESUS, and to serve him constantly.

13. O that thou wert worthy to suffer something for the Name of JESUS! How great glory would remain unto thyself; what joy would arise to all God's saints; how great edification also to thy neighbor!

For all men recommend patience; few, however, they are who are willing to suffer.

With great reason oughtest thou cheerfully to suffer some little for Christ's sake; since many suffer more grievous things for the world.

14. Know for certain that thou oughtest to lead a dying life. And the more any man dieth to himself, so much the more doth he begin to live unto God.

No man is fit to comprehend things heavenly, unless he submit himself to the bearing of adversities for Christ's sake.

Nothing is more acceptable to God, nothing more wholesome to thee in this world, than that thou suffer cheerfully for Christ.

And if thou couldst choose, thou oughtest rather to wish to suffer adversities for Christ, than to be refreshed with many consolations; because thou wouldst thus be more like unto Christ, and more conformable to all the saints.

For our worthiness and the growth of our spiritual estate consisteth not in many sweetnesses and comforts; but rather in the patient enduring of great afflictions and tribulations.

15. Indeed if there had been any better thing, and more profitable to man's salvation, than suffering, surely Christ would have showed it by word and example.

For both the disciples that followed Him, and also all who desire to follow Him, He plainly exhorteth to the bearing of the cross, and saith, "If any man will come after me, let him deny himself, and take up his cross, and follow me."

So that when we have thoroughly read and searched all, let this be the final conclusion, "That through much tribulation we must enter into the kingdom of God."

THE THIRD BOOK

OF INTERNAL CONSOLATION.

1.
Of Christ's speaking inwardly to
the Faithful Soul.

I will hearken what the Lord God will speak in me.

Blessed is the soul which heareth the Lord speaking within her, and receiveth from His mouth the word of consolation.

Blessed are the ears that gladly receive the pulses of the Divine whisper, and give no heed to the many whisperings of this world.

Blessed indeed are those ears which listen not after the voice which is sounding without, but for the Truth teaching within.

Blessed are the eyes which are shut to outward things, but intent on things within.

Blessed are they that enter far into inward things, and endeavor to prepare themselves, more and more, by daily exercises, for the receiving of heavenly secrets.

Blessed are they who are glad to have time to spare for God, and who shake off all worldly hindrances.

2. Consider these things, O my soul, and shut up the door of thy sensual desires, that thou mayest hear what the Lord thy God shall speak in thee.

Thus saith thy Beloved, I am thy Salvation, thy Peace, and thy Life; keep thyself with me, and thou shalt find peace.

Let go all transitory things, and seek those that be everlasting.

What are all temporal things, but snares? And what can all creatures avail thee, if thou be forsaken by the Creator?

Bid farewell therefore to all things else, and labor to please thy Creator, and to be faithful unto Him, that so thou mayest be able to attain unto true blessedness.

2.
That the Truth speaketh inwardly without Noise of Words.

Speak, Lord, for Thy servant heareth.

I am thy servant, grant me understanding, that I may know Thy testimonies.

Incline my heart to the words of Thy mouth: let Thy speech distil as the dew.

The children of Israel in times past said unto Moses, "Speak thou unto us, and we will hear: let not the Lord speak unto us lest we die."

Not so, Lord, not so, I beseech Thee: but rather with the prophet Samuel, I humbly and earnestly entreat, "Speak, Lord, for Thy servant heareth."

Let not Moses speak unto me, nor any of the prophets, but rather do thou speak, O Lord God, the inspirer and enlightener of all the prophets; for thou alone without them canst perfectly instruct me, but they without thee can profit nothing.

2. They indeed may utter words, but they cannot give the Spirit.

Most beautifully do they speak, but if thou be silent, they inflame not the heart.

They teach the letter, but thou openest the sense: they bring forth mysteries, but thou unlockest the meaning sealed things.

They declare thy commandments, but thou helpest us to fulfil them.

They point out the way, but thou givest strength to walk in it.

They work only outwardly, but thou instructest and enlightenest the heart.

They water, but thou givest the increase.

They cry aloud in words, but thou impartest understanding to the hearing.

3. Let not Moses therefore speak unto me, but thou, O Lord my God, the everlasting Truth; lest I die, and prove unfruitful, if I be only warned outwardly, and not inflamed within:

Lest it turn to my condemnation,—the word heard and not fulfilled, known and not loved, believed and not observed.

Speak therefore, Lord, for thy servant heareth; for thou hast the words of eternal life.

Speak thou unto me, to the comfort, however imperfect, of my soul, and to the amendment of my whole life, and to thy praise and glory and honor everlasting.

3.
That the Words of God are to be heard with Humility, and that many weigh them not.

My son, hear my words, words, of greatest sweetness, surpassing all the knowledge of the philosophers and wise men of this world.

"My words are Spirit and Life," and not to be weighed by the understanding of man.

They are not to be drawn forth for vain approbation, but to be heard in silence, and to be received with all humility and great affection.

AND I said, Blessed is the man whom thou shalt instruct, O Lord, and shalt teach out of thy law, that thou mayest give him rest from the evil days, and that he be not desolate upon earth.

2. I TAUGHT the prophets from the beginning (saith the Lord), and cease not, even to this day, to speak to all; but many are hardened, and deaf to my voice.

Most men do more willingly listen to the world than to

God; they sooner follow the desires of their own flesh, than God's good pleasure.

The world promiseth things temporal and mean, and is served with great eagerness: I promise things most high and eternal; and yet the hearts of men remain torpid and insensible.

Who is there that in all things serveth and obeyeth me with so great care as the world and its lords are served withal? Be ashamed, O Sidon, saith the sea. And if thou ask the cause, hear wherefore.

For a small income a long journey is undertaken; for everlasting life many will scarce once lift a foot from the ground.

The most pitiful reward is sought after; for a single bit of money sometimes there is shameful contention; for a vain matter and slight promise men fear not to toil day and night.

3. But, alas! For an unchangeable good, for an inestimable reward, for the highest honor, and glory without end, they grudge even the least fatigue.

Be ashamed, therefore, thou slothful and complaining servant, that they are found to be more ready to destruction than thou to life.

They rejoice more in vanity than thou dost in the truth.

Sometimes, indeed, they are frustrated of their hope; but my promise deceiveth none, nor sendeth him away empty that trusteth in me.

What I have promised, I will give; what I have said I will fulfil; if only any man remain faithful in my love even to the end.

I am the rewarder of all good men, and the strong approver of all who are devoted to me.

4. Write thou my words in thy heart, and meditate diligently on them; for in time of temptation they will be very needful for thee.

What thou understandest not when thou readest, thou shalt know in the day of visitation.

In two ways I am wont to visit mine elect, namely, with temptation and with consolation.

And I daily read two lessons to them, one in reproving their vices, another in exhorting them to the increase of all virtues.

He that hath my words and despiseth them, hath one that shall judge him in the last day.

A PRAYER TO IMPLORE THE GRACE OF DEVOTION.

O Lord my God! Thou art to me whatsoever is good. And who am I, that I should dare to speak to thee? I am thy poorest, meanest servant, and a most vile worm, much more poor and contemptible than I can or dare express.

Yet do thou remember, O Lord, that I am nothing, have nothing, and can do nothing.

Thou alone art good, just and holy; thou canst do all things, thou accomplishest all things, thou fillest all things, only the sinner thou leavest empty.

Remember thy mercies, and fill my heart with thy grace. thou who wilt not that thy works should be void and in vain.

6. How can I bear up myself in this miserable life, unless thou strengthen me with thy mercy and grace?

Turn not thy face away from me; delay not thy visitation; withdraw not thy consolation, lest my soul become as a thirsty land.

Teach me, O Lord, to do thy will; teach me to live worthily and humbly in thy sight; for thou art my wisdom, thou dost truly know me, and didst know me before the world was made, and before I was born into the world.

4.
That we ought to live in Truth and Humility before God.

My son, walk thou before me in truth, and ever seek me in simplicity of thy heart.

He that walketh before me in truth, shall be defended from the assaults of evil, and the truth shall set him free from seducers, and from the slanders of unjust men.

If the truth shall have made thee free, thou shalt be free indeed, and shalt not care for the vain words of men.

O Lord, it is true. According as thou sayest: so, I beseech thee, let it be with me; let thy truth teach me, guard me, and preserve me safe to the end.

Let it set me free from all evil affection and inordinate love; and I shall walk with thee in great liberty of heart.

2. I WILL teach thee (saith the Truth) those things which are right and pleasing in my sight.

Reflect on thy sins with great displeasure and grief; and

never esteem thyself to be anything, because of any good works.

In truth thou art a sinner; thou art subject to and encumbered with many passions. Of thyself thou always tendest to nothing; speedily art thou cast down, speedily overcome, speedily disordered, speedily dissolved.

Thou hast nothing whereof thou canst glory, but many things for which thou oughtest to account thyself vile; for thou art much weaker than thou art able to comprehend.

3. And therefore let nothing seem much unto thee whatsoever thou doest.

Let nothing seem great, nothing precious and wonderful, nothing worthy of estimation, nothing high, nothing truly commendable, and to be desired, but that alone which is eternal.

Let the eternal truth be above all things pleasing to thee: Let thine own extreme unworthiness be always displeasing to thee.

Fear nothing, blame nothing, flee nothing, so much as thy vices and sins; which ought to be more unpleasing to thee than any losses whatsoever of things earthly.

Some walk not sincerely in my sight, but out of curiosity and pride desire to know my secrets, and to understand the high things of God, neglecting themselves and their own salvation.

These oftentimes, when I oppose myself to them, for their pride and curiosity do fall into great temptations and sins.

4. Fear thou the judgments of God, and dread the wrath of the Almighty. Discuss not thou the works of the Most High, but search diligently thine own iniquities, in how great things thou hast offended, and how many good things thou hast neglected.

Some place their devotion only in books, some in pictures, some in outward signs and figures.

Some have me in their mouths, but little in their hearts.

Others there are who, being illuminated in their understandings, and purged in their affection, do always pant after things eternal, are unwilling to hear of the things of this world, and serve the necessities of nature with grief; and these perceive what the Spirit of truth speaketh in them.

For He teacheth them to despise earthly, and to love heavenly things; to neglect the world, and to desire heaven all the day and night.

5.
Of the Wonderful Effect of Divine Love.

I bless thee, O Heavenly Father, Father of my Lord Jesus Christ, for that thou hast vouchsafed to remember me a poor creature.

O Father of mercies, and God of all comfort, thanks be unto thee, who sometimes with thy comfort refreshest me, unworthy as I am of all comfort.

I will always bless and glorify thee, with thine only-begotten Son, and the Holy Ghost, the Comforter, for ever and ever.

Ah, Lord God, thou holy lover of my soul, when thou comest into my heart, all that is within me shall rejoice.

Thou art my glory and the exultation of my heart: Thou art my hope and refuge in the day of my tribulation.

2. But because I am as yet weak in love, and imperfect in virtue, I have need to be strengthened and comforted by thee: visit me therefore often, and instruct me with all holy discipline.

Set me free from evil passions, and heal my heart of all inordinate affections: that being inwardly cured and thoroughly cleansed, I may be made fit to love, courageous to suffer, steady to persevere.

3. Love is a great thing, yea, a great and thorough good; by itself it makes everything that is heavy, light: and it bears evenly all that is uneven.

For it carries a burden which is no burden, and makes everything that is bitter, sweet and savory.

The noble love of JESUS impels a man to do great things, and stirs him up to be always longing for what is more perfect.

Love desires to be on high, and will not be kept back by anything low and mean.

Love desires to be free, and estranged from all worldly affections, that so its inward sight may not be hindered; that it may not be entangled by any temporal prosperity, or subdued by any adversity.

Nothing is sweeter than love, nothing more courageous,

nothing higher, nothing wider, nothing more pleasant, nothing fuller nor better in heaven and earth; because love is born of God, and cannot rest but in God, above all created things.

4. He that loveth, flieth, runneth and rejoiceth; he is free and is not bound.

He giveth all for all, and hath all in all; because he resteth in One Highest above all things, from whom all that is good flows and proceeds.

He respecteth not the gifts, but turneth himself above all goods unto the giver.

Love oftentimes knoweth no bounds, but is fervent beyond all measure.

Love feels no burden, thinks nothing of trouble, attempts what is above its strength; pleads no excuse of impossibility; for it thinks all things lawful for itself and all things possible.

It is therefore able to undertake all things, and it completes many things, and brings them to a conclusion, where he who does not love, faints and lies down.

5. Love watcheth, and, sleeping, slumbereth not.

Though weary, love is not tired; though pressed, it is not straitened; though alarmed, it is not confounded: but as a lively flame and burning torch, it forces its way upwards, and securely passeth through all.

If any man love, he knoweth what is the cry of this voice. For it is a loud cry in the ears of God, this ardent affection of the soul which saith, "My God, my Love, Thou art all mine, and I am all thine."

6. Enlarge thou me in love, that, with the inward palate of my heart, I may taste how sweet it is to love, and to be dissolved, and as it were to bathe myself in thy love.

Let me be possessed by love, mounting above myself, through excessive fervor and admiration.

Let me sing the song of love, let me follow thee, my Beloved, on high; let my soul spend itself in thy praise, rejoicing through love.

Let me love thee more than myself, and love myself only for thee; and in thee all that truly love thee, as the law of love commandeth, shining out from thyself.

7. Love is active, sincere, affectionate, pleasant, and amiable; courageous, patient, faithful, prudent, long-suffering, manly, and never seeking itself.

For in whatever instance a person seeketh himself, there he falleth from love.

Love is circumspect, humble, and upright; not yielding to softness, or to levity, nor attending to vain things; it is sober, chaste, steady, quiet, and guarded in all the senses.

Love is subject, and obedient to its superiors; unto itself mean and despised, unto God devout and thankful, trusting and hoping always in Him, even then when God imparteth no relish of sweetness unto it: for without sorrow none liveth in love.

8. He that is not prepared to suffer all things, and to stand to the will of his Beloved, is not worthy to be called a lover.

A lover ought to embrace willingly all that is hard and distasteful for the sake of his Beloved; and not to turn away from Him on account of any contradictions.

6.

Of the Proving of a True Lover.

My son, thou art not yet a courageous and considerate lover.

WHEREFORE sayest Thou this, O Lord?

BECAUSE for a slight opposition thou givest over thy undertakings, and too eagerly seekest consolation.

A courageous lover standeth firm in temptations, and giveth no credit to the crafty persuasions of the enemy. As I please him in prosperity, so in adversity I am not unpleasing to him.

2. A wise lover regardeth not so much the gift of him who loves him, as the love of the giver.

He esteems the good will rather than the value of the gift, and sets all gifts below him whom he loves.

A noble-minded lover resteth not in the gift, but in me above every gift.

All therefore is not lost, if sometimes thou thinkest less of me or my saints than thou wouldest.

That good and sweet affection which thou sometimes feelest, is the effect of grace present, and a sort of foretaste of thy heavenly home: but hereon thou must not lean too much, for it cometh and goeth.

But to strive against evil faults which may befall thee, and to reject with scorn the suggestions of the devil, is a notable sign of virtue, and shall have great reward.

3. Let no strange fancies therefore trouble thee, which on any subject whatever may crowd into thy mind. Keep thy purpose with courage, and preserve an upright intention towards God.

Neither is it an illusion that sometimes thou art suddenly rapt on high, and presently returnest again unto the accustomed vanities of thy heart.

For these thou dost rather unwillingly suffer, than commit: and so long as they displease thee, and thou strivest against them, it is matter of reward, and not of loss.

4. Know that the old enemy doth strive by all means to hinder thy desire to good, and to divert thee from all religious exercises; particularly, from the reverent estimation of God's saints, from the devout commemoration of my Passion, from the profitable remembrance of thy sins, from the guard of thine own heart, and from the firm purpose of advancing in virtue.

Many evil thoughts does he suggest to thee, that so he may cause a wearisomeness and horror in thee, to call thee back from prayer and holy reading.

Humble confession is displeasing unto him, and if he could, he would cause thee to cease from Holy Communion.

Trust him not, nor heed him, although he should often set snares of deceit to entrap thee.

Charge him with it, when he suggesteth evil and unclean thoughts unto thee; say unto him,

"Away thou unclean spirit! Blush thou miserable wretch! Most unclean art thou that bringest such things unto mine ears.

"Begone from me, thou wicked seducer! Thou shalt have no part in me; but JESUS shall be with me as a strong warrior, and thou shalt stand confounded.

"I had rather die, and undergo any torment, than consent unto thee.

"Hold thy peace and be silent; I will hear thee no more, though thou shouldst work me many troubles. 'The Lord is my Light and my Salvation, whom shall I fear?'

"Though an host of men rose against me, yet should not my heart be afraid. The Lord is my Helper and my Redeemer."

5. Fight like a good soldier: and if thou sometimes fall through frailty, take again greater strength than before, trust-

ing in my more abundant grace: and take great heed of vain pleasing of thyself, and of pride.

Pride brings many into error, and makes them sometimes fall into blindness almost incurable.

Let the fall of the proud, thus foolishly presuming on their own strength, serve thee for a warning, and keep thee ever humble.

7.
That Grace is to be Guarded by Humility.

My son, it is more profitable for thee and more safe, to conceal the grace of devotion, not to lift thyself on high, nor to speak much thereof, nor to dwell much thereon; but rather to despise thyself, and to fear lest the grace have been given to one unworthy of it.

This affection thou must not too earnestly cleave unto, for it may be quickly changed to the contrary.

Think when thou art in grace, how miserable and needy thou art wont to be without grace.

Nor is it in this only that thy progress in spiritual life consists, that thou hast the grace of comfort; but rather that with humility, self-denial, and patience, thou endurest the withdrawing thereof, provided thou do not then become listless in the exercise of prayer, nor suffer the rest of thy accustomed duties to be at all neglected.

Rather do thou cheerfully perform what lieth in thee, according to the best of thy power and understanding; and do not wholly neglect thyself because of the dryness or anxiety of mind which thou feelest.

2. For there are many who, when things succeed not well with them, presently become impatient or slothful.

For the way of man is not always in his power, but it belongeth unto God to give, and to comfort, when He will, and how much He will, and whom He will; as it shall please Him, and no more.

Some unadvised persons, by reason of their over-earnest desire of the grace of a devoted life, have overthrown themselves; because they attempted more than they were able to perform, not weighing the measure of their own weakness, but following the desire of their heart rather than the judgment of their reason.

And because they dwelt on greater matters than was pleasing to God, they therefore quickly lost His grace.

They who had built themselves nests in heaven were made helpless and vile outcasts; to the end that being humbled and impoverished, they might learn not to fly with their own wings, but to trust under my feathers.

They that are yet but novices and inexperienced in the way of the Lord, unless they govern themselves by the counsel of discreet persons, may easily be deceived and broken to pieces.

3. And if they will rather follow their own notions than trust to others who are more experienced, their end will be dangerous, at least if they are unwilling to be drawn away from their own conceit.

It is seldom the case that they who are wise in their own conceit endure humbly to be governed by others.

Better is it to have a small portion of good sense, with humility and a slender understanding, than great treasures of science with vain self-complacency.

Better it is for thee to have little, than much of that which may make thee proud.

He acts not very discreetly, who wholly gives himself over to joy, forgetting his former helplessness, and that chastened fear of the Lord which is afraid of losing the grace which hath been offered.

Nor again is he very valiantly wise who, in time of adversity or any heaviness, at once yields too much to despairing thoughts, and reflects and thinks of me less trustfully than he ought.

4. He who in time of peace is willing to be over secure shall be often found in time of war too much dejected and full of fears.

If thou couldest always continue humble and moderate within thyself, and also couldest thoroughly moderate and govern thy spirit, thou wouldst not so quickly fall into danger and offence.

It is good counsel, that when fervor of spirit is kindled within thee, thou shouldst consider how it will be, when that light shall leave thee.

And when this happeneth, then remember that the light may return again, which, as a warning to thyself, and for mine own glory, I have withdrawn for a time.

5. Such trials are oftentimes more profitable, than if thou shouldst always have things prosper according to thy will.

For a man's worthiness is not to be estimated by the number of visions and comforts which he may have, or by his skill in the Scriptures, or by his being placed in high station.

But if he be grounded in true humility, and full of divine charity; if he be always purely and sincerely seeking God's honor; if he think nothing of and unfeignedly despise himself, and even rejoice more to be despised and made low by others, than to be honored by them.

8.
Of a Mean Conceit of Ourselves in the Sight of God.

Shall I speak unto my Lord, who am but dust and ashes? If I esteem myself to be anything more, behold, Thou standest against me, and my iniquities bear true witness, and I cannot contradict it.

But if I abase myself, and reduce myself to nothing, and shrink from all self-esteem, and grind myself to the dust I am, thy grace will be favorable to me, and thy light near unto my heart; and all self-esteem, how little soever, shall be swallowed up in the valley of my nothingness, and perish forever.

There thou showest thyself unto me, what I am, what I have been, and whither I am come; for I am nothing, and I knew it not.

If I be left to myself, behold, I become nothing but mere weakness; but if thou for an instant look upon me, I am forthwith made strong, and am filled with new joy.

And a great marvel it is, that I am so suddenly lifted up, and so graciously embraced by thee, who of mine own weight am always sinking downward.

2. Thy love is the cause hereof, freely preventing me, and relieving me in so many necessities, guarding me also from pressing dangers, and snatching me (as I may truly say) from evils out of number.

For indeed by loving myself amiss, I lost myself; and by seeking thee alone, and purely loving thee, I have found both myself and thee, and by that love have more deeply reduced myself to nothing.

Because thou, O dearest Lord, dealest with me above all desert, and above all that I dare hope or ask.

3. Blessed be thou, my God: for although I be unworthy of any benefits, yet thy royal bounty and infinite goodness never cease to do good even to the ungrateful, and to those who are turned away far from thee.

Turn thou us unto thee, that we may be thankful, humble, and devout; for thou art our salvation, our courage, and our strength.

9.
That all Things are to be referred unto God, as their last End.

My son, I ought to be thy supreme and ultimate end, if thou desire to be truly blessed.

By this intention thy affections will be purified, which are too often inordinately inclined to selfishness and unto creatures.

For if in anything thou seekest thyself, immediately thou faintest and driest up.

I would therefore thou shouldst refer all things principally unto Me, for I am He who have given all.

Consider everything as flowing from the Highest God; and therefore unto Me as their original all must be brought back.

2. From Me, as from a living fountain, the small and the great, the poor and the rich, do draw the water of life; and they that willingly and freely serve Me shall receive grace for grace.

But he who desires to glory in things out of Me or to take pleasure in some private good, shall not be grounded in true joy, nor be enlarged in his heart, but shall many ways be encumbered and straitened.

Thou oughtest therefore to ascribe nothing of good thyself, nor do thou attribute goodness unto any man; but give all unto God, without whom man hath nothing.

I have given thee all, and My will is to have thee all again;

and with great strictness do I exact from thee a return of thanks.

3. This is the truth whereby vain-glory is put to flight.

And if heavenly grace enter in and true charity, there will be no envy nor narrowness of heart, neither will self-love busy itself.

For divine charity overcometh all things, and enlargeth all the powers of the soul.

If thou rightly judge, thou wilt rejoice in Me alone, in Me alone thou wilt hope; for none is good save God alone, who is to be praised above all things, and in all to be blessed.

10.
That to despise the World and serve God, is sweet.

Now I will speak again, O Lord, and will not be silent; I will say in the ears of my God, my Lord, and my King, who is on high: "O how great is the abundance of thy goodness, O Lord, which thou hast laid up for them that fear thee."

But what art thou to those who love thee? What to those who serve thee with their whole heart?

Truly unspeakable is the sweetness of contemplating thee, which thou bestowest on them that love thee.

In this especially thou hast showed me the sweetness of thy love: that when I was not, thou madest me; when I went far astray from thee, thou broughtest me back again, that I might serve thee; and that thou hast commanded me to love thee.

2. O fountain of love unceasing, what shall I say concerning thee?

How can I forget thee, who hast vouchsafed to remember me, even after I had wasted away and perished?

Thou hast showed mercy to thy servant beyond all expectation: and hast exhibited favor and loving-kindness beyond all desert.

What return shall I make to thee for this grace? For it is not granted to all to forsake all, to renounce the world, and to undertake a life of religious retirement.

Is it any great thing that I should serve thee, whom the whole creation is bound to serve?

It ought not to seem much to me, to serve thee: but rather this doth appear much to me, and wonderful; that thou vouchsafest to receive into thy service one so poor and unworthy, and to make him one with thy beloved servants.

3. Behold, all things are thine which I have, and whereby I serve thee.

And yet contrariwise, thou rather servest me than I thee.

Behold, heaven and earth which Thou has created for the service of man, are ready at hand, and do daily perform whatever thou has commanded.

And this is little: Thou has moreover also appointed angels to minister to man.

But that which excelleth all is this, that thou thyself hast vouchsafed to serve man, and hast promised that thou wouldst give thyself unto him.

4. What shall I give thee for all these thousands of benefits? I would I could serve thee all the days of my life.

I would I were able, at least for one day, to do thee some worthy service.

Truly thou are worthy of all service, of all honor, and everlasting praise.

Truly thou are my Lord, and I thy poor servant, who am bound to serve thee with all my might, neither ought I ever to be weary of praising thee.

And this I wish to do, this I desire; and whatsoever is wanting unto me, do thou, I beseech thee, vouchsafe to supply.

5. It is a great honor, and a great glory, to serve thee, and to despise all things for thee.

For great grace shall be given to those who shall have willingly subjected themselves to thy most holy service.

They who for thy love shall have renounced all carnal delights, shall find the sweetest consolations of the Holy Ghost.

They shall attain great freedom of mind, who for thy Name's sake enter into the narrow way, and have left off all worldly care.

6. O sweet and delightful service of God, by which a man is made truly free and holy!

O sacred state of religious service, which makes a man equal to the angels, pleasing to God, terrible to devils, and worthy to be commended of all the faithful!

O welcome service and ever to be desired, in which we are

rewarded with the Greatest Good, and attain to joy which shall endlessly remain with us!

11.
That the Longings and Desires of our Hearts are to be examined and moderated.

My son, thou must still learn many things, which thou hast not yet well learned.

WHAT are these, O Lord?

THAT thou frame thy desires wholly according to my good pleasure; and that thou be not a lover of thyself, but an earnest follower of my will.

Various longings and desires oftentimes inflame thee, and drive thee forwards with vehemence: but do thou consider whether thou be not moved rather for thine own advantage, than for my honor.

If I be the cause, thou wilt be well content, howsoever I shall ordain; but if there lurk in thee any self-seeking, behold, this it is that hindereth thee and weigheth thee down.

2. Beware therefore thou lean not too much open any desire, conceived without asking my counsel, lest perhaps afterwards it repent thee, or thou be displeased with that which at first pleased thee, and which thou desiredst earnestly, as the best.

For not every affection which seems good is immediately to be followed; nor on the other hand is every contrary affection at the first to be avoided.

It is sometimes expedient to use a restraint even in good desires and endeavors, lest through unseasonable effort thou incur distraction of mind; lest by thy want of self-government thou beget a scandal unto others; or again, being by others thwarted and resisted, thou become suddenly confounded, and so fall.

3. Sometimes however thou must use violence, and resist manfully thine appetite, not regarding what the flesh would or would not; but rather taking pains that even perforce it may be made subject to the Spirit.

And so long ought it to be chastened and to be forced to remain under servitude, until it be prepared for everything, and learn to be content with a little, and to be pleased with plain and simple things, and not to murmur against any inconvenience.

12.
Of the Growth of Patience in the Soul, and of Striving against Concupiscence.

O Lord my God, patience is very necessary for me, for I perceive that many things in this life do fall out as we would not.

For whatsoever plans I shall devise for my own peace, my life cannot be without war and affliction.

It is so, my son. But my will is, that thou seek not that peace which is void of temptations, or which suffereth nothing contrary: but rather think that thou hast found peace, when thou art exercised with sundry tribulations, and tried in many adversities.

2. If thou say, that thou art not able to suffer much, how then wilt thou endure the fire hereafter?

Of two evils the less is always to be chosen. That thou mayest therefore avoid the everlasting punishment that is to come, endeavor to endure present evils patiently, for God's sake.

Dost thou think that the men of this world suffer nothing or but as little? Ask even of those who live most at ease, and thou shalt find it otherwise.

But thou wilt say, they have many delights, and follow their own wills, and therefore they do not much weigh their own afflictions.

Be it so, that they have whatsoever they will; but how long dost thou think that it will last?

3. Behold, the wealthy of this world shall consume away like smoke, and there shall be no memory of their past joys!

Yea, even while they are yet alive, they do not rest in them without bitterness, and weariness, and fear.

For from the self-same thing in which they delight they oftentimes receive the penalty of sorrow.

And it is but just that having inordinately sought and followed after pleasures, they should enjoy them not without shame and bitterness.

4. O how brief, how false, how inordinate and base, are all those pleasures.

Yet so drunken and blind are men, that they understand it not; but like dumb beasts, for the poor enjoyment of a corruptible life, they incur the death of the soul.

Thou therefore, my son, "go not after thy lusts, but refrain thyself from thine appetites." "Delight thyself in the Lord, and He shall give thee the desires of thine heart."

5. For if thou desire true delight, and to be more plentifully comforted by me; behold, in the contempt of all worldly things, and in the cutting of all base delights, shall be thy blessing, and abundant comfort shall be given thee.

And the more thou withdraw thyself from all solace of creatures, so much the sweeter and more powerful consolations shalt thou find in me.

But at the first, thou shalt not without some sadness, nor without a laborious conflict, attain unto them.

Old inbred habit will, for a time, resist, but by a better way it shall be entirely overcome.

The flesh will murmur against thee; but with fervency of spirit thou shalt bridle it.

The old serpent will tempt and trouble thee, but by prayer he shall be put to flight. Moreover also, by useful work thou shalt greatly stop the way against him.

13.
Of Humble Obedience after the Example of Jesus Christ.

My son, he that endeavoreth to withdraw himself from obedience, withdraweth himself from grace: and he who seeketh for himself private benefits, loseth those which are common.

He that doth not cheerfully and freely submit himself to his superior, showeth that his flesh is not as yet perfectly brought into subjection, but oftentimes struggleth and murmureth against thee.

Learn thou therefore quickly to submit thyself to thy superior, if thou desire to keep thine own flesh under the yoke.

For more speedily is the outward enemy overcome, if the inward man be not in disorder.

There is no worse enemy, nor one more troublesome to the

soul, than thou art unto thyself, if thou be not in harmony with the Spirit.

It is altogether necessary that thou conceive a true contempt for thyself, if thou desire to prevail against flesh and blood.

2. Because thou still lovest thyself inordinately, thou art afraid to resign thyself wholly to the will of others.

And yet, what great matter is it, if thou, who art but dust and nothing, subject thyself to a man for God's sake, when I, the Almighty and the Most Highest, who created all things of nothing, humbly subjected myself to man for thy sake?

I became of all men the most humble and the most abject, that thou mightest overcome thy pride with my humility.

O dust, learn to be obedient. Learn to humble thyself, thou earth and clay, and to bow thyself down under the feet of all men.

Learn to break thine own will, and to yield thyself to all subjection.

3. Be zealous against thyself, and suffer no pride to dwell in thee: but show thyself so humble and so lowly, that all may be able to walk over thee, and to tread thee down as the mire of the streets. Vain man, what hast thou to complain of?

What canst thou answer, vile sinner, to them that upbraid thee, thou who hast so often offended God, and hast so many times deserved hell?

But mine eye spared thee, because thy soul was precious in my sight; that thou mightest know my love, and ever be thankful for my benefits;

Also that thou mightest continually give thyself to true subjection and humility, and endure patiently to be despised.

14.
Of considering the Secret Judgments of God,
that so we be not lifted up for anything good in us.

Thou, O Lord, thunderest forth thy judgments over me, thou shakest all my bones with fear and trembling, and my soul is very sore afraid.

I stand astonished; and I consider "That the heavens are not pure in thy sight."

If in angels thou didst find wickedness, and didst not spare even then, what shall become of me?

Even stars fell from heaven, what then can I presume who am but dust?

They whose works seemed commendable, have fallen into the lowest misery; and those who did eat the bread of angels, I have seen delighting themselves with the husks of swine.

2. There is therefore no holiness, if thou, O lord, withdraw thine hand.

No wisdom availeth, if thou cease to guide.

No courage helpeth, if thou leave off to defend.

No chastity is secure, if thou do not protect it.

No vigilance of our own availeth, if thy sacred watchfulness be not present with us.

For, if we be left of thee, we sink and perish; but being visited of thee, we are raised up and live.

Truly we are inconstant, but by thee we are established: we wax lukewarm, but by thee we are inflamed.

3. O how humbly and meanly ought I to think of myself! How ought I to esteem it as nothing, if I seem to have any good in me!

With what profound humility ought I to submit myself to thine unfathomable judgments, O Lord; where I find myself to be nothing else than nothing, and very nothing!

O weight that cannot be measured! O sea that cannot be passed over, where I discover nothing of myself save only and wholly nothing!

Where then can glorying hide itself? Where can be trust in mine own virtue?

All vain-glorying is swallowed up in the deep of thy judgments over me.

4. What is all flesh in thy sight?

Shall the clay boast against Him that formed it?

How can he be lifted up with vain words, whose heart is truly subject to God?

Not all the world will make him proud, whom the Truth hath subjected unto itself: neither shall he, who hath firmly settled his whole hope in God, be moved by the tongues of all his flatterers.

For even they themselves who speak, behold, they all are nothing, for they will pass away with the sound of their words; but the truth of the Lord remaineth for ever.

15.

*In Everything which we desire, how we ought
to feel, and what we ought to say.*

My son, say thou thus in everything: Lord, if this be pleasing unto thee, so let it be.

"Lord, if it be to thy honor, in thy Name let this be done.

"Lord, if thou see it to be expedient, and know it to be profitable for me, then grant unto me that I may use this to thine honor.

"But if thou know it will be hurtful unto me, and no profit to the health of my soul, take away the desire from me."

For not every desire proceedeth from the Holy Spirit, even though it seem unto a man right and good.

It is difficult to judge truly whether a good spirit or the contrary be urging thee to desire this or that; or whether by thine own spirit thou be moved thereunto.

Many have been deceived in the end, who at the first seemed to be led by a good spirit.

2. Therefore whatsoever seemeth to be desirable, must always be desired and prayed for in the fear of God and with humility of heart; and chiefly thou must commit the whole matter to me with special resignation of thyself, and thou must say,

"O Lord, thou knowest what is best for us, let this or that be done, as thou pleasest.

"Give what thou wilt, and how much thou wilt and when thou wilt.

"Deal with me as thou thinkest good, and as best pleaseth thee, and is most for thy honor.

"Set me where thou wilt, and deal with me in all things just as thou wilt.

"I am in thy hand: turn me round, and turn me back again, as thou shalt please.

"Behold, I am thy servant, prepared for all things; for I desire not to live unto myself, but unto thee; and O that I could do it worthily and perfectly!"

A PRAYER THAT THE WILL OF GOD MAY BE FULFILLED.

3. O MOST merciful JESUS, grant to me thy grace, that it

may be with me, and work with me, and continue with me even to the end.

Grant that I may always desire and will that which is to thee most acceptable and most dear. Let thy will be mine, and let my will ever follow thine, and agree perfectly with it.

Let my will be all one with thine, and let me not be able to will, or anything to forego, but what thou willest or dost not will.

4. Grant that I may die to all things that are in the world, and for thy sake may love to be contemned, and not be known in this generation.

Grant to me above all things that I can desire, to desire to rest in thee, and in thee to have my heart at peace.

Thou art the true peace of the heart: thou art its only rest; out of thee all things are full of trouble and unrest. In this peace, that is, in thee, the one chiefest eternal Good, I will lay me down and sleep. *Amen.*

16.
That True Comfort is to be sought in God alone.

Whatsoever I can desire or imagine for my comfort, I look for it not here but hereafter.

For if I alone should possess all the comforts of the world, and might enjoy all the delights thereof, it is certain that they could not long endure.

Wherefore, O my soul, thou canst not be fully comforted, nor have perfect refreshment, except in God, the comforter of the poor, and the helper of the humble.

Wait a little while, O my soul, wait for the divine promise, and thou shalt have abundance of all good things in heaven.

If thou desire beyond measure the things that are present, thou shalt lose those which are heavenly and eternal.

Use temporal things, and desire eternal.

Thou canst not be satisfied by any temporal goods, because thou art not created to enjoy them.

2. Although thou shouldst possess all created good, yet couldst thou not be happy thereby nor blessed; but in God, who created all things, consisteth thy whole blessedness and felicity.

Not such happiness as is seen and commended by the foolish lovers of the world, but such as the good and faithful servants of Christ wait for, and of which the spiritual and pure in heart, whose conversation is in heaven, sometimes have a foretaste.

Vain and brief is all human consolation.

Blessed and true is the consolation which is received inwardly from the truth.

A devout man beareth everywhere about with him his own comforter, JESUS, and saith unto Him, "Be Thou present with me, O Lord JESUS, in every time and place,

"Let this be my comfort, to be willing to lack all human comfort.

"And if thy comfort be wanting, let thy will and just proving of me be unto me as the greatest comfort; for thou wilt not always be angry, neither wilt thou chide forever."

17.
That all our Anxieties are to be rested on God.

MY son, suffer me to do with thee what I please. I know what is expedient for thee.

Thou thinkest as man; thou judgest in many things as human affection persuadeth thee.

O LORD, what thou sayest is true. Thy care for me is greater than all the care that I can take for myself.

For he standeth but very unsafely, who casteth not all his care upon thee.

O Lord, if only my will may remain right and firm towards thee, do with me whatsoever it shall please thee.

For it cannot be anything but good, whatsoever thou shalt do with me.

2. If it be thy will that I should be in darkness, be thou blessed; and if it be thy will that I should be in light, be thou again blessed. If thou vouchsafe to comfort me, be thou blessed; and if thou wilt have me afflicted, be thou blessed also.

MY son, such as this ought to be thy state, if thou desire to walk with Me.

Thou oughtest to be as ready to suffer as to rejoice.

Thou oughtest as cheerfully to be destitute and poor, as to be full and rich.

3. O LORD, for thy sake, I will cheerfully suffer whatsoever shall come on me with thy permission.

From thy hand I am willing to receive indifferently good and evil, sweet and bitter, joy and sorrow; and for all that befalleth me I will be thankful.

Keep me safe from all sin, and I shall fear neither death nor hell.

So thou do not cast me from thee forever, nor blot me out of the book of life, what tribulation soever befalleth me shall not hurt me.

18.
That Temporal Sufferings must be borne patiently after the Example of Christ.

My son, I descended from heaven for thy salvation; I took upon me thy sorrows, not necessity but love drawing me thereto; that thou thyself mightest learn patience, and bear temporal sufferings without repining.

For the hour of my birth, even until my death on the cross, I was not without suffering of grief.

I suffered great want of things temporal; I often heard many murmurings against me; I endured patiently disgraces and revilings; in return for benefits I received ingratitude; for miracles, blasphemies; for heavenly doctrine, reproofs.

2. O LORD, for that thou wert patient in thy lifetime, herein especially fulfilling the commandment of thy Father; it is reason that I, a most miserable sinner, should bear myself patiently according to thy will, and for my soul's welfare endure the burden of this corruptible life as long as thou thyself shalt choose.

For although this present life be burdensome, yet notwithstanding it is now by thy grace made very gainful; and, by thine example and the footsteps of thy saints, more bright and clear, and endurable to the weak.

It is also much more full of consolation than it was formerly under the old law, when the gate of heaven remained shut; and the way also to heaven seemed more dark, when so few cared to seek after the kingdom of heaven.

Moreover also, they who then were just and such as should be saved, could not enter into the heavenly kingdom, before the accomplishment of thy Passion, and the payment of the debt of thy holy death.

3. O how great thanks am I bound to render unto thee, that thou hast vouchsafed to show unto me and to all faithful people the good and the right way to thine eternal kingdom.

For thy life is our way, and by the path of holy patience we walk toward thee, who art our Crown.

If thou hadst not gone before us and taught us, who would have cared to follow!

Alas, how many would remain behind and afar off, if they considered not thy glorious example!

Behold, we are even yet lukewarm, though we have heard of so many of thy miracles and doctrines. What would become of us, if we had not so great light whereby to follow thee!

19.
Of the Endurance of Injuries and of the Proof of True Patience.

What is it thou sayest, my son? Cease to complain, when thou considerest my Passion, and the sufferings of my other saints.

Thou hast not yet resisted unto blood.

It is but little which thou sufferest, in comparison of those who suffered so much, who were so strongly tempted, so grievously afflicted, so many ways tried and exercised.

Thou oughtest therefore to call to mind the more heavy sufferings of others, that so thou mayest the more easily bear thine own very small troubles.

And if they seem unto thee not very small, then beware lest thine impatience be the cause thereof.

However, whether they be small or whether they be great, endeavor patiently to undergo them all.

2. The better thou disposeth thyself to suffering, the more wisely thou doest, and the greater reward shalt thou receive.

Thou shalt also more easily endure it, if both in mind and by habit thou art diligently prepared thereunto.

Do not say, "I cannot endure to suffer these things at the hands of such an one, nor ought I to endure things of this sort; for he hath done me great wrong, and reproacheth me with things which I never thought of; but of another I will willingly suffer, that is, if they are things which I shall see I ought to suffer."

Such a thought is foolish; it considereth not the virtue of patience, nor by whom it will be to be crowned; but rather, weigheth too exactly the persons, and the injuries offered to itself.

3. He is not truly patient, who is willing to suffer only so much as he thinks good, and from whom he pleases.

But the truly patient man minds not by whom he is exercised, whether by his superiors, by one of his equals, or by an inferior; whether by a good and holy man, or by one that is perverse and unworthy.

But indifferently from every creature, how much soever, or how often soever anything adverse befall him, he takes it all thankfully as from the hands of God, and esteems it great gain:

For with God it is impossible that any thing, how small soever, if only it be suffered for God's sake, should pass without its reward.

4. Be thou therefore prepared for the fight, if thou wilt win the victory.

Without a combat thou canst not attain unto the crown of patience.

If thou art unwilling to suffer, thou refusest to be crowned. But if thou desire to be crowned, fight manfully, endure patiently.

Without labor there is no rest, nor without fighting can the victory be won.

O LORD, let that become possible to me by thy grace, which by nature seems impossible to me.

Thou knowest that I am able to suffer but little, and that I am quickly cast down, when a slight adversity ariseth.

For thy Name's sake, let every exercise of tribulation be made pleasant unto me; for to suffer and to be troubled for thy sake, is very wholesome for my soul.

20.
Of the Acknowledging of our own Infirmities; and of the Sufferings of this Life.

I will acknowledge my sin unto thee; I will confess mine infirmity unto thee, O Lord.

Oftentimes a small matter it is that makes me sad and dejected.

I resolve to act with courage, but when even a small temptation comes, I am at once in a great strait.

It is sometimes a very trifle, whence a great temptation arises.

And whilst I think myself safe, and when I least expect it, I sometimes find myself overcome by all but a slight breath.

2. Behold therefore, O Lord, my low estate, and my frailty which is in every way known unto thee.

Have mercy on me, and deliver me out of the mire, that I may not stick fast therein, and may not remain utterly cast down for ever.

This is that which oftentimes strikes me down, and confounds me in thy sight, that I am so subject to fall, and so weak in resisting my passions.

And although I do not altogether consent, yet their continued assaults are troublesome and grievous unto me; and it is very exceedingly irksome to live thus daily in conflict.

Hereby doth my weakness become known unto me, in that hateful fancies do always much more easily invade than forsake me.

3. Most mighty God of Israel, thou zealous lover of faithful souls! O that thou wouldst consider the labor and sorrow of thy servant, and assist him in all things whatsoever he undertaketh.

Strengthen me with heavenly courage, lest the old man, the miserable flesh, not as yet fully subject to the spirit, prevail and get the upper hand. Against this it will be needful for me to fight, as long as I breathe in this miserable life.

Alas, what a life is this, where tribulation and miseries are never wanting; where all is full of snares, and enemies!

For when one tribulation or temptation goeth, another

cometh; yea and while the first conflict is yet lasting, many others come unexpected one after another.

4. And how can a life be loved that hath so many embitterments, and is subject to so many calamities and miseries?

How too can it be called a life, that begetteth so many deaths and plagues?

And yet it is the object of men's love, and its delights are sought of many.

The world is oftentimes blamed for being deceitful and vain, and yet men do not easily part with it, because the desires of the flesh bear so great a sway.

But some things draw us to love the world, others to contemn it.

The lust of the flesh, the lust of the eyes, and the pride of life, do draw us to the love of the world; but the pains and miseries, that justly follow them, cause a hatred of the world and a loathing thereof.

5. But alas, the fondness for vicious pleasures overcometh the mind of him who is given to the world; and he esteemeth it a delight to be ever under thorns, because he hath neither seen nor tasted the sweetness of God, and the inward pleasantness of virtue.

But they who perfectly contemn the world, and study to live to God under holy discipline, these are not ignorant of the divine sweetness promised to those who truly forsake the world. They also very clearly see how grievously the world erreth, and how it is in many ways deceived.

21.
That we are to rest in God above all his Gifts and Benefits.

Above all things, and in all things, O my soul, that shalt rest in the Lord always, for he himself is the everlasting rest of the saints.

Grant me, O most sweet and loving JESUS, to rest in thee, above all creatures, above all health and beauty, above all glory and honor, above all power and dignity, above all knowledge and subtlety, above all riches and arts, above all joy and gladness, above all fame and praise, above all sweetness and comfort, above all hope and promise, above all desert and desire:

Above all gifts and benefits that thou canst give and impart unto us; above all mirth and joy that the mind of man can receive and feel:

Finally, above angels and archangels, and above all the heavenly hosts, above all things visible and invisible, and above all that thou art not, O my God.

2. Because thou, O Lord my God, art supremely good above all; thou alone art most high, thou alone most powerful, thou alone most full and sufficient, thou alone most sweet and most full of consolation.

Thou alone art most lovely and loving, thou alone most noble and glorious above all things, in whom all good things together both perfectly are, and ever have been, and shall be.

And therefore whatsoever thou bestowest on me besides thyself, or revealest unto me of thyself, or promisest, is but mean and unsatisfying, whilst thou art not seen and not fully obtained.

For surely my heart cannot truly rest, nor be entirely contented, unless it rest in thee, and rise above all gifts and all creatures whatsoever.

3. O thou most beloved spouse of my soul, JESUS Christ, thou most pure Lover, thou Lord of all creation; O that I had the wings of true liberty, that I might flee away and rest in thee!

O when shall it be fully granted me, to consider in quietness of mind, and to see how sweet thou art, my Lord God!

When shall I fully gather up myself into thee, that by reason of my love to thee I may not feel myself, but thee alone, above all sense and measure, in a manner not known unto every one!

But now I oftentimes sigh, and bear my unhappiness with grief:

Because many evils occur in this vale of miseries, which do often trouble, grieve, and overcloud me; often hinder and distract me, allure and entangle me, so that I can have no free access unto thee, nor enjoy the sweet welcomings, which are ever ready for the blessed spirits.

O let my sighs move thee and my manifold desolation here on earth.

4. O JESUS, thou brightness of eternal glory, thou comfort of the pilgrim soul, with thee is my tongue without voice, and my very silence speaketh unto thee.

How long doth my Lord delay to come?

Let him come unto me his poor despised servant, and let him make me glad. Let him put forth his hand, and deliver his poor servant from all anguish.

Come, O come; for without thee I shall have no joyful day nor hour; for thou art my joy, and without thee my table is empty.

A wretched creature am I, and as it were imprisoned and loaded with fetters, until thou refresh me with the light of thy presence, and grant me liberty, and show a friendly countenance toward me.

5. Let others seek what they please instead of thee; but for me, nothing else doth nor shall delight me, but thou only, my God, my hope, my everlasting salvation.

I will not hold my peace, nor cease to pray, until thy grace return again, and thou speak inwardly unto me.

BEHOLD, here I am. Behold, I come unto thee, because thou hast called upon me. Thy tears and the desire of thy soul, thy humiliation and thy contrition of heart, have inclined and brought me unto thee.

And I said, LORD, I have called thee, and have desired to enjoy thee, being ready to refuse all things for thy sake.

For thou first hast stirred me up that I might seek thee.

Blessed be thou therefore, O Lord, that hast showed this goodness to thy servant, according to the multitude of thy mercies.

6. What hath thy servant more to say before thee? He can only greatly humble himself in thy sight, ever mindful of his own iniquity and vileness.

For there is none like unto thee in all whatsoever is wonderful in heaven and earth.

Thy works are very good, thy judgments true, and by thy providence the universe is governed.

Praise therefore and glory be unto thee, O wisdom of the Father: let my mouth, my soul, and all creatures together, praise and bless thee.

22.
Of the Remembrance of God's manifold Benefits.

Open, O Lord, my heart in thy law, and teach me to walk in thy commandments.

Grant me to understand thy will, and with great reverence and diligent consideration to remember thy benefits, as well in general as in particular, that henceforward I may be able worthily to give thee thanks.

But I know and confess, that I am not able even in the least matter, to give thee due thanks for the favors which thou bestowest upon me.

I am less than the least of all thy benefits: and when I consider thy noble bounty, the greatness thereof maketh my spirit to faint.

2. All that we have in our soul and body, and whatsoever we possess outwardly or inwardly, naturally or supernaturally, are thy benefits, and do speak thee bountiful, merciful and good, from whom we have received all good things.

Although one have received more, another less, all notwithstanding are thine, and without thee even the least blessing cannot be had.

He that hath received the greatest cannot glory of his own desert, nor extol himself above others, nor exult over the lesser. For he is the greatest and the best who ascribeth least unto himself, and who is rendering thanks is the most humble and most devout.

And he that esteemeth himself viler than all men, and judgeth himself most unworthy, is fittest to receive greater blessings.

2. But he that hath received fewer, ought not to be out of heart, nor to take it grievously, nor to envy them that are enriched with greater store; but rather to turn his mind to thee, and highly to praise thy goodness, for that thou bestowest thy gifts so bountifully, so freely, and so willingly, without respect of persons.

All things proceed from thee, and therefore in all things thou art to be praised.

That knowest what is fit to be given to every one. And why this man hath less and that man more, it is not for us to judge, but for thee, who dost exactly know what is meet for every one.

4. Wherefore, O Lord God, I even esteem it a great mercy, not to have much of that which outwardly and in the opinion of men seems worthy of glory and applause.

He who considereth the poverty and unworthiness of his own person, should be so far from conceiving grief or sadness, or from being cast down thereat, that he rather should take great comfort and be glad.

For thou, O God, hast chosen the poor and humble and the despised of this world for thyself, to be thy familiar friends and servants.

Witnesses are thine apostles themselves, whom thou hast made princes over all the earth.

And yet they lived in the world without complaint, so humble and simple, without all malice and deceit, that they even rejoiced to suffer reproach for thy name; and what the world abhorreth, they embraced with great affection.

5. When therefore a man loveth thee and acknowledgeth thy benefits, nothing ought so to rejoice him as thy will toward him, and the good pleasure of thine eternal appointment.

And herewith he ought to be so contented and comforted, that he would as willingly be the least, as another would wish to be the greatest.

He would too be as peaceable and contented in the last place as in the first; as willing to be a despised castaway, of no name or character, as to be preferred in honor before others, and to be greater in the world than they.

For thy will and the love of thy glory ought to be preferred before all things, and to comfort him more, and to please him better, than all the benefits which either he hath received or may receive.

23.
Of Four Things that bring great Inward Peace.

My son, now will I teach thee the way of peace and of true liberty.

O Lord, I beseech thee, do as thou sayest, for this is delightful to me to hear.

Be desirous, my son, to do the will of another rather than thine own.

Choose always to have less rather than more.

Seek always the lowest place, and to be beneath every one.

Wish always, and pray, that the will of God may be wholly fulfilled in thee.

Behold, such a man entereth within the borders of peace and rest.

2. O LORD, this short discourse of thine containeth within itself much perfection.

It is little in words, but full of meaning, and abundant in fruit.

For it could faithfully be kept by me, I should not be so easily disturbed.

For as often as I feel myself unquiet and weighed down, I find that I have strayed from this doctrine.

But thou who canst do all things, and ever lovest the profiting of my soul, increase in me thy grace, that I may be able to fulfil thy words, and to work out mine own salvation.

A PRAYER AGAINST EVIL THOUGHTS.

3. O LORD, my God, be not thou far from me; my God, haste thee to help me; for there have risen up against me sundry thoughts, and great fears, afflicting my soul.

How shall I pass through unhurt? How shall I break them to pieces?

"I, saith he, will go before thee and will humble the great ones of the earth; I will open the doors of the prison, and reveal unto thee hidden secrets."

Do, O Lord, as thou sayest, and let all evil thoughts fly from before thy face.

This is my hope, my one only consolation, to flee unto thee in every tribulation, to trust in thee, to call upon thee from my inmost heart, and to wait patiently for thy consolation.

A PRAYER FOR MENTAL ILLUMINATION.

4. O merciful JESUS, enlighten thou me with the brightness of thine inward light, and take away all darkness from the habitation of my heart.

Repress thou my many wandering thoughts, and break in pieces those temptations which so violently assault me.

Fight thou strongly for me, and vanquish these evil beasts, these alluring desires of the flesh; that so peace may be obtained by thy power, and that thine abundant praise may resound in a holy temple, that is, in a pure conscience.

Command the winds and tempests; say unto the sea, be still; say to the north wind, blow not; and there shall be a great calm.

5. Send out thy light and thy truth, that they may shine upon the earth; for until thou enlighten me, I am but as earth without form and void.

Pour forth thy grace from above, steep my heart in thy heavenly dew, supply fresh streams of devotion to water the face of the earth, that it may bring forth fruit good and excellent.

Lift thou up my mind which is pressed down by a load of sins, and draw up my whole desire to things heavenly; that having tasted the sweetness of heavenly happiness, it may be irksome to me even to think of earthly things.

6. Do thou pluck me away, and deliver me from all the unlasting comfort of creatures; for no created thing can fully comfort and quiet my desires.

John thou me to thyself with an inseparable band of love; for thou, even thou alone, dost satisfy him that loveth thee, and without thee all things are vain and empty.

24.
Of avoiding Curious Enquiry into the Lives of Others.

My son, be not curious, nor trouble thyself with idle cares. What is this or that to thee? Follow thou me.

For what is it to thee, whether that man be such or such, or whether this man do or speak this or that?

Thou shalt not need to answer for others, but shalt give account for thyself; why therefore dost thou thus entangle thyself?

Behold, I know every one, and do see all things that are done under the sun; also I understand how it is with every one, what he thinks, what he wishes, and at what his intentions aim.

Unto me therefore all things are to be committed; but do thou keep thyself in peace, and leave the unquiet to be as unquiet as they will.

Whatsoever they shall have done or said, shall come upon themselves, for me they cannot deceive.

2. Be not careful for the shadow of a great name, or for the familiar friendship of many, or for the particular and separate affection of men.

For these things both distract the heart, and greatly darken it.

Willingly would I speak my word, and reveal my secrets unto thee, if thou wouldst diligently watch for my coming, and open unto me the door of thine heart.

Be thou circumspect, and watchful in prayer, and in all things humble thyself.

25.
Wherein firm Peace of Heart and true spiritual Progress consisteth.

My son, I have said: "Peace I leave with you, my peace I give unto you: not as the world giveth, give I unto you."

Peace is what all desire, but all do not care for the things that pertain unto true peace.

My peace is with the humble and gentle of heart; in much patience shall thy peace be.

If thou wilt hear me and follow my voice, thou shalt be able to enjoy much peace.

WHAT then shall I do, Lord?

IN every matter look to thyself, as to what thou doest and what thou sayest; and direct thy whole attention into this, to please me alone, and neither to desire nor to seek anything besides me.

But of the words or deeds of others judge nothing rashly; neither do thou entangle thyself with things not entrusted unto thee. Thus it may come to pass that thou mayest be little or seldom disturbed.

2. But never to feel any disturbance at all, nor to suffer any trouble of mind or body, belongs not to this life, but to the state of eternal rest.

Think not therefore that thou hast found true peace, if thou feel no heaviness; nor that all is well, when thou art vexed with no adversary; nor that all is perfect, if all things be done according to thy desire.

Neither do thou think at all highly of thyself, nor account thyself to be specially beloved, if thou be in a state of great devotion and sweetness; for it is not by these things that a true lover of virtue is known, nor doth the spiritual progress and perfection of a man consist in these things.

3. WHEREIN then, O Lord, doth it consist?

IN giving thyself up with all thy heart to the divine will, not seeking thine own interest, either in great matters or in small, either in time or in eternity.

So shalt thou keep one and the same countenance, always giving thanks both in prosperity and adversity, weighing all things in an equal balance.

Be thou so full of courage, and so patient in hope, that when inward comfort is withdrawn, thou mayest prepare thy heart to suffer even greater things; and do not justify thyself, as though thou oughtest not to suffer such and so great afflictions, but justify me in whatsoever I appoint, and cease not to praise my holy name.

Then thou walkest in the true and right way of peace, and thou shalt have a sure hope to see my face again with great delight.

Now if thou attain to the full contempt of thyself, know that thou shalt then enjoy abundance of peace, as great as this thy state of sojourning is capable of.

26.
Of the Excellency of a Free Mind, which is sooner gained by Humble Prayer than by Study

O Lord, it is the business of a perfect man never to withdraw his mind from attentive thought of heavenly things, and thus to pass amidst many cares without care; not as one destitute of all feeling, but, by the privilege of a free mind, cleaving to no creature with inordinate affection.

2. I beseech thee, my most gracious God, preserve me from the cares of this life, lest I should be too much entangled therein; and from the many necessities of the body, lest I should be ensnared by pleasure; and from whatsoever is an obstacle to the soul, lest, broken with troubles, I should be overthrown.

I speak not of those things which worldly vanity so earnestly desireth, but of those miseries, which, as punishments and as the common curse of mortality, do weigh down and hinder the soul of thy servant, that it cannot enter into the freedom of the Spirit so often as it would.

3. O my God, thou sweetness ineffable, turn into bitterness for me all that carnal comfort, which draws me away from the love of eternal things, and in evil wise allures me to itself by the view of some present good.

Let me not be overcome, O Lord, let me not be overcome by flesh and blood; let not the world and the brief glory thereof deceive me; let not the devil and his subtle fraud trip me up.

Give me strength to resist, patience to endure and constancy to persevere.

Give me, instead of all the comforts of the world, the most sweet unction of thy Spirit, and, in place of carnal love, pour into my heart the love of thy name.

4. Behold, meat, drink, clothing, and other necessaries for the support of the body, are burdensome to a fervent spirit.

Grant me to use such refreshments moderately, and not to be entangled with an undue desire of them.

It is not lawful to cast away all things, because nature needs to be sustained; but to require superfluities and those things that are merely pleasureable, the holy law forbiddeth us; for then the flesh would rebel against the Spirit. Herein, I beseech thee, let thy hand govern me and teach me, that I may not exceed in anything.

27.
That it is Love of Self which most hindereth from the Chiefest Good.

My son, thou oughtest to give all for all, and to be in nothing thine own.

Know thou that the love of thyself doth hurt thee more than any thing in the world.

According to the love and affection thou bearest to any thing, so doth it cleave unto thee more or less.

If thy love be pure, simple, and well-ordered, thou shalt be free from bondage.

Do not covet that which it is not lawful for thee to have. Do not have that which may hinder thee, and may deprive thee of inward liberty.

Strange it is that thou committest not thyself wholly unto me from the bottom of thy heart, together with all things thou canst have or desire.

2. Why dost thou consume thyself with vain grief? Why dost thou weary thyself with needless cares?

Submit to my good will, and thou shalt suffer no hurt.

If thou seek this or that, and wouldst be here or there, the better to enjoy thine own profit and pleasure, thou shalt never be at peace, nor free from trouble of mind. For in every case somewhat will be wanting, and in every place there will be some one to cross thee.

It profiteth thee not therefore to obtain and multiply any outward things, but rather to despise them, and utterly to root them out from thy heart.

And this thou must understand not only of revenues and wealth, but of seeking after honor also, and of the desire of vain praise, which all must pass away with this world.

No place availeth if the spirit of fervor be wanting, neither shall that peace long continue, which is sought from without. If the state of thy heart be destitute of a true foundation, that is, if thou stand not steadfast in me, thou mayest change, but shalt not better thyself.

For when occasion ariseth and is laid hold of, thou wilt find that which thou didst flee from, and yet more.

A PRAYER FOR A CLEAN HEART AND HEAVENLY WISDOM.

4. STRENGTHEN me, O God, by the grace of thy holy spirit.

Grant me to be strengthened with might in the inner man, and to empty my heart of all useless care and anguish; so that I be not drawn away with sundry desires of anything whatever, whether mean or precious, but that I look on all things as passing away, on myself also as soon to pass away with them.

For nothing abideth under the sun, where all things are vanity and vexation of spirit. O how wise is he that so considereth them!

5. O Lord, grant me heavenly wisdom, that I may learn above all things to seek and to find thee, above all things to enjoy and to love thee, and to think of all other things as they really are, according to thy wise ordering.

Grant me prudence to avoid him that flattereth me, and to endure patiently him that contradicteth me.

Because it is a great part of wisdom not to be moved with every wind of words, nor to give ear to an evil flatterer; for thus I shall walk securely in the way which I have begun.

28.
Against the Tongues of Slanderers.

My son, take it not grievously if some think ill of thee, and speak that which thou wouldest not willingly hear.

Thou oughtest to be the hardest judge of thyself, and to think no man weaker than thyself.

If thou dost walk spiritually, thou wilt not much weigh fleeting words.

It is no small wisdom to keep silence in an evil time, and in the heart to turn thyself to me, and not be troubled by the judgment of men.

2. Let not thy peace depend on the tongues of men; for, whether they judge well of thee or ill, thou art not on that account other than thyself. Where are true peace and true glory? Are they not in me?

And he that careth not to please men, nor feareth to displease them, shall enjoy much peace.

From inordinate love and vain fear ariseth all disquietness of heart and distraction of the mind.

29.
How that we ought to call upon God, and to bless Him, when Tribulation is upon us.

Blessed be thy name, O Lord, for ever; for that it is thy will that this temptation and tribulation should come upon me.

I cannot escape it, but must needs flee unto thee, that thou mayest help me, and turn it to my good.

Lord, I am now in affliction, and it is not well with me, but I am much troubled with the present suffering.

And now, O beloved Father, what shall I say? I am in a straight; save thou me from this hour.

Yet therefore came I unto this hour that thou mightest be

glorified, when I shall have been greatly humbled, and by thee delivered.

Let it please thee, Lord, to deliver me; for, wretched that I am, what can I do, and whither shall I go without thee?

Grant me patience, O Lord, even now in this my strait. Help me, my God, and then I will not fear how grievously soever I be afflicted.

2. And now in these my troubles what shall I say?

Lord, thy will be done! I have well deserved to be afflicted and grieved.

Surely I ought to bear it; and O that I may bear it with patience, until the tempest be overpast, and all be well again, or even better!

But thine omnipotent hand is able to take even this temptation from me, and to assuage the violence thereof, that I utterly sink not under it; as oftentimes heretofore thou hast done unto me, O my God, my Mercy!

And the more difficult it is to me, so much the more easy to thee is this change of the right hand of the most High.

30.
Of Craving the Divine Aid, and of Confidence of Recovering Grace.

My son, I am the Lord that giveth strength in the day of tribulation.

Come thou unto me, when it is not well with thee.

This is that which most of all hindereth heavenly consolation, that thou art too slow in turning thyself unto prayer.

For before thou dost earnestly supplicate me, thou seekest in the meanwhile many comforts, and lookest for refreshment in outward things.

And hence it cometh to pass that all doth little profit thee, until thou well consider that I am he who doth rescue them that trust in him; and that out of me there is neither powerful help, nor profitable counsel, nor lasting remedy.

But do thou, having now recovered breath after the tempest, gather strength again in the light of my mercies; for I am at hand (saith the Lord) to repair all, not only entirely, but also abundantly and in most plentiful measure.

2. Is there anything hard to me? Or shall I be like unto one that promiseth and performeth not?

Where is thy faith? Stand firmly and with perseverance; take courage and be patient; comfort will come to thee in due time.

Wait, wait, I say, for me: I will come and heal thee.

It is a temptation, this that vexeth thee, and a vain fear, this that affrighteth thee.

What else doth anxiety about the future bring to thee, but sorrow upon sorrow? "Sufficient for the day is the evil thereof."

It is a vain thing and unprofitable, to be either disturbed or pleased about future things, which perhaps will never come to pass.

3. But it is in the nature of man to be deluded with such imaginations; and it is a sign of a mind as yet weak to be so easily drawn away by the suggestions of the enemy.

For so that he may but delude and deceive thee, he careth not whether it be by true things or by false; whether he overthrow thee with the love of present things, or the fear of future things.

Let not therefore thy heart be troubled, neither let it be afraid.

Trust in me, and put thy confidence in my mercy.

When thou thinkest thyself farthest off from me, oftentimes I am nearest unto thee.

When thou judgest that almost all is lost, then oftentimes the greatest gain of reward is close at hand.

All is not lost, when a thing falleth out against thee.

Thou must not judge according to present feeling, nor so take any grief, or give thyself over to it, from whencesoever it cometh, as though all hopes of escape were quite taken away.

4. Think not thyself wholly left, although for a time I have sent thee some tribulation, or even have withdrawn thy desired comfort; for this is the way to the kingdom of heaven.

And without doubt it is more expedient for thee and for the rest of My servants, that ye be exercised with adversities, than that ye should have all things according to your desires.

I know the secret thoughts of thy heart, and that it is very expedient for thy welfare, that thou be left sometimes without spiritual enjoyment, lest perhaps thou shouldst be puffed up with the prosperous estate, and shouldst be puffed up with thy prosperous estate, and shouldst be willing to please thyself in that which thou art not.

That which I have given, I can take away; and can restore it again when I please.

5. When I give it, it is still Mine; when I withdraw it, I take not anything that is thine; for every good and every perfect gift is Mine.

If I send thee affliction, or any cross whatsoever, repine not, nor let thy heart fail thee; I can quickly succor thee, and turn all thy heaviness into joy.

Nevertheless I am righteous and greatly to be praised, when I deal thus with thee.

6. If thou be wise, and consider this rightly, thou wilt never mourn so dejectedly for any adversity, but rather wilt rejoice and give thanks.

Yea, thou wilt account this thine special joy, that I afflict thee with sorrows, and do not spare thee.

"As my Father hath loved me, so have I loved you," said I unto my beloved disciples; whom doubtless I sent not out to temporal joys, but to great conflicts; not to honor, but to contempt; not idleness, but to labors; not to rest, but that they should bring forth much fruit with patience. Remember thou these words, O my son!

31.
Of the Contempt of all Creatures, in order to find out the Creator.

O LORD, I stand much in need of yet greater grace, if it be thy will that I should attain to that state, where neither man nor any creature shall be a hindrance unto me.

For as long as anything holds me back, I cannot freely take my flight to thee.

He desired to fly freely that said, "Oh, that I had wings like a dove, for then would I flee away and be at rest!"

What is more quiet than the single eye? And who more free than he that desireth nothing upon earth?

A man ought therefore to mount above all creatures, and perfectly to renounce himself, and to be in a sort of ecstasy of mind, and to see that thou, the Creator of all things, hast nothing amongst creatures like unto thyself.

Unless a man be set free from all creatures, he cannot wholly attend unto divine things.

And therefore are there so few contemplative, for that few can wholly withdraw themselves from things created and perishing.

2. To obtain this, there is need of much grace, to elevate the soul, and carry it away above itself.

And unless a man be uplifted in spirit, and be freed from all creatures, and wholly united unto God, whatsoever he knoweth, and whatsoever he hath, is of small account.

A long while shall he be little, and lie grovelling below, whoever he be that esteemeth anything great, save the one only infinite eternal Good.

And whatsoever is not God, is nothing, and ought to be accounted of as nothing.

There is great difference between the wisdom of a man devout and taught of God, and the knowledge of a man learned and studious.

Far more noble is that learning which floweth from above, from the divine influence, than that which is painfully gotten by the wit of man.

3. There are many that desire contemplation, but they endeavor not to practice those things that are needful thereunto.

A great hindrance it is, that men rest in signs and in the things of sense, and little heed perfect mortification.

I know not what it is, by what spirit we are led, nor what we pretend, we that seem to be called spiritual, that we take so much pains, and are so full of anxiety about transitory and mean things, and so rarely think of our own inward concernments with full recollection of mind.

4. Alas, presently, after a slight recollection, we rush into outward things again, and weigh not our works with diligent examination.

We heed not where our affections lie, nor bewail the impurity that is in all our actions.

For "all flesh had corrupted his way," and therefore did the great deluge ensue.

Since, then, the inward affection is much corrupted, the action thence proceeding must needs be corrupted also, a proof of the absence of all inward strength.

From a pure heart proceedeth the fruit of a good life.

5. We ask how much a man has done: but from what principle he acts, is not so diligently considered.

We enquire whether he be courageous, rich, handsome, skilful, a good writer, a good singer, or a good laborer; but how poor he is in spirit, how patient and meek, how devout and spiritual, is seldom spoken of.

Nature respecteth the outward things of a man, grace turneth itself to the inward.

The one is often disappointed; the other hath her trust in God, and so is not deceived.

32.
Of Self-Denial, and renouncing every Evil Appetite.

My son, thou canst not possess perfect liberty unless thou wholly renounce thyself.

They all are but in fetters who merely seek their own interest, and are lovers of themselves. Covetous are they, curious, wanderers, always seeking what is soft and delicate, not the things of JESUS Christ, but oftentimes devising and framing that which will not continue.

For all that is not of God shall perish.

Keep this short and complete saying: "Forsake all and thou shalt find all." Forego desire and thou shalt find rest.

Consider this well, and when thou hast fulfilled it, thou shalt understand all things.

O LORD, this is not the work of one day, nor children's sport; yea rather in this short word is included all perfection.

MY son, thou oughtest not to turn back, nor at once to be cast down, when thou hearest of the way of the perfect; but rather to be stirred up to higher things, and at least in longing desire to sigh after them.

I would it were so with thee, that thou wert arrived at this, to be no longer a lover of thyself, but to stand merely at my beck, and at his whom I have appointed a father over thee; then thou shouldst exceedingly please Me, and all thy life shall pass away in joy and peace.

Thou hast yet many things to part with, which unless thou wholly resign unto Me, thou shalt not attain to that which thou desirest.

"I counsel thee to buy of Me gold tried in the fire, that

thou mayest become rich;" that is, heavenly wisdom, which treadeth under foot all lower things.

Set little by earthly wisdom, and study not to please others or thyself.

3. I said, that mean things must be bought with things which, among men, seem precious and of great esteem.

For true heavenly wisdom doth seem very mean, of small account, and almost forgotten among men, as having no high thoughts of itself, nor seeking to be magnified upon earth. Many indeed praise it with their lips, but in their life they are far from it; yet is it the precious pearl, which is hidden from many.

33.
Of Inconstancy of Heart, and of having our Final Intent directed unto God.

My son, trust not to thy feelings, for whatever they be now, they will quickly be changed towards some other thing.

As long as thou livest, thou art subject to change, even against thy will; so that thou art at one time merry, at another sad; at one time quiet, at another troubled; now devout, now undevout; now diligent, now listless; now grace, and now light.

But he that is wise and well instructed in the Spirit standeth fast upon these changing things; not heeding what he feeleth in himself, or which way the wind of instability bloweth; but that the whole intent of his mind may be to the right and the best end.

For thus he will be able to continue one and the same and unshaken, in the midst of so many various events directing continually the single eye of his intent unto me.

2. And the purer the eye of the intent is, with so much the more constancy doth a man pass through the several kinds of storms which assail him.

But in many the eye of a pure intent waxes dim, for it is quickly drawn aside to any pleasurable object which meets it.

For it is rare to find one who is wholly free from all blemish of self-seeking.

So of old the Jews came to Bethany to Martha and Mary,

not for Jesus' sake only, but that they might see Lazarus also.

The eye of our intent therefore is to be purified, that it may be single and right, and is to be directed unto me, beyond all the various earthly objects which come between.

34.
That God is precious, above all Things, and in all Things, to him that loveth him.

Behold! My God, and my All." What would I more, and what greater happiness can I desire?

O sweet and delightful word! But to him only that loveth the word, not the world nor the things that are in the world.

"My God, and my All!" To him that understandeth, enough is said: And to repeat it again and again, is pleasant to Him that loveth.

For when thou art present, all things do yield delight; but when thou art absent, everything becometh irksome.

Thou givest quietness of heart, and much peace, and pleasant joy.

Thou makest us to take delight in all things, and in all to praise thee; neither can anything please long without thee; but if it be pleasant and grateful, thy grace must needs be present, and it must be seasoned with the sweetness of thy wisdom.

2. What will not be pleasant to the taste unto him who hath a true relish for thee?

And to him that hath no relish for thee, what can be pleasant?

But the wise men of the world, and they also who relish the things of the flesh, come short of thy wisdom; for in the former is found much vanity, and in the latter death.

But they that follow thee in contempt of worldly things, and mortification of the flesh, are known to be truly wise: for they are brought over from vanity to truth, from the flesh to the spirit.

These relish God; and what good soever is found in creatures, they wholly refer unto the praise of their Maker.

Great, however, yea, very great is the difference between the sweetness of the Creator and of the creature, of eternity and of time, of light uncreated and of the light that receiveth its light therefrom.

3. O thou everlasting Light, surpassing all created lights, dart the beams of thy brightness from above, to pierce all the most inward parts of my heart.

Purify, rejoice, enlighten and enliven my spirit with all the powers thereof, that I may cleave unto thee with abundance of joy and triumph.

O when will that blessed and desired hour come, that thou mayest satisfy me with thy presence, and mayest be unto me all in all.

So long as this is not granted me, I shall not have perfect joy.

Still alas! The old man doth live in me: he is not wholly crucified, he is not perfectly dead.

Still doth he mightily strive against the Spirit, and stirreth up inward wars, and suffereth not the kingdom of my soul to be in peace.

4. But thou that rulest the power of the sea, and stillest the rising of the waves thereof, arise and help me!

Scatter the nations that delight in war, crush thou them in thy might.

Display thy greatness, I beseech thee, and let thy right hand be glorified, for there is no other hope or refuge for me, save in thee, O Lord my God.

35.
That there is no Security from Temptation in this Life.

My son, thou art never secure in this life, but, as long as thou livest, thou shalt always need spiritual armor.

Thou dwellest among enemies, and art assaulted on the right hand and on the left.

If therefore thou defend not thyself on every side with the shield of patience, thou canst not be long without a wound.

Moreover, if thou fix not thy heart on me with sincere willingness to suffer all things for me, thou wilt not be able to bear the heat of this combat, nor to attain to the palm of the blessed.

Thou oughtest therefore manfully to go through all, and to secure a strong hand against whatsoever withstandeth thee.

For to him that overcometh is manna given, but for the indolent there remaineth much misery.

2. If thou seek rest in this life, how wilt thou then attain to the everlasting rest?

Dispose not thyself for much rest, but for great patience.

Seek true peace, not in earth, but in heaven; not in men, nor in any other creature, but in God alone.

For the love of God thou oughtest cheerfully to undergo all things, that is to say, all labor, grief, temptation, vexation, anxiety, necessity, infirmity, injury, detraction, reproof, humiliation, shame, correction, and contempt.

These help to virtue; these are the trial of a babe in Christ; these form the heavenly crown.

I will give an everlasting reward for a short labor, and infinite glory for transitory shame.

3. Thinkest thou that thou shalt always have spiritual consolations at will?

My saints had not such always, but they had many afflictions, and sundry temptations, and great discomforts.

But in all these they did bear up themselves patiently, and trusted rather in God than in themselves, knowing that the sufferings of this time are not worthy to be compared to the future glory.

Wilt thou have that at once, which many after many tears and great labors have hardly obtained?

Wait for the Lord, behave thyself manfully, and be of good courage; be not faithless, do not leave thy place, but steadily expose both body and soul for the glory of God.

I will reward thee in most plentiful wise; I will be with thee in every tribulation.

36.
Against the Vain Judgments of Men.

My son, rest thy heart firmly on the Lord, and fear not the judgment of men, when conscience testifieth of thy dutifulness and innocency.

It is a good and happy thing to suffer in such a way; nor

will this be grievous to a heart which is humble, and which trusteth rather in God than in itself.

The most part of men are given to talk much, and therefore little trust is to be placed in them.

Moreover also, to satisfy all is not possible.

Although Paul endeavored to please all in the Lord, and made himself all things unto all men, yet with him it was a very small thing that he should be judged of man's judgment.

2. He did for the edification and salvation of others what lay in him, and as much as he was able; yet could he not hinder but that he was sometimes judged and despised by others.

Therefore he committed all to God, who knew all; and with patience and humility he defended himself against unjust tongues, and against such as thought vanities and lies, and spake boastfully whatever they listed.

Sometimes notwithstanding he made answer, lest the weak should be offended by his silence.

3. Who art thou that fearest a mortal man? Today he is, and tomorrow he is not seen.

Fear God, and thou shalt not need to shrink from the terrors of men.

What harm can the words or injuries of any man do thee? He hurteth himself rather than thee, nor shall he be able to avoid the judgment of God, whosoever he be.

Do thou have God before thine eyes, and contend not with peevish words.

And if for the present thou seem to be worsted and to suffer shame undeservedly, do not therefore repine, neither do thou by impatience lessen thy crown.

But rather lift thou up thine eyes to me in heaven, who am able to deliver thee from all shame and wrong, and to render to every man according to his works.

37.
Of Pure and Entire Resignation for the obtaining Freedom of Heart.

My son, forsake thyself, and thou shalt find me.

Choose not anything, nor appropriate anything whatever to thyself, and thou shalt always be a gainer.

For greater grace shall be added to thee, the moment thou hast resigned thyself, and hast not resumed thy claim.

LORD, how often shall I resign myself, and wherein shall I forsake myself?

ALWAYS and at every hour; as well in small things as in great. I expect nothing, but do desire that thou be found stripped of all things.

Otherwise, how canst thou be mine, and I thine, unless thou be stripped of all self-will, both within and without?

The sooner thou doest this, the better it will be with thee; and the more fully and sincerely thou doest it, so much the more shalt thou please me, and so much the greater shall be thy gain.

2. Some there are who resign themselves, but with exceptions: for they put not their whole trust in God, therefore they study how to provide for themselves.

Some also at first do offer all, but afterwards, being assailed with temptation, they return again to their own ways, and therefore make no progress in the way of virtue.

These shall not attain to the true liberty of a pure heart, nor to the favor of my sweetest friendship, unless they first make an entire resignation and a daily oblation of themselves. Without this, there neither is nor can be a fruitful union.

3. I have very often said unto thee, and now again I say the same, Forsake thyself, resign thyself, and thou shalt enjoy much inward peace.

Give all for all; seek nothing, ask back nothing; abide purely and with a firm confidence in me, and thou shalt possess me; thou shalt be free in heart, and darkness shall not tread thee down.

Let this be thy whole endeavor, let this be thy prayer, this thy desire; that, being stripped of all selfishness, thou mayest with entire simplicity follow JESUS only, and, dying to thyself, mayest live eternally to me.

Then all vain imaginations, evil perturbations, and superfluous cares shall fly away.

Then also immoderate fear shall leave thee, and inordinate love shall die.

38.
Of Good Government of Ourselves in Things Outward, and of Recourse to God in Dangers.

My son, thou oughtest with all diligence to endeavor, that, in every place and action, and in all outward business, thou be inwardly free, and thoroughly master of thyself; and that all things be under thee, and not thou under them.

Thou must be lord and master of thine own actions, not a servant or a hireling.

Rather shouldst thou be as a freed man and a true Hebrew, passing over into the lot and freedom of the sons of God.

For they stand above things present, and contemplate the things eternal.

They look on transitory things with the left eye and with the right do behold the things of heaven.

Temporal things cannot draw them to cleave unto them: rather do they draw temporal things to serve them, and this in such way as they are ordained by God, and are appointed by the great Work-master, who hath left nothing in his creation without due order.

2. If too thou stand steadfast in all things, and do not estimate what thou seest and hearest by the outward appearance, nor with a carnal eye; but at once in every affair dost enter with Moses into the tabernacle to ask counsel of the Lord; thou shalt sometimes hear the divine oracle, and shall return instructed concerning many things, both present and to come.

For Moses always had recourse to the tabernacle for the deciding of doubts and questions, and fled to the help of prayer for support under dangers and the iniquity of men.

So oughtest thou in like manner to fly to the closet of thine heart, very earnestly craving the divine favor.

For we read, that for this cause Joshua and the children of Israel were deceived by the Gibeonites, because they asked not counsel at the mouth of the Lord, but, giving credit too lightly to their fair words, were deluded by their counterfeit piety.

39.
That a Man should not be over-careful in Matters of Business.

My son, always commit thy cause to me. I will dispose well of it in due time.

Wait for my ordering of it, and thou shalt find it will be for thy good.

O Lord, I do most cheerfully commit all unto thee, for my care can little avail.

Would that I did not so much dwell on future things, but gave myself up without a struggle to thy good pleasure.

2. My son, oftentimes a man vehemently struggleth for somewhat he desireth, and when he hath arrived at it, he beginneth to be of another mind; for man's affections do not long continue fixed on one object, but rather do urge him from one thing to another.

It is therefore no small benefit for a man to forsake himself; even in the smallest things.

3. The *true* profiting of a man considereth in the denying of himself; and he that thus denieth himself, liveth in great freedom and security.

But the old enemy, who always setteth himself against all that are good, ceaseth at no time from tempting, but day and night lieth grievously in wait, to cast the unwary, if he can, headlong into the snare of deceit.

Therefore "Watch ye, and pray," saith our Lord, "that ye enter not into temptation."

40.
That Man hath of himself no Good Thing, nor Anything whereof he can glory.

Lord, what is man, that thou art mindful of him, or the son of man, that thou visitest him?"

What hath man deserved that thou shouldest grant him thy favor?

O Lord, what cause have I to complain, if thou forsake

me? Or if thou do not that which I desire, what can I justly say against it?

Surely this I may truly think and say: Lord, I am nothing, I can do nothing, I have nothing that is good of myself, but in all things I am wanting, and do ever tend to nothing.

And unless thou help me, and inwardly instruct me, I must become altogether lukewarm and careless.

2. But Thou, O Lord, art always the same, and endurest for ever, always good, just, and holy, doing all things well, justly, and holily, and disposing all things with wisdom.

But I, that am more ready to go backward than forward, do not ever continue in one estate, for "seven times are passed over me."

Yet it is soon better with me, when it so pleaseth thee, and when thou vouchsafest to stretch forth thy helping hand; for thou canst help me alone without human aid, and canst so strengthen me, that my countenance shall be no more changed, but my heart shall be turned to thee alone, and be at rest.

3. Wherefore, if I could once perfectly cast off all human comfort, either for the attainment of devotion, or because of mine own necessities enforcing me to seek after thee (because that no mortal man could comfort me), then might I well hope in thy grace, and rejoice for the gift of fresh consolation.

4. Thanks be unto thee, from whom all things proceed, whensoever it is well with me.

But I am in thy sight mere vanity and nothing, a man weak, and never continuing in one stay.

Whereof then can I glory? Or for what do I desire to be respected? Is it for that I am nothing? Yet this is most vain.

Mere empty glory is in truth an evil pest, a very great vanity; because it draweth a man from true glory, and robbeth him of heavenly grace.

For whilst he pleaseth himself, he displeaseth thee; whilst he gapeth after the praise of men, he is deprived of true virtues.

5. But the true glory and holy exultation is for a man to glory in thee, and not in himself; to rejoice in thy name, not in his own strength, and not to delight in any creature but for thy sake.

Praised be thy Name, not mine; magnified be thy work, not mine. Let thy holy Name be blessed, but to me let no part of men's praises be given.

Thou art my glory, thou art the joy of my heart.

In thee will I glory and rejoice all the day, but as for myself, I will not glory, but in my infirmities.

6. Let the Jews seek honor one of another, I will seek that which cometh from God alone.

For all human glory, all temporal honor, all worldly height, compared to thy eternal glory, is vanity and folly.

O my God, my Truth, and my Mercy, O Blessed Trinity, to thee alone be praise, honor, power, and glory for ever and ever.

41.
Of the Contempt of all Temporal Honor.

My son, trouble not thyself, if thou see others honored and advanced, whilst thou art contemned and debased.

Lift up thy heart into heaven to me, and the contempt of men on earth shall not grieve thee.

LORD, we are blind, and are quickly misled by vanity.

If I look rightly into myself, I cannot say that any creature hath ever done me wrong; and therefore I cannot justly complain before thee.

2. But because I have often and grievously sinned against thee, all creatures do justly take arms against me.

Unto me, therefore, shame and contempt is justly due, but unto thee praise, honor, and glory.

And unless I prepare myself with cheerful willingness to be despised and forsaken of all creatures, and to be esteemed altogether nothing, I cannot obtain inward peace and stability, nor be spiritually enlightened, nor be fully united unto thee.

42.
That our Peace is not to be set on Men.

My son, if thou rest thy peace on any because of the opinion which thou hast of him, or because of thine intimate acquaintance with him, thou shalt ever be inconstant and enthralled.

But if thou have recourse unto the ever-living and abiding Truth, the departure of death of a friend shall not grieve thee.

Thy regard for thy friend ought to be grounded in me; and for my sake is he to be beloved, whosoever he be that thou thinkest well of, and who is very dear unto thee in this life.

Without me friendship hath no strength, and no continuance; neither is that love true and pure, which is not knit by me.

Thou oughtest to be so dead to such affections towards thy friends, that (as much as appertaineth unto thee) thou shouldst be willing to be without all human friendship.

Man approacheth so much the nearer unto God, the farther he departeth from all earthly comfort.

And the lower he descendeth in himself, and the meaner he becometh in his own sight, the higher he ascendeth towards God.

But he that attributeth any good unto himself, hindereth the entry of God's grace; for the grace of the Holy Spirit ever seeketh an humble heart.

If thou knewest perfectly to annihilate thyself, and to empty thyself of all created love, then should I be constrained to flow into thee with great abundance of grace.

When thou hast regard unto creatures, the sight of the Creator is withdrawn from thee.

Learn in all things to overcome thyself, for the love of thy Creator, and then shalt thou be able to attain to divine knowledge.

How small soever anything be, if it be inordinately loved and regarded, it keepeth thee back from the highest good, and defileth the soul.

43.
Against Vain and Secular Knowledge.

My son, let not the sayings of men move thee, however fair and ingenious they may be, "For the kingdom of God consisteth not in word, but in power."

Observe well my words, for they inflame the heart, and enlighten the mind; they cause compunction, and carry with them many a consolation.

Never read the word of God in order to appear more learned or more wise.

Be studious for the mortification of thy sins; for this will profit thee more than the knowledge of many difficult questions.

2. When thou shalt have read and known many things, thou oughtest ever to return to the one beginning and principle.

I am He that teacheth man knowledge; and I give unto little children a clearer understanding than can be taught by man.

He therefore, to whom I speak, shall quickly be wise, and shall profit much in the Spirit.

Woe be to them that enquire many curious things of men, and little care about the way of serving me!

The time will come, when the Master of masters shall appear, Christ the Lord of angels, to hear the lessons of all, that is, to examine the consciences of every one.

And then will he search Jerusalem with candles; and the hidden things of darkness shall be laid open, and the arguings of men's tongues shall be silent.

3. I am he who in one instant do raise up the humble mind, so that a man shall understand more reasonings of eternal truth, than if he had studied ten years in the schools.

I teach without noise of words, without confusion of opinions, without the desire of honor, without bandying of arguments.

I am he who instructeth men to despise earthly things, to loathe things present, to seek things heavenly, to relish things eternal, to flee honors, to endure offences, to place all hope in me, out of me to desire nothing, and above all things ardently to love me.

4. A certain one by loving me entirely, became instructed in divine things, and was wont to speak that which was admirable.

He profiteth more by forsaking all things, than by studying subtleties.

But to some men I speak common things, to others things uncommon; to some I appear sweetly by signs and figures, but to some I reveal mysteries with much light.

The voice of books is indeed one, but it instructs not all alike; for I am the teacher of the truth within, I am the searcher of the heart, the discerner of the thoughts, the mover of actions, distributing to every man as I judge meet.

44.
Of not attracting to Ourselves Outward Things.

My son, in many things it is thy duty to be ignorant, and to esteem thyself as dead upon earth, and as one to whom the whole world is crucified.

Thou must also pass by many things with a deaf ear, and rather think of those which belong unto thy peace.

It is more useful to turn away one's eyes from unpleasing things, and to leave every one to his own opinion, than to be a slave to contentious discourses.

If all stand well betwixt thee and God, and if thou hast his judgment in thy mind, thou shalt the more easily endure to be overcome.

2. O LORD, to what a pass are we come! Behold, we bewail a temporal loss: for a pitiful gain we toil and run; and the spiritual losses of our soul are forgotten, and hardly at last return to the memory.

That which little or nothing profiteth we heed; and that which is especially necessary, we slightly pass over; because the whole man doth slide off into outward things; and unless he speedily repent, he settleth down in them, and that willingly.

45.
That Credit is not to be given to All: and that Man is prone to offend in Words.

Grant me help, O Lord, in tribulation, for vain is the help of man!

How often have I been deceived, finding want of faithfulness where I thought myself sure!

And how often have I found it, where beforehand I least expected it.

It is in vain therefore to trust in men, but the salvation of the righteous is of thee, O God!

Blessed be thou, O Lord my God, in all things that befall us.

We are weak and unstable; we are quickly deceived, and soon changed.

2. Who is he, that is able in all things so warily and circumspectly to keep himself, as never to fall into any deceit or perplexity?

But he that trusteth in thee, O Lord, and seeketh thee with a single heart, doth not so easily fall.

And if he do fall into any tribulation, be he never so much entangled, yet he shall quickly either through thee be delivered, or by thee be comforted; for thou wilt not forsake him that trusteth in thee, even to the end.

A friend is rarely to be found that continueth faithful in all his friend's distresses.

Thou, O Lord, even thou alone art most faithful at all times, and there is none like unto thee.

3. O how wise was that holy soul that said, "My mind is firmly settled and grounded in Christ."

If it were so with me, then would not human fear easily vex me, nor the darts of words move me.

Who can foresee all things? Who is able to beware beforehand of evils to come? If things even foreseen do oftentimes hurt us, how can things unlooked for do otherwise than wound us grievously?

But wretched that I am, why did I not provide better for myself? Why also have I so easily trusted others?

But we are men, nothing else but frail men, although by many we may be reputed and called angels.

To whom shall I give credit, O lord? To whom but to thee? Thou art the truth, which neither doth deceive, nor can be deceived.

And on the other side, "every man is a liar," weak, inconstant, and subject to fall, especially in words; and therefore we must not immediately give credit to that which in the outward show seemeth at the first to sound aright.

4. O with what wisdom hast thou warned us to beware of men; and, because a man's foes are they of his own household, not forwith to believe if one should say, Lo here, or Lo there.

My hurt has been my instructor, and O that I might thereby increase my caution, and not my folly.

"Be wary," saith one, "be wary, keep to thyself what I tell

thee;" and whilst I hold my peace, and think it a secret, he cannot himself keep that which he desired me to keep, but presently betrayeth both me and himself, and is gone.

From such tales and such indiscreet persons protect me, O Lord, that I neither fall into their hands, nor ever commit such things myself.

Grant me to observe truth and constancy in my words, and remove far from me a crafty tongue.

What I am not willing to suffer in others, I ought by all means to avoid myself.

5. O how good is it, and how it tendeth to peace, to be silent about other men, and not to believe at random all that is said, nor eagerly to report what we have heard.

How good it is to lay one's self open to few, and always to be seeking after thee who are the searcher of the heart.

Nor should we be carried about with every wind of words, but we should desire that all things, both within and without, be accomplished according to the pleasure of thy will.

How safe is it, for the keeping of heavenly grace, to avoid appearances, and not to seek those things that seem to cause admiration abroad, but to follow with all diligence the things which bring amendment of life, and zeal.

6. To how many hath virtue itself, known and over hastily commended, been hurtful!

How profitable hath grace been when preserved in silence in this frail life, which is temptation and warfare.

46.
Of putting our Trust in God when Evil Words arise.

My son, stand steadily, and put thy trust in me; for what are words, but words?

They fly through the air, but hurt not the rock.

If thou be guilty, see that thou be willing to amend thyself; if conscience reproach thee not, resolve to suffer willingly for God's sake.

It is but a small matter to suffer sometimes a few words, if thou hast not yet the courage to endure hard stripes.

And why do such small matters go to thy heart, but because thou art yet carnal, and regardest men more than thou oughtest?

For because thou art afraid to be despised, therefore thou art not willing to be reproved for thy faults, but seekest the shelter of excuses.

2. But look better into thyself, and thou shalt acknowledge that the world is yet alive in thee, and a vain desire to please men.

For when thou shunnest to be abased and reproved for thy faults, it is evident that thou art neither truly humble, nor truly dead to the world, nor the world crucified to thee.

But give diligent ear to my words, and thou shalt not regard ten thousand words spoken by men.

Behold, if all should be spoken against thee that could be most maliciously invented, what would it hurt thee, if thou sufferedst it to pass entirely away, and madest no more reckoning of it than a mote? Could it pluck so much as one hair from thy head?

3. But he that hath no heart within him, and hath not God before his eyes, is easily moved with a word of dispraise.

Whereas he that trusteth in me, and hath no wish to trust in his own judgment, shall be free from the fear of men.

For I am the judge and the discerner of all secrets: I know how the matter was; I know him that offered the injury, and him that suffered it.

From me hath this proceeded; this hath happened by my permission, that the thoughts of many hearts might be revealed.

I shall judge the guilty, and the innocent; but by a secret judgment I would beforehand prove them both.

4. The testimony of men oftentimes deceiveth; but my judgment is true; it shall stand and not be overthrown.

It is commonly hidden; and not known in all respects, but to few: notwithstanding it never erreth, neither can it err, although to the eyes of the foolish it seemeth not right.

Men ought therefore to have recourse to me in every judgment, and not to lean on their own opinion.

For the just man will not be moved, whatsoever befalleth him from God; and if any unjust charge be brought against him, he will not be much troubled.

Neither will he rejoice with a foolish exultation, if by means of others he be reasonably vindicated.

For he considereth that I am he that searcheth the heart and reins, and judgeth not according to the outside, nor according to human appearance.

For that oftentimes in my sights found worthy of blame, which in the judgment of men is thought to be commendable.

O LORD GOD, the just judge, strong and patient, thou who knowest the frailty and wickedness of men, be thou my strength, and all my trust, for mine own conscience sufficeth me not.

Although I know nothing against myself, yet I cannot hereby justify myself; for without thy mercy, in thy sight shall no man living be justified.

47.
That all Grievous Things are to be endured for the Sake of Eternal Life.

My son, be not dismayed by the painful labors which thou hast undertaken for me, neither be thou utterly cast down because of any tribulations which befall thee; but let my promise strengthen and comfort thee in all events.

I am able to reward thee above all measure and degree.

Thou shalt not long toil here, and shalt not always be oppressed with grief.

Wait a little while, and thou shalt see a speedy end of thine evils.

There will come an hour when all labor and trouble shall cease.

Poor and brief is all that which passeth away with time.

2. Do with thy might what thou doest; labor faithfully in my vineyard; I will be thy reward.

Write, read, mourn, keep silence, pray, suffer crosses manfully; life everlasting is worthy of all these, yea, and of greater combats.

Peace shall come in the day which is known unto the Lord, and it shall be neither day nor night, such as now is but everlasting light, infinite brightness, steadfast peace, and secure rest.

Then thou shalt not say, "Who shall deliver me from the body of this death?" Nor cry, "Woe is me, that I sojourn in Mesech!" For death shall be cast down headlong, and there shall be salvation which cannot fail: there shall be no more anxious thoughts, but blessed joy, sweet and lovely company.

3. O if thou hadst seen the everlasting crowns of the saints in heaven, and with how great glory they rejoice, who in times past were contemptible to this world, and esteemed unworthy of life itself; truly thou wouldst presently humble thyself even unto the dust, and wouldst rather seek to be under the feet of all, than to have command so much as over one.

Neither wouldst thou desire the pleasant days of this life, but rather wouldst rejoice to suffer affliction for God, and esteem it thy greatest gain to be reputed as nothing amongst men.

4. O if thou hadst a relishing of these things, and didst suffer them to sink into the bottom of thy heart, how couldst thou so much as once complain?

Are not all painful labors to be endured for the sake of life eternal?

It is no small matter to lose or to gain the kingdom of God.

Life up thy face therefore unto heaven; behold, I and all my saints with me, who in this world had great conflicts, do now rejoice, are now comforted, now secure, now at rest, and they shall remain with me everlastingly in the kingdom of my Father.

48.
Of the Day of Eternity, and this Life's Straitnesses.

O most blessed mansion of the city which is above! O most clear day of eternity, which night obscureth not, but the highest truth ever enlighteneth! O day ever joyful, ever secure, and never changing into a contrary state!

O that that day would once appear, and that all these temporal things were at an end!

To the saints it shineth, glowing with everlasting brightness, but to those that are pilgrims on the earth, it appeareth only afar off, and as it were through a glass.

2. The citizens of heaven do know how joyful that day is; but the banished children of Eve bewail the bitterness and tediousness of this.

The days of this life are short and evil, full of sorrow and straitnesses.

Here a man is defiled with many sins, ensnared with many passions, held fast by many fears, racked with many cares, distracted with many curiosities, entangled with many vanities, compassed about with many errors, worn with many labors, burdened with temptations, enervated by pleasures, tormented with want.

3. O when shall these evils be at an end? When shall I be delivered from the miserable bondage of my sins? When shall I be mindful, O Lord, of thee alone? When shall I fully rejoice in thee?

When shall I enjoy true liberty without any hindrances without any trouble of mind and body?

When shall I have solid peace, peace secure and undisturbed peace within and peace without, peace every way assured?

O merciful JESUS, when shall I stand to behold thee? When shall I contemplate the glory of thy kingdom? When wilt thou be unto me in all?

O when shall I be with thee in thy kingdom, which thou hast prepared for they beloved from all eternity?

I am left, a poor and banished man, in the land of mine enemies, where there are daily wars and great calamities.

4. Comfort my banishment, assuage my sorrow; for my whole desire sigheth after thee.

For all is burdensome to me, whatsoever this world offereth for my consolation.

I long to enjoy thee in my inmost soul, but I cannot attain unto it.

My desire is, that I may be wholly given up to things heavenly, but temporal things and unmortified passions weigh me down.

With the mind I wish to be above all things, but with the flesh I am enforced against my will to be beneath all.

Thus, unhappy man that I am, I fight against myself, and am become grievous to myself, whilst my spirit seeketh to be above, and my flesh to be below.

5. O what do I inwardly suffer, whilst in my mind I dwell on things heavenly, and presently in my prayers a multitude of carnal fancies rise up to me! O my God, be not thou far from me, nor turn away in wrath from thy servant.

Cast forth thy lightning and disperse them; shoot out thine arrows, and let all the imaginations of the enemy be confounded.

Gather in and call home my senses unto thee; make me to

forget all worldly things; enable me to cast away speedily, and to despise all the imaginations of wickedness.

Succor me, O thou the everlasting truth, that no vanity may move me.

Come to me, thou heavenly sweetness, and let all impurity flee from before thy face.

Pardon me also, and in mercy deal gently with me, as often as in prayer I think on aught beside thee.

I must truly confess, that I am wont to be subject to many distractions.

For oftentimes I am not there, where I stand or sit, but rather I am there, whither my thoughts do carry me.

Where my thoughts are, there am I; and commonly there are my thoughts, where my affection is.

That too readily occurs to me, which is by nature delightful, or by custom is pleasing.

6. And for this cause, thou art truth itself hast plainly said, Where thy treasure is, there will thy heart be also.

If I love heaven, I willingly muse on heavenly things.

If I love the world, I rejoice at the felicity of the world, and grieve for the adversity thereof.

If I love the flesh, I shall fancy oftentimes those things that are pleasing to the flesh.

If I love the Spirit, I shall delight to think on things spiritual.

For whatsoever I love, thereof do I willingly speak and hear, and carry home with me the images thereof.

But blessed is the man, who for thy sake, O Lord, is willing to part with all creatures, who does violence to his nature, and through fervor of Spirit crucifieth the lusts of the flesh; that so with a serene conscience he may offer pure prayers unto thee, and, all earthly things both outwardly and inwardly being excluded, he may be meet to be admitted into the angelical choirs.

49.
Of the Desire of Everlasting Life, and how Great Rewards are promised to those that strive resolutely.

My son, when thou perceivest the desire of everlasting bliss to be given thee from above, and longest to depart out of the tabernacle of this body, that thou mayest contemplate my brightness without shadow of turning; open thy heart wide, and receive this holy inspiration with thy whole desire.

Give greatest thanks to the heavenly goodness, which treateth thee with such condescension, visiting thee mercifully, stirring thee up fervently, powerfully sustaining thee, lest through thine own weight thou fall down to earthly things.

Neither dost thou obtain this by thine own thought or endeavor, but by the mere condescension of heavenly grace and divine favor; to the end that thou mayest make further progress in all virtue, and obtain greater humility, and prepare thyself for future conflicts, and endeavor to cleave unto me with the whole affection of thy heart, and to serve me with fervent willingness.

2. My son, oftentimes the fire burneth, but the flame ascendeth not up without smoke.

So likewise the desires of some men burn towards heavenly things, and yet they are not free from the temptations of carnal affection.

And therefore it is not altogether purely for the honor of God, that they make such earnest requests to him.

So also oftentimes are thy desires, which thou hast pretended to be so serious and earnest.

For those desires are not pure and perfect, which are tainted with self-love.

3. Ask not for that which is delightful and profitable to thee, but for that which is acceptable to me, and which tendeth to my honor; for if thou judgest aright, thou oughtest to prefer and follow my appointment, rather than thine own desire, or anything whatever that is to be desired.

I know thy desire, and have heard thy frequent groanings.

Now thou longest to enjoy the glorious liberty of the sons

of God; now dost thou delight in the everlasting habitation, thy heavenly home full of joy; but that hour is not yet come; there still remaineth another time, and that a time of war, a time of labor and of trial.

Thou desirest to be filled with the chiefest good, but thou canst not attain it yet.

I AM he; wait thou for me (saith the Lord) until the kingdom of God shall come.

4. Thou art still to be tried upon earth, and to be exercised in many things.

Comfort shall be sometimes given thee, but the abundant fulness thereof shall not be granted.

Take courage therefore, and be valiant, as well in doing as in suffering things contrary to nature.

It is thy duty to put on the new man, and to be changed into another man.

It is thy duty oftentimes to do what thou wouldst not; thy duty to leave undone what thou wouldst do.

That which pleaseth others shall go well forward; that which pleaseth thee shall not speed.

That which others say shall be heard; what thou sayest shall be accounted nothing; others shall ask and shall receive; thou shalt ask but shalt not obtain.

5. Others shall be great in the praise of men, but about thee there shall be no word.

To others this or that shall be committed, but thou shalt be accounted a thing of no use.

At this nature will sometimes be troubled, and it is a great thing if thou bear it with silence.

In these and many such like things, the faithful servant of the Lord is wont to be tried how far he can deny and break his will in all things.

These is scarcely anything wherein thou hast such need to die to thyself, as in seeing and suffering those things that are contrary to thy will; especially when that is commanded to be done, which seemeth unto thee inconvenient, or useless.

And because thou being under authority darest not resist the higher power, therefore it seems hard to thee to walk at another's beck, and to feel that thou must give up all thine own will.

6. But consider, my son, the fruit of these labors, the end near at hand, and the reward exceeding great; and thou wilt

not grudge to bear them: rather thou wilt have the strongest comfort of thy patience.

For instead of that little of thy will, which now thou so readily forsakest, thou shalt always have thy will in heaven.

Yea, there thou shalt find all that thou canst wish, all that thou shalt be able to desire.

There thou shalt have within thy reach all good, without fear of losing it.

There shall thy will be ever one with me; it shall not covet any outward or selfish thing.

There none shall withstand thee, no man shall complain of thee, no man hinder thee, nothing come in thy way; but all things thou canst desire shall be there altogether present, and shall refresh thy whole affection, and fill it up to the brim.

There I will give thee glory for the reproach which here thou sufferedst, the garment of praise for heaviness, for the lowest place a kingly throne for ever.

There shall the fruit of obedience appear, the labor of repentance shall rejoice, and humble subjection shall be gloriously crowned.

7. At present then bend thyself humbly under all, and care not who said this or commanded it.

But take especial care, that whether thy superior, or thine inferior, or thine equal, require anything of thee, or do but insinuate their desire, thou take it all in good part, and with a sincere will endeavor to fulfil it.

Let one seek this, another that; let this man glory in this, the other in that, and be praised a thousand, thousand times; but do thou rejoice neither in this, nor in that, but in the contempt of thyself, and in the good pleasure and honor of me alone.

This is what thou art to wish, whether it be by life or by death, God may be always glorified in thee.

50.
How the Desolate ought to give up himself into the Hands of God.

O Lord God, holy Father, be thou blessed both now and for evermore, because as thou wilt, so is it done, and what thou doest is good.

Let thy servant rejoice in thee, not in himself nor in anything else; for thou alone art the true gladness, thou art my hope and my crown, thou art my joy and my honor, O Lord.

What hath thy servant, but what he hath received from thee, even without any merit of his?

Thine are all things, both what thou hast given, and what thou hast made.

I am poor, and in trouble, from my youth; and sometimes my soul is sorrowful even unto tears; sometimes also it is disturbed within itself by reason of sufferings which hang over me.

2. I long after the joy of peace, the peace of thy children I earnestly crave, who are fed by thee in the light of thy comfort.

If thou give peace, if thou pour into my heart holy joy, the soul of thy servant shall be full of melody, and shall become devout in thy praise.

But if thou withdraw thyself (as many times thou dost), he will not be able to run the way of thy commandments; but rather he will bow his knees, and smite his breast, because it is not now with him as it was in times past, when thy candle shined upon his head, and under the shadow of thy wings he was protected from the temptations which assaulted him.

3. O righteous Father, and ever to be praised, the hour is come that thy servant is to be proved.

O beloved Father, meet and right it is that in this hour thy servant should suffer somewhat for thy sake.

O Father, evermore to be honored, the hour is come, which from all eternity thou didst foreknow should come; that for a short time thy servant should outwardly be oppressed, but inwardly should ever live with thee.

That he should be for a little while despised, and humbled, and in the sight of men should fail, and be wasted with sufferings and languors; that he might rise again with thee in the morning dawn of the new light, and be glorified in heaven.

Holy Father, thou hast so appointed it, and so wilt have it; and that is fulfilled which thyself hast commanded.

4. For this is a favor to thy friend, that for love of thee he may suffer and be afflicted in the world, how often soever and by whom soever thou permittest such trials to befall him.

Without thy counsel and providence, and without cause, nothing cometh to pass in the earth.

It is good for me, Lord, that thou hast humbled me, that I

may learn thy righteous judgments, and may cast away all haughtiness of heart, and all presumption.

It is profitable for me, that shame hath covered my face, that I may seek to thee for consolation rather than to men.

I have learned also hereby to dread thine unsearchable judgments, who afflictest the just with the wicked, though not without equity and justice.

5. I give thee thanks, for that thou hast not spared my sins, but hast worn me down with bitter stripes, inflicting sorrows and sending anxieties upon me within and without.

There is none else under heaven who can comfort me, but thou only, O Lord my God, the heavenly physician of souls, who woundest and healest, who bringest down to hell and bringest back again.

Thy discipline shall be over me, and thy rod itself shall instruct me.

6. Behold, O beloved Father, I am in thy hands, I bow myself under the rod of thy correction.

Strike my back and my neck too, that my crookedness may be conformed to thy will.

Make me a dutiful and humble disciple of thine (as thou hast been wont to do me good), that I may be ready at every beck of thy divine pleasure.

Unto thee I commend myself and all mine to be corrected: it is better to be punished here than hereafter.

Thou knowest all and everything, and there is nothing in the conscience of man which can be hidden from thee.

Before anything is done, thou knowest that it will come to pass, and hast no need that any should teach thee, or admonish thee of those things which are being done on the earth.

Thou knowest what is expedient for my spiritual progress, and how greatly tribulation serves to scour off the rust of my sins.

Do with me according to thy good pleasure, and disdain me not for my sinful life, known to none so thoroughly and clearly as to thee alone.

7. Grant me, O Lord, to know that which is worth knowing, to love that which is worth loving, to praise that which pleaseth thee most, to esteem that highly which to thee is precious, to abhor that which in thy sight is filthy and unclean.

Suffer me not to judge according to the sight of the eyes, nor to give sentence according to the hearing of the ears of ignorant men: but with a true judgment to discern between things visible and spiritual, and above all to be ever searching after the good pleasure of thy will.

8. The minds of men are often deceived in their judgments; the lovers of the world too are deceived in loving only things visible.

What is a man ever the better, for being esteemed great by man?

The deceitful in flattering the deceitful, the vain man in extolling the vain, the blind in commending the blind, the weak in magnifying the weak, deceiveth him; and in truth doth rather put him to shame, while he so vainly praiseth him.

For what every one is in thy sight, that is he, and no more.

51.
That a Man ought to employ himself in Works of Humility, when Strength is wanting for Higher Employment.

My son, thou art not able always to continue in the more fervent desire of virtue, nor to persist in the higher pitch of contemplation; but thou must needs sometimes, by reason of original corruption, descend to inferior things, and bear the burden of this corruptible life, though against thy will, and with wearisomeness.

As long as thou carriest a mortal body, thou shalt feel weariness and heaviness of heart.

Thou oughtest therefore in the flesh oftentimes to bewail the burden of the flesh; for that thou canst not employ thyself unceasingly in spiritual studies and divine contemplation.

2. Then it is expedient for thee to flee to humble and outward works, and to refresh thyself with good actions, to await with a firm confidence my coming and heavenly visitation, to bear patiently thy banishment and the dryness of thy mind, till I shall again visit thee, and set thee free from all anxieties.

For I will cause thee to forget thy painful toils, and to enjoy thorough inward quietness.

I will spread open before thee the pleasant fields of holy scripture, that with an enlarged heart thou mayest begin to run the way of my commandments.

And thou shalt say, "The sufferings of this present time are not worthy to be compared with the glory that shall be revealed in us."

52.

That a Man ought not to account Himself as worthy of Comfort, but rather as deserving of Chastisement.

O Lord, I am not worthy of thy consolation nor of any spiritual visitation; and therefore thou dealest justly with me, when thou leavest me poor and desolate.

For though I could shed a sea of tears, still I should not be worthy of thy consolation.

I am not worthy of any thing but to be scourged and punished, because I have grievously and often offended thee, and in many things have greatly sinned.

Wherefore, all things duly considered, I am not worthy even of the least comfort.

But thou, O gracious and merciful God, who willest not that thy works should perish, to show the riches of thy goodness upon the vessels of mercy, vouchsafest even beyond all his desert to comfort thy servant above the manner of men.

For thy consolations are not like to the discourses of men.

2. What have I done, O Lord, that thou shouldst bestow any heavenly comfort upon me?

I remember not that I have done any good, but that I have been always prone to sin and slow to amendment.

This is true, and I cannot deny it. If I should say otherwise, thou wouldst stand against me, and there would be none to defend me.

What have I deserved for my sins, but hell and everlasting fire?

I confess in very truth that I am worthy of all scorn and contempt, nor is it fit that I should be remembered amongst thy devout servants.

And although I be unwilling to hear this, yet notwithstanding, for the truth's sake, I will lay open my sins against myself, that so the more readily I may be counted worthy to obtain thy mercy.

3. What shall I say, in that I am guilty and full of all confusion?

My mouth can utter nothing but this word only, "I have

sinned, O Lord! I have sinned; have mercy on me, pardon me."

Spare me a little that I may bewail my griefs, before I go into the land of darkness, a land covered with the shadow of death.

What dost thou so much require of a guilty and miserable sinner, as that he be contrite, and that he humble himself for his offences?

Of true contrition and humbling of the heart ariseth hope of forgiveness; the troubled conscience is reconciled; the favor of God, which was lost, is recovered; man is preserved from the wrath to come; and God and the penitent soul meet together with a holy kiss.

4. Humble contrition for sins is an acceptable sacrifice unto thee, O Lord, savoring much sweeter in thy presence than the perfume of frankincense.

This is also the pleasant ointment, which thou wouldst to be poured upon thy sacred feet; for a contrite and humbled heart thou never hast despised.

Here is the place of refuge from the angry face of the enemy here is amended and washed away whatever defilement and pollution hath been anywhere contracted.

53.
That the Grace of God is not given to those who relish Earthly Things.

My son, my grace is precious, it suffereth not itself to be mingled with outward things, nor with earthly consolations.

Thou oughtest therefore to cast away all hindrances to grace if thou desire to receive the inpouring thereof.

Choose therefore a secret place to thyself, love to live alone with thyself, desire the conversation of none; but rather pour out devout prayer unto God, that thou mayest keep thy soul contrite, and thy conscience pure.

Esteem thou the whole world as nothing, prefer attendance upon God before all outward things.

For thou wilt not be able to attend upon me, and at the same time to take delight in things transitory.

Thou oughtest to remove thyself away from thine acquaintance and friends, and not to depend on any temporal comfort.

So the blessed apostle Peter beseecheth, that the faithful of Christ would keep themselves in this world as strangers and pilgrims.

2. O how great a confidence shall he have at the hour of death, whom no affection to any earthly thing detaineth in the world.

But the having a heart so retired from all, the unspiritual mind doth not as yet comprehend; nor doth the carnal man know the liberty of him that is spiritual.

Notwithstanding, if he desire to be truly spiritual, he ought to renounce those who are far off, as well as those who are near unto him, and to beware of no man more than of himself.

If thou perfectly overcome thyself, thou shalt very easily bring all else under the yoke.

The perfect victory is, to triumph over ourselves.

For he that keepeth himself subject, in such sort that his affections be obedient to reason, and his reason in all things obedient to me; he truly is conqueror of himself, and lord of the world.

3. If thou desire to mount unto this height, thou must set out courageously, and lay the axe to the root, that thou mayest pluck up and destroy both that hidden inordinate inclination to self, and all love of private and earthly good.

On this sin almost all dependeth, whatsoever is thoroughly to be overcome; which evil being once vanquished and subdued, there will presently ensue great peace and tranquillity.

But because few labor perfectly to die unto themselves, or altogether to go out of themselves, therefore in themselves they remain entangled, nor can be lifted up in spirit above themselves.

But for him that desireth to walk freely with me, it is necessary that he mortify all his corrupt and inordinate affections and that he do not earnestly cleave to any creature with particular love.

54.
Of the different Stirrings of Nature and Grace.

My son, mark diligently the stirrings of nature and grace; for in a very contrary yet subtle manner do they move, so that they can hardly be distinguished but by him that is spiritually and inwardly enlightened.

All men indeed desire that which is good, and pretend some good in their words and deeds: and therefore under the show of good, many are deceived.

Nature is crafty, and seduceth many, ensnareth and deceiveth them, and always proposeth herself for her end and object.

But grace walketh in simplicity, abstaineth from all show of evil, sheltereth not herself under deceits, doeth all things purely for God's sake, in whom also she finally resteth.

2. Nature is unwilling and loth to die, or to be kept down, or to be overcome, or to be in subjection, or readily to be subdued:

But grace studieth self-mortification, resisteth sensuality, seeketh to be in subjection, is desirous to be kept under, and wisheth not to use her own liberty. She loveth to be kept under discipline, and desireth not to rule over any, but always to live and remain and be under God, and for God's sake is ready humbly to bow down unto all.

Nature striveth for her own advantage, and considereth what profit she may reap by another.

Grace considereth not what is profitable and convenient unto herself, but rather what may be for the good of many.

Nature willingly receiveth honor and reverence.

Grace faithfully attributeth all honor and glory unto God.

3. Nature feareth shame and contempt.

Grace rejoiceth to suffer reproach for the name of JESUS.

Nature loveth leisure and bodily ease.

Grace cannot be unemployed, but cheerfully embraceth labor.

Nature seeketh to have things that are curious and beautiful, and abhorreth those which are cheap and coarse.

Grace delighteth in what is plain and humble, despiseth not

rough things, and refuseth not to be clothed in that which is old and worn.

Nature respecteth temporal things, rejoiceth at earthly gain, sorroweth for loss, is irritated by every little injurious word.

Grace looketh to things eternal, cleaveth not to things temporal, is not disturbed at losses, nor soured with hard words; because she hath placed her treasure and joy in heaven, where nothing of it perisheth.

4. Nature is covetous, doth more willingly receive than give, and loveth to have things private and her own.

Grace is kind of heart, and ready to share with others, shunneth private interest, is content with a little, judgeth that it is more blessed to give than to receive.

Nature inclineth a man to the creature, to his own flesh, to vanities, and to wandering hither and thither.

Grace draweth him unto God and to every virtue, renounceth the creature, avoideth the world, hateth the desires of the flesh, restraineth wanderings abroad, blusheth to be seen in public.

Nature is willing to have some outward solace, whereby she may receive delight of the senses.

Grace seeketh consolation in God alone, and to have delight in the highest good above all visible things.

5. Nature turneth everything to her own gain and profit, she cannot bear to do anything without reward, but for every kindness she hopeth to obtain either what is equal, or what is better, or at least praise or favor; and is very earnest to have her works and gifts much valued.

Grace seeketh no temporal thing, nor desireth any other reward save God alone, and asketh not more of temporal necessaries, than what may serve her for the obtaining of things eternal.

6. Nature rejoiceth to have many friends and kinsfolk, she glorieth of noble place and noble birth, she smileth on the powerful, fawneth upon the rich, applaudeth those who are like herself.

Grace loveth even her enemies, and is not puffed up with multitude of friends; and thinketh not greatly of high birth, unless it be joined with more exalted virtue.

Grace favoreth the poor rather than the rich, sympathizeth more with the innocent than with the powerful, rejoiceth with the true man, not with the deceitful.

She is ever exhorting good men to strive for the best gifts; and by all virtue to become like to the Son of God.

Nature quickly complaineth of want and of trouble.

Grace endureth need with firmness and constancy.

7. Nature referreth all things to herself, striveth and argueth for herself.

Grace bringeth back all to God, from whence originally they proceed; she ascribeth no good to herself, nor doth she arrogantly presume; she contendeth not, nor preferreth her own opinion before others; but in every matter of sense and understanding she submitteth herself unto the eternal wisdom and the divine judgment.

Nature is eager to know secrets and to hear news; she loveth to appear abroad and to make proof of many things by her own senses; she desireth to be acknowledged, and to do things for which she may be praised and admired.

Grace careth not to hear news, nor to understand curious matters (because all this taketh its rise from the old corruption of man), seeing that upon earth there is nothing new, nothing durable.

Grace teacheth therefore to restrain the senses, to shun vain complacency and ostentation, humbly to hide those things that are worthy of admiration and praise, and from everything and in every knowledge to seek profitable fruit, and the praise and honor of God.

She will not have herself nor that which pertaineth to her publicly praised, but desireth that God should be blessed in his gifts, because that of mere love he bestoweth all things.

8. This grace is a supernatural light, and a certain special gift of God, and the proper mark of the elect, and a pledge of everlasting salvation. It raiseth up a man from earthly things to love the things of heaven, and from being carnal maketh him a spiritual man.

The more therefore nature is depressed and subdued, so much the more is grace infused, and every day by new visitations the inward man is created anew according to the image of God.

55.
Of the Corruption of Nature, and the Efficacy of Divine Grace.

O Lord my God, who hast created me after thine own image and likeness, grant me this grace, which thou hast showed to be so great and so necessary to salvation; that I may overcome my most evil nature, which draweth me to sin and to perdition.

For I feel in my flesh the law of sin contradicting the law of my mind, and leading me captive to the obeying of sensuality in many things; neither can I resist the passions thereof, unless thy most holy grace being infused into my heart do assist me.

2. There is need of thy grace, O Lord, and of large supplies thereof, that nature may be overcome, which is ever prone to evil from her youth.

For through Adam the first man, nature being fallen and corrupted by sin, the penalty of this stain hath descended upon all mankind, in such sort that "nature" itself, which by thee was created good and upright, is now taken for the sin and infirmity of corrupted nature; because the inclination thereof left unto itself draweth to evil and to lower things.

For the small power which remaineth is, as it were, a spark lying hid in the ashes.

This is natural reason itself, encompassed about with great darkness, yet still retaining power to discern the difference between true and false, good and evil; although it be unable to fulfil all that it approveth, and enjoyeth no longer the full light of the truth, nor soundness in its own affections.

3. Hence it is, O my God, that I delight in thy law after the inward man, knowing thy commandment to be good, just and holy, reproving also all evil and sin, as things to be avoided.

But with the flesh I serve the law of sin, in that I obey my senses rather than my reason.

Hence it is, that to will what is good is present with me, but how to perform it I find not.

Hence it is that I often purpose many good things, but because grace is wanting to help my infirmity, upon a light resistance I start back and faint.

Hence it cometh to pass that I know the way of perfection, and see clearly enough what I ought to do; but being pressed down by the weight of mine own corruption, I rise not to that which is more perfect.

4. O Lord, how entirely needful is thy grace for me, to begin any good work, to go on with it, and to accomplish it.

For without that grace I can do nothing, but in thee I can do all things, when thy grace doth strengthen me.

O grace heavenly indeed! Without which our most worthy actions are nothing, nor are any gifts of nature to be esteemed.

Neither arts nor riches, beauty nor strength, wit nor eloquence, are of any value before thee, without thy grace, O Lord.

For gifts of nature are common to good and bad, but the peculiar gift of the elect is grace or love; and they that bear this honorable mark, are accounted worthy of everlasting life.

So eminent is this grace that neither the gift of prophecy, nor the working of miracles, nor any speculation, how high soever, is of any esteem without it.

No, not even faith, nor hope, nor any other virtues, are unto thee acceptable, without charity and grace.

5. O most blessed grace, that makest the poor in spirit rich in virtues, and renderest him who is rich in many goods humble in heart!

Come thou down unto me, come and replenish me early with thy comfort, lest my soul faint for weariness and dryness of mind.

I beseech thee, O Lord, that I may find grace in thy sight; for thy grace is sufficient for me, though other things that nature desireth be not obtained.

Although I be tempted and vexed with many tribulations, yet I will fear no evil, so long as thy grace is with me.

This alone and by itself is my strength; this alone giveth advice and help.

This is stronger than all enemies, and wiser than all the wise.

6. Thy grace is the mistress of truth, the teacher of discipline, the light of the heart, the solace in affliction, the driver away of sorrow, the expeller of fear, the nurse of devotion, the mother of tears.

Without this, what am I but a withered branch, and an unprofitable stock only meet to be cast away!

Let thy grace therefore, O Lord, always prevent and follow me, and make me to be continually given to good works, through the Son Jesus Christ. Amen.

56.
That we ought to deny Ourselves, and imitate Christ by the Cross.

My son, the more thou canst go out of thyself, so much the more wilt thou be able to enter into me.

As to desire no outward thing produceth inward peace, so the forsaking of ourselves inwardly, joineth us into God.

I will have thee learn perfect resignation of thyself to my will, without contradiction or complaint.

Follow thou me: "I AM the way, the truth, and the life." Without the way, there is no going; without the truth, there is no knowing; without the life, there is no living. I AM the way, which thou oughtest to follow, the truth, which thou oughtest to trust; the life, which thou oughtest to hope for.

I AM the way inviolable, the truth infallible, the life that cannot end.

I AM the straitest way, the highest truth, the true life, the blessed life, the life uncreated.

If thou remain in my way, thou shalt know the truth, and the truth shall make thee free, and thou shalt lay hold on eternal life.

2. If thou wilt enter into life, keep the commandments.

If thou wilt know the truth, believe me.

If thou wilt be perfect, sell all.

If thou wilt be my disciple, deny thyself utterly.

If thou wilt possess a blessed life, despise this life present.

If thou wilt be exalted in heaven, humble thyself in this world.

If thou wilt reign with me, bear the cross with me.

For only the servants of the cross can find the way of blessedness and of true light.

3. O Lord Jesus, forasmuch as thy life was narrow and despised by the world, grant me to imitate thee, though the world despise.

For the servant is not greater than his Lord, nor the disciple above his Master.

Let thy servant be exercised in thy life, for therein consisteth my salvation and my true holiness.

Whatsoever I read or hear besides it, doth not give me full refreshment or delight.

4. My son, inasmuch as thou knowest and hast read all these things, happy shalt thou be, if thou do them.

"He that hath my commandments and keepeth them, he it is that loveth me; and I will love him, and will manifest myself unto him," and will make him sit together with me in my Father's kingdom.

O LORD JESUS, as thou hast said and promised, so let it come to pass, and grant that I may not be wholly undeserving of this favor.

I have received the cross from thy hand; I have borne it, and will bear it even unto death, even as thou hast laid it upon me.

Verily the life of a Christian is a cross, yet is it also a guide to paradise.

I have begun, I may not go back, neither is it fitting to leave that which I have undertaken.

5. Courage, then, brethren, let us go forward together! JESUS will be with us.

For the sake of JESUS we have undertaken this cross, for the sake of JESUS let us persevere in the cross.

He will be our helper, who is also our guide and forerunner.

Behold, our king entereth in before us, and he will fight for us.

Let us follow manfully, let no man fear any terrors; let us be prepared to die valiantly in battle, nor bring shame on our glory by flying from the cross.

57.
That a man should not be too much dejected, even when he falleth into some Defects.

My son, patience and humility in adversity are more pleasing to me, than much comfort and devotion in prosperity.

Why art thou so grieved for every little matter spoken against thee?

Although it had been much more, thou oughtest not to have been moved.

But now let it pass; it is not the first that hath happened, nor is it anything new; neither shall it be the last, if thou live long.

Thou art courageous enough so long as nothing adverse befalleth thee.

Thou canst give good counsel also, and canst strengthen others with thy words; but when any tribulation suddenly cometh to thy door, thou failest in counsel and in strength.

Observe then thy great frailty, of which thou too often hast experience in small matters.

It is notwithstanding intended for thy good, when these and such like trials happen to thee.

2. Put it out of thy heart as well as thou canst; and if it touch thee, yet let it not cast thee down, nor long perplex thee.

At least bear it patiently, if thou canst not bear it joyfully.

Although thou be unwilling to hear it, and conceive indignation thereat, yet restrain thyself, and suffer no ill-advised word to pass out of thy mouth, whereby Christ's little ones may be offended.

The storm which is now raised shall quickly be appeased and inward grief shall be sweetened by the return of grace.

I yet live, saith the Lord, and am ready to help thee, and to give thee greater comfort than before, if thou put thy trust in me, and call devoutly upon me.

3. Be more patient of soul, and gird thyself to greater endurance.

All is not lost, although thou feel thyself very often afflicted or grievously tempted.

Thou art a man, and not God; thou art flesh, not an angel.

How canst thou look to continue always in the same state of virtue, when an angel in heaven hath fallen, as also the first man in paradise?

I am he who lift up the mourners in safety and soundness, and those that know their own weakness I advance to mine own divine glory.

4. O LORD, blessed be thy word, more sweet unto my mouth than honey and the honey-comb.

What should I do in these so great tribulations and straits, unless thou didst comfort me with thy holy words?

What matter is it, how much or what I suffer, so I may at length attain to the haven of salvation?

Grant me a good end, grant me a happy passage out of this world.

Be mindful of me, O my God, and direct me in the right way to thy kingdom. Amen.

58.
That High Matters and God's Secret Judgments are not to be narrowly inquired into.

My son, beware thou dispute not of high matters, nor of the secret judgments of God, why this man is so left, and that man taken into such great favor; why also one man is so much afflicted, and another so greatly advanced.

These things are beyond the reach of man, neither is it in the power of any reason or disputation to search out the judgments of God.

When therefore the enemy suggesteth these things unto thee, or some curious people raise the question, let thy answer be that of the prophet, "Thou art just, O Lord, and thy judgment is right."

And again, "The judgments of the Lord are true and righteous altogether."

My judgments are to be feared, not to be discussed; for they are such as cannot be comprehended by the understanding of man.

2. In like manner I advise thee not to inquire, nor dispute of the merits of holy men, which of them is holier than the other, or which shall be the greater in the kingdom of heaven.

These things oftentimes breed strife and unprofitable contentions, they also nourish pride and vain-glory; from whence spring envy and dissensions, whilst one will proudly prefer this, and the other another.

To desire to know and search out such things answereth no good end, and is painful to righteous souls; for I am not the God of dissension, but of peace; which peace consisteth rather in true humility, than in self-exaltation.

3. Some are carried with zeal of affection towards these or those; but this is rather human love than divine.

I am he who made all the saints; I gave them grace; I obtain for them glory.

I know what every one hath deserved; I have prevented them with the blessings of my goodness.

I foreknew my beloved ones before the beginning of the world.

I chose them out of the world: they chose not me first.

I called them by grace, I drew them by mercy, I led them safely through sundry temptations.

I have poured into them glorious consolations, I give them perseverance, I crown their patience.

4. I acknowledge both the first and the last; I embrace all with love inestimable.

I am to be praised in all my saints; I am to be blessed above all things, and to be honored in every one whom I have thus gloriously exalted and predestinated, without any merits of their own.

He therefore that despiseth one of the least of mine, honoreth not the greatest; for that I made both the small and the great.

And he that dispraiseth any of my saints, dispraiseth me also, and all the rest in the kingdom of heaven.

These all are one through the bond of love; their thought is the same, their will is the same, and they all love one another.

5. But still (which is a far higher thing), they love me more than themselves or any merits of their own.

For being ravished above self and self-love, they are wholly carried out to love me, in whom also they rest with full fruition.

Nothing can turn them back, nothing can press them down; for being full of the eternal truth, they burn with the fire of unquenchable charity.

Let therefore carnal and natural men who can love nothing but their own selfish joys, forbear to dispute of the state of God's saints. Such men add and take away according to their own fancies, not as it pleaseth the eternal truth.

6. Many are ignorant, especially those who are but little enlightened; and these can seldom love any with a perfect spiritual love.

They are as yet much drawn by a natural affection and human friendship to this man or to that. And according to the experience they have of themselves in their earthly affections, so do they frame imaginations of things heavenly.

But there is an incomparable distance between the things which the imperfect imagine and the things which they that are enlightened are enabled to behold through revelation from above.

7. Beware therefore, my son, that thou handle not with vain curiosity things which exceed thy knowledge; but rather let this be thy great business and endeavor, to attain if it be but the meanest place in the kingdom of God.

Even if any man should know who exceeds another in sanctity, or who is accounted the greatest in the kingdom of heaven; what would this wisdom profit him, unless he should humble himself the more in my sight, and then should rise up to give the greater praise to my name, in proportion to this his knowledge?

Far more acceptable to God is he that thinketh of the greatness of his own sins, and the smallness of his virtues, and how far he is from the perfection of saints, than he who disputeth of their greatness or littleness.

8. They are well, yea right well, contented, if men would but content themselves, and refrain from vain discourses.

They glory not of their own merits, inasmuch as they ascribe no goodness to themselves, but attribute all to me, who of mine infinite love have given them all things.

They are filled with so great love of God, and with such an overflowing joy, that there is no glory nor happiness that is or that can be wanting unto them.

All the saints, the higher they are in glory, the more humble are they in themselves, and the nearer and dearer unto me.

And therefore it is written, "That they did cast their crowns before God, and fell down on their faces before the Lamb, and adored him that liveth for ever and ever."

9. Many inquire, who is the greatest in the kingdom of God, who know not whether they shall ever be numbered among the least.

It is a great thing to be even the least in heaven, where all are great; for they all shall be called, and shall be, the sons of God.

"The least shall become a thousand," and "the sinner of an hundred years shall die."

For when the disciples asked who should be greatest in the kingdom of heaven, they received such an answer as this:

"Except ye be converted, and become as little children, ye shall not enter the kingdom of heaven; whosoever therefore shall humble himself as this little child, the same is greatest in the kingdom of heaven."

10. Woe be unto them who disdain to humble themselves willingly with little children; because the low gate of the kingdom of heaven will not give them entrance.

Woe also to the rich, who have here their consolation; for whilst the poor enter into the kingdom of God, they shall stand lamenting without.

Rejoice ye that be humble, and ye poor be ye filled with joy, for yours is the kingdom of God, if at least ye walk according to the truth.

59.
That all our Hope and Trust are to be fixed in God alone.

Lord, what is my confidence which I have in this life? Or what is the greatest comfort I can derive from anything under heaven?

Is it not thou, O Lord my God, whose mercies are without number?

Where hath it ever been well with me without thee? Or when could it be ill with me, when thou wert present?

I had rather be poor for thy sake, than rich without thee.

I rather choose to be a pilgrim on earth with thee, than without thee to possess heaven. Where thou art, there is heaven: and where thou art not, there is death and hell.

Thou art all my desire, and therefore I must needs sigh and call and earnestly pray unto thee.

For I have none fully to trust to, none that can seasonably help me in my necessities, but only thee, my God.

Thou art my hope, thou my confidence; thou art my comforter, and in all things most faithful unto me.

2. All men seek their own gain. Thou settest forward my salvation and my profit only, and turnest all things to my good.

Although thou exposest me to divers temptations and adversities, yet thou orderest all this to mine advantage, who art wont to try thy beloved ones in a thousand ways.

In which trial of me thou oughtest no less to be loved and praised, than if thou didst fill me full of heavenly consolations.

3. In thee therefore, O Lord God, I place my whole hope and refuge: on thee I rest in my tribulation and anguish: for I find all to be weak and inconstant, whatsoever I behold save in thee.

For many friends cannot profit, nor strong helpers assist, nor prudent counsellors give a profitable answer, nor the books of the learned afford comfort, nor any precious substance deliver, nor any place, however retired and lovely, give shelter, unless thou thyself dost assist, help, strengthen, console, instruct, and guard us.

4. For all things, that seem to belong to the attainment of peace and felicity, without thee are nothing, and do bring in truth no felicity at all.

Thou therefore art the end of all that is good, the height of life, the depth of all that can be spoken; and to hope in thee above all things, is the strongest comfort of thy servants.

To thee therefore do I lift up mine eyes; in thee my God, the Father of mercies, do I put my trust.

Bless and sanctify my soul with thy heavenly blessings, that it may become thy holy habitation, and the seat of thine eternal glory; and let nothing be found in this temple of thy dignity, which shall offend the eyes of thy majesty.

According to the greatness of thy goodness and the multitude of thy mercies look upon me, and hear the prayer of thy poor servant, who is exiled far from thee in the land of the shadow of death.

Protect and keep the soul of me, the meanest of thy servants, amidst the many dangers of this corruptible life, and by thy grace accompanying direct me along the way of peace to the land of everlasting light. *Amen.*

THE FOURTH BOOK

CONCERNING THE COMMUNION.

A Devout Exhortation to the Holy Communion.

"Come unto me all ye that labor and are heavy laden, and I will refresh you," saith the Lord.

"The bread which I will give is my flesh, which I will give for the life of the world."

"Take ye and eat; this is my body which is given for you: do this in remembrance of me."

"He that eateth my flesh and drinketh my blood; dwelleth in me, and I in him."

"The words which I have spoken unto you are spirit and life."

1.

With how great Reverence Christ ought to be received.

These are thy words, O Christ, the everlasting truth, though not spoken all at one time, nor written in one place.

Because therefore they are thine and true, they are all thankfully and faithfully to be received by me.

They are thine, and thou hast pronounced them: and they are mine also, because thou hast spoken them for my salvation.

I cheerfully receive them from thy mouth, that they may be the more deeply implanted in my heart.

They arouse me, those most gracious words, so full of sweetness and of love; but mine own offences do dishearten me, and an impure conscience driveth me back from the receiving of so many mysteries.

The sweetness of thy words doth encourage me, but the multitude of my sins weigheth me down.

2. Thou commandest me to come confidently unto thee, if I would have part with thee; and to receive the food of immortality, if I desire to obtain everlasting life and glory.

"Come unto me (sayest thou), all ye that labor and are heavy laden, and I will refresh you."

O sweet and loving word in the ear of a sinner, that thou, my Lord God, shouldst invite the poor and needy to the participation of thy most holy body and blood!

But who am I, Lord, that I should presume to approach unto thee?

Behold the heaven of heavens cannot contain thee, and thou sayest, "Come ye all unto me."

3. What meaneth this so gracious a condescension and this so loving invitation?

How shall I dare to come, who know not any good in myself, whereupon I may presume?

How shall I bring thee into my house, I that have so often offended thy most gracious countenance?

Angels and archangels stand in awe of thee: holy and righteous men do fear thee: and sayest thou, "Come ye all unto me?"

Unless thou, O Lord, didst say this, who would believe it to be true?

And unless thou didst command it, who could attempt to draw near?

Behold, Noah that just man labored a hundred years in the making of the ark, that he might be saved with a few; and how can I in one hour's space prepare myself to receive with reverence the maker of the world?

4. Moses, thy great servant, and thine especial friend, made an ark of incorruptible wood, which also he covered over with the finest gold, wherein to lay up the tables of the law: and I a corrupted creature, how shall I dare so unconcernedly to receive the maker of the law and the giver of life?

Solomon the wisest of the kings of Israel bestowed seven years in building a magnificent temple to the praise of thy name.

He also celebrated the feast of dedication thereof eight days together; he offered a thousand peace-offerings, and he solemnly set the ark of the covenant in the place prepared for it with the sound of trumpets, and great joy.

And I the most miserable and poorest of men, how shall I bring thee into my house, I that can scarce spend one half hour in true devotion? And would that I could even once spend something like one half hour in worthy and due manner!

5. O my God, how earnestly did they study and endeavor to please thee!

Alas, how little is that which I do! How short a time do I spend when I am preparing myself to receive the communion!

Seldom am I wholly collected; very seldom indeed am I cleansed from all distraction.

And yet surely in the life-giving presence of thy Godhead no unbecoming thought ought to intrude itself, nor should any creature occupy my heart; for it is not an angel, but the Lord of angels, whom I am about to entertain.

6. And yet very great is the difference between the ark of the covenant with its relics, and thy most pure body with its unspeakable virtues; between those legal sacrifices, figures of things to come, and the true sacrifice of thy body, the fulfillment of all ancient sacrifices.

Why therefore am I not more ardent and zealous in seeking thine adorable presence?

Why do I not prepare myself with greater solicitude to receive thy holy things? Whereas those holy ancient patriarchs and prophets, yea kings also and princes, with the whole people, showed such an affectionateness of devotion to thy divine service.

7. The most devout king David danced before the ark of God with all his might, calling to mind the benefits bestowed in time past upon his forefathers. He made instruments of sundry kinds, he set forth psalms, and appointed them to be sung with joy; he also oftentimes himself sang to the harp, being inspired with the grace of the Holy Ghost. He taught the people of Israel to praise god with their whole hearts, and with voices full of harmony to bless and praise him every day.

If so great devotion was then used, and such celebrating of divine praise was kept up before the ark of the testament; what reverence and devotion ought now to be preserved by me and all Christian people, during the ministration of this sacrament, in receiving the most precious body and blood of Christ.

8. Many run to divers places to visit the memorials of saints departed, are full of admiration at hearing of their deeds, behold with awe the spacious buildings of their temples, and find their affections moved by whatever is connected with their memory.

But behold, thou art thyself here present with me on thine altar, my God, Saint of saints, Creator of men, and Lord of the angels.

Often in looking after such memorials, men are moved by curiosity, and by the novelty of fresh sights, whilst little or no fruit of amendment is carried home; particularly when they go from place to place with levity, without a true penitent heart.

But here, in this holy sacrament, thou art wholly present, my God, the man Christ JESUS: here, to all worthy and devout receivers, is granted an abundant fruit of eternal salvation.

There is here to attract men nothing that savors of levity, of curiosity, or of sense; nothing but firm faith, devout hope, and sincere charity.

9. O God, the invisible creator of the world, how wonderfully dost thou deal with us; how sweetly and graciously dost

thou dispose of all things with thine elect, to whom thou offerest thyself to be received in this sacrament!

For this verily exceedeth all understanding. This specially draweth the hearts of the devout, and inflameth their affections.

For even thy true faithful ones, who dispose their whole life to amendment, by this most precious sacrament oftentimes gain much of the grace of devotion, and love of virtue.

10. O the admirable and hidden grace of this sacrament, which only the faithful ones of Christ do know. But the unbelieving and such as are slaves unto sin cannot have experience thereof!

In this sacrament spiritual grace is conferred, and the strength which was lost is restored in the soul, and the beauty which by sin had been disfigured again returneth.

This grace is sometimes so great, that out of the fulness of devotion here given, not the mind only, but the weak body also, feeleth great increase of strength bestowed on it.

11. Nevertheless our coldness and negligence is much to be bewailed and pitied, that we are not drawn with greater affection to receive Christ, in whom doth consist all the hope of those that are to be saved, and all their merit.

For he himself is our sanctification and redemption; he himself is the comfort of those who are here but travellers, and the everlasting fruition of saints.

It is therefore much to be lamented that many do so little consider this salutary mystery, which causeth joy in heaven, and preserveth the whole world.

Alas for the blindness and hardness of man's heart, that doth not more deeply weigh so unspeakable a gift; but rather cometh by the daily use thereof to regard it little or nothing!

12. For if this most holy sacrament were to be celebrated in one place only, and consecrated by one only priest in the world; with how great desires dost thou think would men be affected to that place, and toward such a priest of God, that they might be witnesses of the celebration of these divine mysteries?

But now many are made priests, and in many places Christ is offered; that the grace and love of God to man may appear so much the greater, the more widely this sacred communion is spread over the world.

Thanks be unto thee, O merciful JESUS, thou eternal shepherd, that thou hast vouchsafed to refresh us, who are poor and in a state of banishment, with thy precious body and blood, and to invite us to the receiving of these mysteries with the words even of thine own mouth, saying, "Come unto me all ye that labor and are heavy laden, and I will refresh you."

2.

That the great Goodness and Love of God is exhibited to Man in this Sacrament.

In confidence of thy goodness and great mercy, O Lord, I draw near, as one sick to the healer, as one hungry and thirsty to the fountain of life, needy to the king of heaven, a servant unto my Lord, a creature to my creator, a desolate soul to my merciful comforter.

But whence is this to me, that thou vouchsafest to come unto me? What am I, that thou shouldst grant thine own self unto me?

How dare a sinner appear before thee? And how is it that thou dost vouchsafe to come unto a sinner?

Thou knowest thy servant, thou knowest that he hath in him no good thing, for which thou shouldst grant him this favor.

I confess therefore mine own unworthiness, I acknowledge thy goodness, I praise thy tender mercy, and give thee thanks for this thy transcendent love.

For thou doest this for thine own sake, not for any merits of mine; to the end that thy goodness may be better known unto me, thy love more abundantly poured down, and thy gracious humility more eminently set forth.

Since therefore it is thy pleasure, and thou hast commanded that it should be so, this that seemeth to thee good pleaseth me also, and would that mine iniquity might be no hindrance!

2. O most sweet and most merciful Jesus, how great reverence and thanksgiving, together with perpetual praise, is due unto thee for the receiving of thy sacred body and blood, whose preciousness no man is able to express!

But on what shall my thoughts dwell at this communion, in thus approaching unto my Lord, whom I am not able duly to honor, and yet whom I cannot but desire devoutly to receive?

3. What can I think on better, and more profitable, than utterly to humble myself before thee, and to exalt thine infinite goodness over me?

I praise thee, my God, and will exalt thee forever. I do despise myself, and cast myself down before thee, into the deep of mine own unworthiness.

Behold, thou art the Holy of Holies, and I the scum of sinners!

Behold, thou inclinest thyself unto me, and I am not worthy so much as to look up unto thee!

Behold, thou comest unto me; it is thy will to be with me; thou invitest me to thy banquet.

Thou art willing to give me heavenly food and bread of angels to eat, which is indeed no other than thyself the living bread, which camest down from heaven, and givest life unto the world.

4. Behold, from whence doth this love proceed! What gracious condescension shineth forth herein! How great thanks and praises are due unto thee for these benefits?

O how great and profitable was thy counsel, when thou didst ordain it! How sweet and pleasant the banquet, when thou gavest thyself to be our food!

O how admirable is this thy working, O Lord, how mighty is thy power, how unspeakable thy truth!

For thou didst speak the word and all things were made; and this was done which thou thyself commandest.

5. A thing much to be admired, worthy of all faith, and surpassing man's understanding, that thou, my Lord God, true God and man, shouldst offer thyself wholly to us in a little bread and wine, and therein become our inexhaustible support.

Thou who art the Lord of the universe, and standest in need of none, art pleased to dwell in us by means of this thy sacrament.

Do thou preserve my heart and body undefiled, that with a cheerful and pure conscience I may be able often to receive to my everlasting health, those mysteries which thou didst specially ordain and institute for thine own honor, and for a never-ceasing memorial of thyself.

6. Rejoice, O my soul, and give thanks unto God, for so noble a gift, and so precious a consolation, left unto thee in this vale of tears.

For as often as thou callest to mind this mystery, and receivest the body of Christ, so often dost thou go over the work of thy redemption, and art made partaker of all the merits of Christ.

For the love of Christ is never diminished, and the greatness of his propitiation is never exhausted.

Therefore thou oughtest to dispose thyself hereunto by a constant fresh renewing of thy mind, and to weigh with attentive consideration the great mystery of salvation.

So great, so new, and so joyful ought it to seem unto thee, when thou comest to these holy mysteries, as if on this same day Christ first descending into the womb of the virgin were become man, or hanging on the cross did this day suffer and die for the salvation of mankind.

3.
That it is profitable to Communicate often.

Behold, O Lord, I come unto thee, that I may be comforted in thy gift, and be delighted in thy holy banquet, which thou, O God, hast of thy goodness prepared for the poor.

Behold in thee is all whatsoever I can or ought to desire; and thou art my salvation and my redemption, my hope and my strength, my honor and glory.

Make therefore this day the soul of thy servant joyful; for unto thee, O Lord JESUS, have I lifted up my soul.

I desire to receive thee now with devotion and reverence. I desire to bring thee into my house, that with Zaccheus I may be blessed by thee, and be numbered amongst the children of Abraham.

My soul thirsteth to receive thy body and blood, my heart longeth to be joined to thee.

2. Give thyself to me, and it sufficeth; for beside thee there is no comfort.

Without thee I cannot be; without thy visitation I cannot endure to live.

And therefore I must needs often draw near unto thee, and receive thee for the medicine of my soul; lest haply I faint by the way, if I be deprived of this heavenly food.

For so, most merciful JESUS, thou once didst say, when preaching to the people, and curing divers diseases, "I will not send them home fasting, lest they faint in the way."

Deal thou therefore in like manner now with me, who hast vouchsafed to leave thyself in this sacrament for the comfort of the faithful.

For thou art the sweet refection of the soul; and he that eateth thee worthily shall be partaker and heir of everlasting glory.

It is needful for me, who so often fall into error and sin, and so quickly wax dull and faint, that by frequent prayer and confession, and receiving of thy holy body and blood, I renew, cleanse, and inflame myself, lest haply, by long abstaining, I fall away from my holy purposes.

3. For the imaginations of man are prone unto evil from his youth, and unless some divine remedy help him, he quickly falleth away to worse things.

This holy communion therefore draweth men back from evil, and strengtheneth them in good.

For if I be now so often negligent and cold when I communicate; what would become of me if I received not this remedy and sought not after so great a help?

Although every day I be not fit nor well prepared; I will endeavor notwithstanding at due times to receive the divine mysteries, and to be partaker of so great a grace.

For this is the one chief consolation of faithful souls, so long as they are absent from thee in this mortal body, that being mindful of their God, they often receive their beloved with devout mind.

4. O the wonderful condescension of thy tender mercy towards us that thou, O Lord God, the creator and giver of life to all spirits, doth vouchsafe to come unto a poor soul, and with thy whole deity and humanity to appease the hunger thereof!

O happy minds and blessed souls, who have the privilege of receiving thee, their Lord God, with devout affection, and in so receiving thee are permitted to be filled with spiritual joy!

Oh how great a Lord they entertain! How beloved a guest do they harbor! How delightful a companion do they receive! How faithful a friend do they welcome! How lovely and noble a spouse do they embrace! Even him who is to be loved above all things that are loved, and above all things that can be desired.

O thou the most sweet, most beloved, let heaven and earth, and all that adorns them, be silent in thy presence. For what praise and beauty soever they have, it is received from thy bounteous condescension, and shall never equal the grace and beauty of thy name, whose wisdom is infinite.

4.
That many Benefits are bestowed upon those that communicate devoutly.

Lord, my God, do thou present thy servant with the blessings of thy goodness, that I may approach worthily and devoutly to thy glorious sacrament.

Stir up my heart unto thee, and deliver me from all dulness. Visit me with thy salvation, that I may taste in spirit thy sweetness, which plentifully lieth hid in this sacrament as in a fountain.

Enlighten also mine eyes to behold so great a mystery, and strengthen me with undoubting faith to believe it.

For it is thy work, and no human power; thy sacred institution, not man's invention.

For of himself no man is able to comprehend and understand these things, which surpass the understanding even of angels.

What portion then of so high and sacred a mystery shall I, unworthy sinner, dust and ashes, be able to search out and comprehend?

2. O Lord, in the simplicity of my heart, with a good and firm faith, and at thy commandment, I draw near unto thee with hope and reverence; and do truly believe that thou art here present in this sacrament, both God and man.

Thy will is, that I should receive thee, and that I should unite myself unto thee in charity.

Wherefore I implore thy mercy, and do crave thy special grace, to the end I may wholly be dissolved and overflow with love unto thee, and never hereafter suffer any external consolation to enter in.

For this most high and precious sacrament is the health both of soul and body, the medicine for all spiritual languor; hereby my vices are cured, my passions bridled, my temptations overcome or at least weakened; greater grace is infused, virtue begun is increased, faith is confirmed, hope strengthened, and love inflamed and enlarged.

3. For thou hast bestowed, and still oftentimes dost bestow many benefits in this sacrament upon thy beloved ones that communicate devoutly, O my God, the protector of my soul, the strengthener of human frailty, and the giver of all inward comfort.

Thou impartest unto them much comfort against sundry tribulations; and liftest them up from the depth of their own dejected state, to hope in thy protection; and dost inwardly refresh and enlighten them with new grace, so that they who at first and before communion felt themselves full of anxiety and heartlessness, afterwards, being refreshed with heavenly meat and drink, do find in themselves a change for the better.

And in such a way of dispensation thou dealest with thine elect, that they may truly acknowledge, and clearly prove, how great their infirmity is, and what goodness and grace they obtain from thee.

For they of themselves are cold, dull and undevout; but by thee they are made fervent, cheerful, and full of devotion.

For who is there, that approaching humbly unto the fountain of sweetness, doth not carry away from thence at least some little sweetness?

Or who standing by a great fire, receiveth not some small heat thereby?

And thou art a fountain always full and overflowing, a fire ever burning and never decaying.

4. Wherefore if I am not permitted to draw out of the full fountain itself, nor to drink my fill, I will notwithstanding set my lips to the mouth of this heavenly conduit, that I may receive from thence at least some small drop to refresh my thirst, that so I may not be wholly dried up.

And though I cannot as yet be altogether heavenly, nor so full of love as the cherubim and seraphim, yet notwithstanding I will endeavor to apply myself earnestly to devotion, and prepare my heart to obtain if it be but some small spark of divine fire, by the humble receiving of this life-giving sacrament.

And whatsoever is hereunto wanting in me, O merciful JESUS, most holy Saviour, do thou bountifully and graciously supply for me, thou who hast vouchsafed to call us all unto thee, saying, "Come unto me all ye that labor and are heavy laden, and I will refresh you."

5. I indeed labor in the sweat of my brows, I am vexed with grief of heart, I am burdened with sins, I am troubled

with temptations, I am entangled and oppressed with many evil passions; and there is none to help me, none to deliver and save me, but thou O Lord God my Saviour, to whom I commit myself and all that is mine, that thou mayest keep watch over me, and bring me safe to life everlasting.

Receive me for the honor and glory of thy name, thou who hast prepared thy body and blood to be my meat and drink.

Grant, O Lord God, my Saviour, that by frequenting the celebration of thy mysteries, the zeal of my devotion may grow and increase.

5.
Of the Dignity of this Sacrament, and of the Ministerial Function.

If thou hadst the purity of an angel, and the sanctity of St. John Baptist, thou wouldst not be worthy to receive or to administer this sacrament.

For it is not within the compass of the deserts of men, that man should consecrate and administer this sacrament of Christ, and receive for food the bread of angels.

Great is this mystery; and great is the dignity of those to whom is granted that which is not permitted to angels.

For only priests rightly ordained in the church have power to celebrate this sacrament, and to consecrate the body of Christ.

The priest is indeed the minister of God, using the word of God, by God's command and appointment: but God is there the principal author, and invisible worker; to whom is subject all that he shall please, and whom everything that he commandeth doth obey.

2. Thou oughtest therefore more to believe God Almighty in this most excellent sacrament, than thine own sense or any visible sign.

And therefore thou are to approach this holy work with fear and reverence.

Consider attentively with thyself, and see what that is, whereof the ministry is delivered unto thee by the laying on of the bishop's hand.

Behold, thou art made a priest, and consecrated to celebrate the Lord's sacrament; take heed now that thou offer this sacrifice to God faithfully and devoutly, and at fit opportunities, and conduct thyself so as thou mayest be without reproof.

Thou hast not lightened thy burden, but art now bound with a straiter band of discipline, and art obliged to a more perfect degree of sanctity.

A priest ought to be adorned with all graces, and to give example of good life to others.

His life and conversation should not be in the common ways of mankind, but with the angels in heaven, or with perfect men on earth.

3. A priest clad in sacred garments is Christ's deputy, that with all supplication and humility he may beseech God for himself and for the whole people.

Neither ought he to cease from prayer and holy oblation, till he prevail to obtain grace and mercy.

When a priest doth celebrate the holy eucharist, he honoreth God, he rejoiceth the angels, he edifieth the church, he helpeth the living, he maketh mention of the departed, and maketh himself partaker of all good things.

6.
An Enquiry concerning Spiritual Exercise before Communion.

When I weigh thy worthiness, O Lord, and mine own vileness, I tremble exceedingly, and am confounded within myself.

For if I come not unto thee, I fly from life, and if I unworthily intrude myself, I incur thy displeasure.

What therefore shall I do, O my God, my helper, and my counsellor in all necessity?

2. Teach thou me the right way, appoint me some brief exercise, suitable to this holy communion.

For it is good for me to know how I should reverently and religiously prepare my heart for thee, for the profitable receiving of this sacrament of thine, or for the celebrating of so great and divine a sacrifice.

7.

Of thoroughly searching our own Conscience, and of Holy Purposes of Amendment.

Above all things, God's priest ought to come to celebrate and to receive this sacrament with very great humility of heart, and with reverential supplication, with a full faith and a dutiful regard for God's honor.

Examine diligently thy conscience, and to the uttermost of thy power purify and cleanse it with true contrition and humble confession; so as there may be nothing in thee, that may be burdensome unto thee, or that may breed in thee remorse of conscience, and hinder thy free access to the throne of grace.

Be grieved at the recollection of all thy sins in general, and in particular bewail and lament thy daily transgressions.

And if thou hast time, confess unto God in the secret of thine heart all the miserable evils of thy disordered passions.

2. Lament thou and grieve, that thou art yet so carnal and worldly, so unmortified in thy passions, so full of the motions of concupiscence:

So unwatchful over thy outward senses, so often entangled with many vain fancies:

So much inclined to outward things, so negligent in things inward and spiritual:

So prone to laughter and unbridled mirth, so indisposed to tears and compunction:

So prompt to ease and pleasures of the flesh, so dull to strictness of life and zeal:

So curious to hear news and to see beautiful sights, so slack to embrace what is humble and low:

So covetous of abundance, so niggardly in giving, so fast in keeping:

So inconsiderate in speech, so reluctant to keep silence:

So uncomposed in manners, so fretful in action:

So eager about food, so deaf to the word of God:

In such a hurry to rest, so slow to labor:

So wakeful in vain conversation, so drowsy at sacred services:

So hasty to arrive at the end thereof, so inclined to be wandering and inattentive:

So negligent in the prayers, so lukewarm in celebrating the holy eucharist, so dry and heartless in receiving it:

So quickly distracted, so seldom wholly gathered into thyself:

So suddenly moved to anger, so apt to take displeasure against another:

So ready to judge, so severe to reprove:

So joyful in prosperity, so weak in adversity:

So often making good resolutions, and yet bring them at last to so poor effect.

3. These and other thy defects being confessed and bewailed with sorrow and great displeasure at thine own infirmity, make thou a firm resolution always to be amending thy life, and to be endeavoring always after a farther progress in holiness.

Then with full resignation and with thy whole will, do thou, to the honor of my name, offer up thyself a perpetual whole burnt-offering on the altar of thy heart, faithfully committing thy body and soul unto me.

And then thou mayest be accounted worthy to draw near to celebrate this eucharistical sacrifice unto God, and to receive profitably the sacrament of my body and blood.

4. For man hath no oblation more worthy, nor any means greater for the destroying of sin, than to offer himself unto God purely and wholly, in the holy communion of the body and blood of Christ.

And when a man shall have done what lieth in him, and shall be truly penitent, how often soever he shall come to me for pardon and grace, "As I live," saith the Lord, "who will not the death of a sinner, but rather that he be converted and live, I will not remember his sins any more, but they shall all be forgiven him."

8.
Of the Oblation of Christ on the Cross, and of Resignation of Ourselves.

Of my own will did I offer up myself unto God the Father for thy sins. My hands were stretched forth on the cross, and my body laid bare, so that nothing remained in me that was not wholly turned into a sacrifice for the appeasing of the divine majesty.

In like manner oughtest thou also to offer thyself willingly unto me in the holy communion, as a pure and sacred oblation, with all thy strength and affections, and to the utmost of thine inward faculties.

What do I require of thee more, than that thou study to resign thyself entirely unto me?

Whatsoever thou givest besides thyself is of no value in my sight, for I seek not thy gifts, but thee.

2. As it would not suffice thee to have all things whatsoever, without me; so neither can it please me, whatsoever thou givest, if thou give not thyself.

Offer up thyself unto me, and give thyself wholly for God, and thine offering shall be acceptable.

Behold I offered up myself wholly unto my Father for thee, and gave my whole body and blood for thy food, that I might be wholly thine, and that thou mightest continue mine to the end.

But if thou abidest in thyself, and dost not offer thyself up freely unto my will, thine oblation is not entire, neither will there be perfect union between us.

Therefore a free offering of thyself into the hands of God ought to go before all thine actions, if thou desire to obtain liberty and grace.

For this cause so few become inwardly free and enlightened, because they are loath wholly to deny themselves.

My sentence standeth sure, "Unless a man forsake all, he cannot be my disciple." If thou therefore desire to be my disciple, offer up thyself unto me with thy whole heart.

9.
That we ought to offer up Ourselves and All that is Ours unto God, and to pray for All.

Thine, O Lord, are all things that are in heaven, and that are in earth.

I desire to offer up myself unto thee, as a free oblation, and to continue thine forever.

O Lord, in the simplicity of my heart I offer myself unto

thee this day, in humble submission, for a sacrifice of perpetual praise, and to be thy servant forever.

Receive thou me, with this holy oblation of thy precious body; which offering I make to thee this day in the presence of angels invisibly attending; and may this be for my good and the good of all thy people.

2. I offer unto thee, O Lord, all my sins and offences, which I have committed before thee, from the day wherein I first could sin, to this hour. I offer them upon thy merciful altar, that thou mayest consume and burn them all with the fire of thy love; that thou mayest wash out all the stains of my sins. Cleanse my conscience from all offences, and restore to me again thy grace which I have lost by sin, forgiving me all my offences, and receiving me mercifully to the kiss of peace.

3. What can I do for my sins, but humbly confess and bewail them, and unceasingly entreat thy favor and propitiation?

I beseech thee, hear me graciously, when I stand before thee my God.

All my sins are very displeasing unto me. I will never commit them any more; but I grieve, and will grieve for them as long as I live, and am purposed to repent and according to the utmost of my power to make restitution.

Forgive me, O God, forgive me my sins for the sake of thy holy name; save thou my soul which thou hast redeemed with thy most precious blood.

Behold I commit myself unto thy mercy, I resign myself into thy hands.

Deal with me according to thy goodness, not according to my wickedness and iniquity.

4. I offer up also unto thee all whatsoever is good in me, although it be very small and imperfect, that thou mayest amend and sanctify it. Make it grateful and acceptable unto thee, and always perfect it more and more; and bring me also, who am a slothful and unprofitable creature, to a good and blessed end.

5. I offer up also unto thee all the pious desires of devout persons, the necessities of parents, friends, brethren, sisters, and of all those that are dear unto me, and that have done good either to myself or to others for thy love.

Also all that have desired of me to pray for them and theirs.

Grant that all may receive the help of thy grace, the aid of thy consolation, protection from dangers, deliverance from pain; that they being freed from all evils, may with joy return abundant thanksgivings unto thee.

6. I offer up also unto thee my prayers and intercessions for those especially who have in any thing wronged, grieved, or slandered me, or have done me any damage or displeasure.

I pray for all those also, whom I have at any time vexed, troubled, grieved, and scandalized by words or deeds, knowingly or in ignorance; that it may please thee to forgive us all our sins and offences, one against another.

Take away from our hearts, O Lord, all suspiciousness, indignation, wrath, and contention, and whatsoever may hurt charity, and lessen brotherly love.

Have mercy, O Lord, have mercy on those that crave thy mercy, give grace unto them that stand in need thereof, and make us such as that we may be counted worthy to enjoy thy grace and go forward to life eternal. *Amen.*

10.
That the Holy Communion is not lightly to be forborne.

Thou oughtest often to have recourse to the fountain of grace and of divine mercy, to the fountain of goodness and of all purity; that thou mayest be healed of thy sins and passions, and be made more strong and vigilant against all the temptations and deceits of the devil.

The enemy, knowing what exceeding great profit and restoring power cometh by the holy communion, endeavoreth by all means and occasions to withdraw and hinder faithful and devout persons from partaking therein.

2. Thus it is that some persons, when they are prepared to fit themselves for holy communion, suffer from the suggestions of Satan worse than before.

That wicked spirit himself (as it is written in Job) cometh amongst the sons of God, to trouble them according to his accustomed malice, or to render them over-fearful and perplexed; that so he may diminish their affections, or by direct assaults take away their faith, to the end he may prevail on them, if possible, either altogether to forbear communicating, or at least to come with lukewarmness.

But there is no heed at all to be taken of these his crafty and fanciful suggestions, be they never so filthy and hideous, but all such vain imaginations are to be turned back upon his own head.

Thou must despise him and laugh him to scorn, nor dare to omit the holy communion on account of his assaults, or for the troubles which he raiseth within thee.

3. Oftentimes also a too great solicitude for the obtaining a certain height of devotion, and a kind of anxiety about the confession of sins, hindereth thee. Follow herein the counsel of the wise, and lay aside all anxiety and scrupulousness; for it hindereth the grace of God, and overthroweth the devotion of the mind.

Do not omit the holy communion for every small vexation and trouble, but rather proceed at once to confess thy sins, and cheerfully forgive others whatever offences they have done against thee.

And if thou hast offended any, humbly crave pardon, and God will readily forgive thee.

4. What availeth it to delay long the confession of thy sins, or to defer the holy communion?

Make thyself thoroughly clean as soon as possible. Spit out the poison with all speed, make haste to apply this sovereign remedy, and thou shalt find it to be better with thee than if thou long defer it.

If thou omit it today for one cause, perhaps tomorrow another of greater force may occur to thee; and so thou mayest be hindered a long time from communion, and grow more and more unfit.

As quickly as ever thou canst, shake off from thyself all present heaviness and sloth. For it is of no use to continue long in disquietude, or to be going on long with a disturbed conscience, and so for every day impediments to separate thyself from this divine service.

Yea, it is very hurtful to defer the communion long, for this usually brings on heavy spiritual drowsiness.

Alas, some lukewarm undisciplined persons do willingly delay confessing their sins, and defer the holy communion, lest they should be engaged to keep a stricter watch over themselves.

5. O how poor and mean is their love, how weak their devotion, who so easily put off the holy communion!

How happy is he and how acceptable to God, who so ordereth his life, and in such purity keepeth his conscience, that he is prepared and well-disposed to communicate even every day, if it were in his power, and if it might be done without being seen of men.

If a person do sometimes abstain out of humility, or by reason of some lawful cause preventing him, he is to be commended so far as it ariseth from a feeling of reverence.

But if a spiritual drowsiness have crept over him, he must bestir himself, and do what lieth in him; and the Lord will assist his desire, for the good will he hath thereto, which is what God doth chiefly respect.

6. But when any lawful hindrance doth happen, he will yet always have a good will, and a pious intention to communicate, and so shall he not lose the fruit of this sacrament.

For any devout person may every day and every hour profitably and without let draw near to Christ in spiritual communion.

And yet on certain days, and at times appointed, he ought to receive sacramentally, with affectionate reverence, the body and blood of his Redeemer, and rather seek the honor and glory of God, than his own comfort.

For he communicateth mystically, and is invisibly refreshed, as often as he devoutly calleth to mind the mystery of the incarnation and the passion of Christ, and is inflamed with the love of him.

7. He that prepareth not himself, except only when a festival draweth near, or when custom compelleth him thereunto, shall too often be unprepared.

Blessed is he that offereth up himself as a whole burnt offering to the Lord, as often as he doth administer or receive the holy communion.

Be not too slow nor yet hurried in celebrating, but keep the accustomed manner of those with whom thou livest.

Thou oughtest not to be tedious and troublesome to others, but to observe the received custom; according to the appointment of our fathers; and rather to yield thyself up to the edification of others, than to thine own devotion or feelings.

11.

That the Body and Blood of Christ and the Holy Scriptures are most necessary unto a Faithful Soul.

Blessed Lord JESUS, how great is the happiness of a devout soul that feasteth with thee in thy banquet; where there is set no other food to be eaten but thyself, the only Beloved, and most to be desired above all he desires of the heart!

And verily it would be a sweet thing unto me in thy presence to pour out tears from the very bottom of my heart, and with grateful Magdalene to wash thy feet with tears.

But where now is that devotion? Where that plentiful effusion of holy tears?

Surely in the sight of thee and thy holy angels, my whole heart ought to be inflamed, and even to weep for joy.

For in this sacrament I have thee truly present, though hidden under another representation.

2. For to behold thee in thine own divine brightness mine eyes would not be able to endure, nor could even the whole world stand in the splendor of the glory of thy majesty.

Herein then dost thou have regard to my weakness, that thou dost veil thyself under this outward sacramental sign.

Him I do really possess and adore whom the angels adore in heaven; but I, for the present and in the meantime, by faith: they, by sight, and without a veil.

I ought to be content with the light of true faith, and to walk therein, until the day of everlasting brightness dawns, and the shadows of figures pass away.

But when that which is perfect is come, the use of sacraments shall cease; because the blessed, in their heavenly glory, need not any sacramental remedy.

For they rejoice without end in the presence of God, beholding his glory face to face; and being transformed from glory to glory into his image, they taste the WORD of God made flesh, as he was from the beginning, and as he abideth forever.

3. Whilst I am mindful of these wonderful things, it becometh tedious unto me, even all spiritual comfort whatso-

ever, because so long as I behold not my Lord openly in his own glory, I make no account at all of whatsoever I see or hear in this world.

Thou art witness unto me, O God, that nothing can comfort me, no creature can give me rest, but thou only, my God, whom I long to contemplate everlastingly.

But this is not possible, so long as I linger in this mortality.

Therefore I must frame myself to much patience; and submit myself to thee in all my desires.

For even thy saints, O Lord, who now rejoice with thee in the kingdom of heaven whilst they lived, waited in faith and in great patience for the coming of thy glory. What they believed, I believe also; what they hoped for, I hope for; whither they are arrived, I trust I shall arrive by thy grace.

In the meantime I will walk in faith, strengthened by the examples of the saints.

I have also holy books for my comfort and for the glass of my life, and above all these, thy most holy body and blood for a remedy and refuge.

4. For I perceive two things to be very particularly necessary for me in this life, without which it would be unsupportable unto me.

Whilst I am detained in the prison of this body, I acknowledge myself to stand in need of two things, namely, food and light.

Unto me then thus weak and helpless thou hast given thy sacred body, for the refreshment both of my soul and body; and thy word thou hast set as a light unto my feet.

Without these two I should not be able to live; for the word of God is the light of my soul, and thy sacrament the bread of life.

These also may be called the two tables, set on the one side and on the other, in the treasury and jewel-house of the holy church.

One table is that of the sacred altar, having the holy bread, that is the precious body of Christ; the other is that of the divine law, containing holy doctrine, teaching men the right faith, and steadily conducting them forward even to that within the veil, where is the holy of holies.

Thanks be unto thee, O Lord JESUS, thou light of everlasting light for that table of holy doctrine which thou hast prepared for us by thy servants the prophets and apostles and other teachers.

5. Thanks be unto thee, O thou Creator and Redeemer of mankind, who to manifest thy love to the whole world, hast prepared a great supper, wherein thou hast set before us to be eaten, not the typical lamb, but thine own most sacred body and blood, rejoicing all the faithful with this holy banquet, and replenishing them to the full with the cup of salvation, in which are all the delight of paradise; and the holy angels do feast with us, but yet with a more happy sweetness.

6. O how great and honorable is the office of God's priests, to whom it is given with sacred words to consecrate this sacrament of the LORD of glory; with their lips to bless, with their hands to hold, with their own mouth to receive, and also to administer to others!

O how clean ought those hands to be, how pure that mouth, how holy that body, how unspotted that heart, where the author of purity so often entereth!

Nothing but what is holy, no word but what is good and profitable, ought to proceed from the mouth of him who so often receiveth this sacrament of Christ.

7. Simple and chaste ought to be the eyes that are wont to behold the body of Christ; the hands should be pure and lifted up to heaven, that use to touch these emblems of the Creator of heaven and earth.

Unto the priests especially it is said in the law, "Be ye holy, for that I the LORD your God am holy."

8. O Almighty God, do thou assist us with thy grace, that we who have undertaken the office of the priesthood, may be able to serve thee worthily and devoutly, in all purity, and with a good conscience.

And if we live not in so great innocency as we ought to do, grant to us at the least worthily to lament the sins which we have committed; and in the spirit of humility, and with the full purpose of a good will, to serve thee more earnestly for the time to come.

12.

*That he who is about to communicate with Christ
ought to prepare himself with great Diligence.*

I am the lover of purity and the giver of all sanctity.

I seek a pure heart, and there is the place of my rest.

Make ready for me a large upper room furnished, and I will keep the passover at thy house with my disciples.

If thou wilt have me come unto thee, and remain with thee, purge out the old leaven, and make clean the habitation of thy heart.

Shut out the whole world, and all the throng of sins: sit thou as it were a sparrow alone upon the house-top, and think over thy transgressions in the bitterness of thy soul.

For every one that loveth will prepare the best and fairest place for his beloved; for herein is known the affection of him that entertaineth his beloved.

2. Know thou notwithstanding, that the merit of no action of thine is able to make this preparation sufficient, although thou shouldst prepare thyself a whole year together, and have nothing else in thy mind.

But it is out of my mere grace and favor that thou art permitted to come to my table. As if a beggar were invited to a rich man's dinner, and he hath no other return to make to him for his benefits, but to humble himself and give him thanks.

Do what lieth in thee, and do it diligently; not for custom, not for necessity; but with fear and reverence and affection receive the body and blood of thy beloved Saviour, when he vouchsafeth to come unto thee.

I am he that have called thee, I have commanded it to be done, I will supply what is wanting in thee; come thou and receive me.

3. When I bestow on thee the grace of devotion, give thanks to thy God; not because thou art worthy, but because I have had mercy on thee.

If thou have it not, but rather dost feel thyself dry: be instant in prayer, sign and knock, and give not over until thou have received some crumb or drop of saving grace.

Thou hast need of me, I have no need of thee.

Neither comest thou to sanctify me, but I come to sanctify and make thee holy.

Thou comest that thou mayest be sanctified by me, and united unto me, that thou mayest receive new grace, and be stirred up anew to amendment of life.

Neglect not this grace, but prepare thy heart with all diligence, and receive thy beloved into thy soul.

4. But thou oughtest not only to prepare thyself to devo-

tion before communion, but carefully also to preserve thyself therein, after thou hast received this sacrament.

Nor is the careful guard of thyself afterwards less required, than devout preparation before.

For a good guard afterwards is the best preparation against for the obtaining of greater grace.

For if a person gives himself up at once too much to outward consolations, he is rendered thereby greatly indisposed to devotion.

Beware of much talk, remain in some secret place, and enjoy thy God; for thou hast him, whom all the world cannot take from thee.

I am he, to whom thou oughtest wholly to give up thyself, that so thou mayest now live the rest of thy time, not in thyself, but in me, and be free from all anxious care.

13.

That the Devout Soul with the whole Heart to seek Union with Christ in this Sacrament.

How shall I obtain this favor, O Lord, to find thee alone and by thyself, to open unto thee my whole heart, and to enjoy thee even as my soul desireth? So that henceforth none may look upon me, nor any creature move me, nor have regard to me: but that thou alone mayest speak unto me, and I to thee, as the beloved is wont to speak to his beloved, and a friend to banquet with his friend.

This I beg, this I long for, that I may be wholly united unto thee, and may withdraw my heart from all created things, and may learn more and more by means of this sacred communion, and the often celebrating thereof, to relish things heavenly and eternal.

Ah, Lord God, when shall I be wholly united to thee, and absorbed by thee, and become altogether forgetful of myself?

"Thou in me, and I in thee!" so also grant that we may both continue together in one.

2. Verily, thou art my beloved, the choicest among thousands, in whom my soul is well pleased to dwell all the days of her life.

Verily, thou art my peacemaker, in whom is highest peace

and true rest, out of whom is labor and sorrow and infinite misery.

Verily, thou art a God that hidest thyself, and thy counsel is not with the wicked, but thy speech is with the humble and simple of heart.

O how sweet is thy spirit, O Lord, who to the end thou mightest show forth thy sweetness toward thy children, dost vouchsafe to feed them with the bread which is full of all sweetness, even that which cometh down from heaven.

Surely there is no other nation so great, that hath God so nigh unto them, as thou our God art present to all thy faithful ones, unto whom, for their daily comfort and for the raising up of their hearts to heaven, thou bestowest thyself.

3. For what other nation is there of such high renown, as the Christian people?

Or what creature under heaven, is there so beloved, as the devout soul, into which God himself entereth, to nourish it with himself?

O unspeakable grace! O admirable condescension! O immeasurable love specially bestowed on man!

But what return shall I make to the Lord for this grace, for charity so unparalleled?

There is nothing else that I am able to present more acceptable, than to offer my heart wholly to my God, and to unite it most inwardly unto him.

Then shall all my inward parts rejoice, when my soul shall be perfectly united unto God.

Then will he say unto me, "If thou art willing to be with me, I am willing to be with thee."

And I will answer him, "Vouchsafe, O Lord, to remain with me, for I will gladly be with thee.

"This is my whole desire, that my heart be united unto thee."

14.
Of the Fervent Desire of some Devout Persons to receive the Body and Blood of Christ.

How great is the abundance of thy goodness, O Lord, which thou hast laid up for them that fear thee!

When I call to mind some devout persons, who approach to this thy sacrament, O Lord, with the greatest devotion and affection, I am oftentimes confounded and blush within myself, that I come with such lukewarmness, yea, coldness, to thine altar and the table of sacred communion.

I grieve that I remain so dry, and without hearty affection; that I am not wholly inflamed in thy presence, O my God, and not so earnestly drawn and affected as many devout persons have been.

For there have been some who out of a vehement desire of the holy communion, and strong affection of heart could not restrain themselves from weeping. And these with desire, both of soul and body, earnestly longed after thee, O God, the fountain of life: not being otherwise able to allay or satisfy their hunger, but by receiving thy body and blood with all delight and spiritual eagerness.

2. O the truly ardent faith of such a clear argument of thy sacred presence!

For they truly know their Lord in the breaking of bread, whose heart within them so vehemently burneth, whilst thou, O blessed JESUS, dost walk and converse with them.

Such affection and devotion as this, love and fervency so vehement, are too often far from me.

Be thou favorable unto me, O merciful JESUS, sweet and gracious Lord, and grant to me, thy poor needy creature, sometimes at least in this holy communion to feel if it be but a small portion of thy hearty love, that my faith may become more strong, my hope in thy goodness may be increased, and that charity once perfectly kindled within me, after the tasting of this heavenly manna, may never decay.

3. But thy mercy is able to grant me the grace which I long for, and in the day when it shall please thee to visit me most mercifully with the spirit of fervor.

For although I burn not with such vehement desire as those who are so specially devoted to thee; yet notwithstanding by thy grace I long for this great and burning desire, praying from the heart that I may participate with all such thy fervent lovers, and be numbered among them in their holy company.

15.
That the Grace of Devotion is obtained by Humility and Denial of Ourselves.

Thou oughtest to seek the grace of devotion instantly, to ask it earnestly, to wait for it with patience and confidence, to receive it with thankfulness, to keep it humbly, to work with it diligently, and to commit the term and manner of this heavenly visitation to God, until it shall please him to come unto thee.

Thou oughtest especially to humble thyself when thou feelest inwardly little or no devotion; and yet not to be too much dejected, nor to grieve inordinately.

God often giveth in one short moment that which he for a long time hath denied: he giveth sometimes in the end, that which in the beginning of thy prayer he deferred to grant.

2. If grace were always presently given, and were ever at hand with a wish, weak man could not well bear it.

Therefore the grace of devotion is to be waited for with good hope and humble patience.

Nevertheless, do thou impute it to thyself, and to thine own sins, when this grace is not given thee, or when it is secretly taken away.

It is sometimes but a small matter that hindereth and hideth grace from us; at least if anything can be called small, and not rather a weighty matter, which hindereth so great a good.

But if thou remove this, be it great or small, and perfectly overcome it, thou shalt have thy desire.

3. For immediately, as soon as thou givest thyself to God from thy whole heart, and seekest not this nor that, according to thine own pleasure or will, but settlest thyself wholly in him, thou shalt find thyself united to him, and at peace; for nothing can afford so sweet a relish, nothing can be so delightful, as the good pleasure of the divine will.

Whosoever therefore, with a single heart, lifteth up his intention to God, and keepeth himself clear of all inordinate love or dislike of any created thing, he shall be the most fit to receive grace, and meet for the gift of true devotion.

For the Lord bestoweth his blessings there, where he findeth the vessels empty.

And the more perfectly a man forsaketh these low things, and the more he dieth to himself by contempt of himself, the more speedily shall grace come, and shall enter in the more plentifully, and shall lift up the free heart higher.

4. Then shall he see, and flow together, and wonder, and his heart shall be enlarged within him, because the hand of the Lord is with him, and he hath put himself wholly into his hand, even for ever and ever.

Behold, thus shall the man be blessed, who seeketh God with his whole heart, and receiveth not his soul in vain.

This man in receiving the holy eucharist, obtaineth the great favor of divine union; for that he looketh not to his own devotion and comfort, but above all devotion and comfort to the honor and glory of God.

16.

That we ought to lay open our Necessities to Christ, and to crave His Grace.

Thou most sweet and loving Lord, whom I now desire to receive with all devotion, thou knowest my infirmities, and the necessities which I endure; in how many sins and evils I am involved; how often I am weighed down, tempted, disturbed, and defiled.

Unto thee I come for remedy, I entreat of thee consolation and support.

I speak to thee who knowest all things, to whom all my inward thoughts are open, and who alone canst perfectly comfort and help me.

Thou knowest what good things I stand in most need of, and how poor I am in all virtue.

2. Behold, I stand before thee poor and naked, calling for grace, and imploring mercy.

Refresh thy hungry supplicant, inflame my coldness with the fire of thy love, enlighten my blindness with the brightness of thy presence.

Do thou for me turn all earthly things into bitterness, all things grievous and contrary into patience, all low and created things into contempt and oblivion.

Lift up my heart to thee in haven, and do not send me away to wander over the earth.

Be thou alone sweet unto me from henceforth for evermore; for thou alone art my meat and drink, my love and my joy, my sweetness and all my good.

3. O that with thy presence thou wouldst wholly inflame, burn, and conform me unto thyself; that I might be made one spirit with thee, by the grace of inward union, and by the meltings of ardent love!

Suffer me not to go away from thee hungry and dry, but deal mercifully with me, as oftentimes thou hast dealt wonderfully with thy saints.

What marvel is it if I should be wholly inflamed by thee, and from myself fail and come to nothing; since thou art a fire always burning and never decaying, a love purifying the heart and enlightening the understanding.

17.

Of Fervent Love and Vehement Desire to receive Christ.

With deep devotion and ardent love, with all affection and fervor of heart, I desire to receive thee, O Lord, as many saints and devout persons have desired thee, when they were partakers of thy holy communion; who in holiness of life were to thee most pleasing, and who in devotion also were most fervent.

O my God, my everlasting love, my whole good, my never ending happiness, I desire to receive with the most earnest affection and the most worthy awe and reverence, that any of the saints ever had, or could feel toward thee.

2. And although I be unworthy to entertain all those feelings of devotion, nevertheless I offer unto thee the whole affection of my heart, as if I alone had all these most ardent longings.

Yea, and all that a dutiful mind can conceive and desire, do I with the deepest reverence and most inward affection, offer and present unto thee.

I desire to reserve nothing to myself, but freely and most cheerfully to sacrifice unto thee myself and all that is mine.

O Lord my God, my Creator and my Redeemer, I do

desire to receive thee this day with such affection, reverence, praise and honor, with such gratitude, worthiness and love, with such faith, hope and purity, as thy most holy mother, the glorious virgin Mary, received and desired thee, when to the angel who declared unto her glad tidings of the mystery of the incarnation she humbly and devoutly answered, "Behold the handmaid of the Lord, let it be done unto me according to thy word."

3. And as thy blessed forerunner, the most excellent among the saints, John Baptist, rejoicing in thy presence, leaped for joy of the Holy Ghost, whilst he was yet shut up in his mother's womb; and afterwards seeing JESUS walking among men, humbled himself very greatly, and said with devout affection, "The friend of the bridegroom that standeth and heareth him rejoiceth greatly because of the voice of the bridegroom" in like manner I also wish to be inflamed with great and holy desires, and to offer myself up to thee from my whole heart.

Wherefore also I offer and present unto thee the triumphant joys, the fervent affections, the ecstasies, the supernatural illuminations and celestial visions of all devout hearts, with all the virtues and praises ever celebrated by all creatures in heaven, and in earth, for myself, and for all such as are commended to me in prayer; that by all thou mayest worthily be praised and for ever glorified.

4. Receive, O Lord my God, my wishes and desires of giving thee infinite praise, and blessing that hath no bounds, which according to the measure of thine ineffable greatness, are most justly due unto thee.

These praises I render unto thee, and long to render them every day and every moment. And with all entreaty and affectionateness I do invite and beseech all heavenly spirits, and all thy faithful servants, to render with me thanks and praises unto thee.

5. Let all people, nations, and languages praise thee, and magnify thy holy and precious name with highest joy and ardent devotion.

And let all who reverently and devoutly celebrate thy most high sacrament, and receive it with full faith, be accounted worthy to find grace and mercy at thy hands, and pray with humble supplication in behalf of me a sinner.

And when they shall have attained to their desired devotion, and joyful union with thee, and shall have departed from thy holy heavenly table, well comforted and marvellously refreshed, O let them vouchsafe to remember my poor soul.

18.

That a Man should not be a Curious Searcher into the Holy Sacrament, but an Humble Follower of Christ, submitting his Sense to Divine Faith.

Thou oughtest to beware of curious and unprofitable searching into this most profound sacrament, if thou wilt not be plunged into the depths of doubt. .

He that is a searcher of my majesty shall be overpowered by its glory. God is able to work more than man can understand.

A dutiful and humble inquiry after the truth is allowable, provided we be always ready to be taught, and study to walk in the sound doctrine of the church.

2. It is a blessed simplicity when a man leaves the difficult ways of questions and disputings, and goes forward in the plain and firm path of God's commandments.

Many have lost devotion, whilst they sought to search into things too high.

Faith is required at thy hands, and a sincere life; not height of understanding, nor deep enquiry into the mysteries of God.

If thou dost not understand, nor conceive these things that are beneath thee, how shalt thou be able to comprehend those which are above thee?

Submit thyself unto God, and humble thy sense to faith, and the light of knowledge shall be given thee, in such degree as shall be profitable and necessary for thee.

3. Some are grievously tempted about faith and this holy sacrament; but this is not to be imputed to themselves, but rather to the enemy.

Be not thou anxious herein; do not dispute with thine own thoughts, nor give any answer to doubts suggested by the devil; but trust the words of God, trust his saints and prophets, and the wicked enemy will flee from thee.

It oftentimes is very profitable to the servant of God to endure such things.

For the devil tempteth not unbelievers and sinners, whom he has already secure possession of; but faithful and religious persons he in various ways tempteth and vexeth.

4. Go forward therefore with simple and undoubting faith, and with the reverence of a supplicant approach thou this holy sacrament; and whatsoever thou art not able to understand, commit without care to Almighty God.

God deceiveth thee not. He is deceived that trusteth too much to himself.

God walketh with the simple, revealeth himself to the humble, giveth understanding to the little ones, openeth the sense to pure minds, and hideth grace from the curious and proud.

Human reason is feeble and may be deceived, but true faith cannot be deceived.

5. All reason and natural search ought to follow faith, not to go before it, nor to break in upon it.

For faith and love do here specially take the lead, and work in hidden ways, in this most holy, most supremely excellent sacrament.

God, who is eternal, and incomprehensible, and of infinite power, doeth things great and unsearchable in heaven and in earth, and there is no tracing out of his marvellous works.

If the works of God were such, as that they might be easily comprehended by human reason, they could not be justly called marvellous or unspeakable.

Heartwarming Books
of
Faith and Inspiration

INSPIRATIONAL FAVORITES

EUGENIA PRICE
St. Simon's Trilogy

☐	13682	Beloved Invader	$2.25
☐	14089	Maria	$2.50
☐	14406	New Moon Rising	$2.50
☐	14195	Lighthouse	$2.50
☐	13305	St. Simon's Memoir	$1.95

HAL LINDSEY

☐	14096	The Late Great Planet Earth	$2.50
☐	14735	The Liberation of Planet Earth	$2.95
☐	14374	Satan Is Alive And Well On Planet Earth	$2.75
☐	14571	The Terminal Generation	$2.50
☐	14698	There's A New World Coming	$2.95

Buy them at your local bookstore or use this handy coupon for ordering: